Cwmbrân New Town
An Urban Characterisation Study

Comisiwn Brenhinol Henebion Cymru
Royal Commission on the Ancient and Historical Monuments of Wales

Susan Fielding
Senior Investigator (Historic Buildings)

Front cover: Building the New Town: the first residents of Pontnewydd West explore Maendy Square.

Back cover: The Cwmbrân Water Gardens looking north towards Monmouth House.

Comisiwn Brenhinol
Henebion Cymru
Royal Commission on the Ancient
and Historical Monuments of Wales

British Library Cataloguing in Publication Data.
A catalogue record for this book is available from the British Library.

ISBN: 978-1-871184-61-7

DOI: 10.52405/RCW9781871184594

Royal Commission on the Ancient and Historical Monuments of Wales,
Ffordd Penglais,
Aberystwyth,
Ceredigion SY23 3BU

Telephone: 01970 621200
Email: nmr.wales@rcahmw.gov.uk
Website: https://rcahmw.gov.uk/
Coflein: https://coflein.gov.uk

Noddir gan
Lywodraeth Cymru
Sponsored by
Welsh Government

Contents

1 Crynodeb Cymraeg (Welsh Summary)

Cwmbrân, Torfaen, yw'r unig Dref Newydd Marc 1 yng Nghymru. Nod yr astudiaeth hon yw darganfod natur y Dref Newydd drwy adrodd ei hanes a disgrifio ei chymeriad cyffredinol, tynnu sylw at agweddau ar ddatblygiad y Dref Newydd y dylid ymchwilio ymhellach iddynt, ac ystyried nodweddion y dylid eu diogelu a'u cadw. Pwrpas yr adroddiad yw helpu i gynllunio datblygiadau yn y dyfodol sy'n parchu rhinweddau'r Dref Newydd, ei chefndir hanesyddol a'i threftadaeth, a'i hamgylchedd a'i chyd-destun ffisegol. Gobeithir hefyd y bydd yn fan cychwyn ar gyfer ymchwil a thrafodaeth bellach ynghylch lle Cwmbrân yn nhreftadaeth adeiledig Cymru.

Gardd-ddinasoedd dechrau'r ugeinfed ganrif oedd yr ysbrydoliaeth ar gyfer y Trefi Newydd. Arweiniodd trefoli cyflym at gynllunio ar gyfer cymunedau a oedd yn gymdeithasol gyfiawn ac yn gorfforol iach drwy ddarparu tai a swyddi o safon uchel a lleoedd gwyrdd agored i weithwyr diwydiannol, gan ddilyn syniadau'r diwygiwr Ebenezer Howard. Er i'r rhaglenni adeiladu mawr rhwng y rhyfeloedd fynd yn erbyn y delfrydau hyn, fe'u rhoddwyd yn ôl ar yr agenda gwleidyddol gan Patrick Abercrombie a'i gynllun ar gyfer Llundain Fwyaf ym 1944 i adeiladu wyth tref newydd o gwmpas y ddinas. Ym 1945 fe gafodd y Pwyllgor Trefi Newydd ei greu, ac ym 1946 fe basiwyd Deddf y Trefi Newydd a'i gwnaeth hi'n bosibl i ddynodi aneddiadau newydd a phenodi Corfforaethau Datblygu Tref Newydd.

Cafodd Cwmbrân ei dynodi ar 4 Tachwedd 1949, a sefydlwyd Corfforaeth Datblygu Cwmbrân. Yn wahanol i Drefi Newydd eraill, y pwrpas oedd darparu tai o safon, ysgolion a chanol tref wedi'i gynllunio'n dda i wasanaethu'r rheiny a oedd yn gweithio yn niwydiannau de-ddwyrain Cymru ac a oedd yn gorfod teithio'n bell iawn i'r gwaith. Cafodd y Prif Gynllun strategol, a luniwyd gan yr ymgynghorwyr cynllunio Minoprio & Spencely & P. W. Macfarlane, ei gyhoeddi ym mis Mawrth 1951.

Mae gan y dref ardal siopa a dinesig ganolog wedi'i hamgylchynu gan 'gymdogaethau' preswyl, ac ardaloedd diwydiannol mewn parthau. O dan y system cymdogaethau, cafodd cymunedau o ryw 5,000 o bobl eu creu a darparwyd siopau, ysgolion, canolfannau iechyd, neuaddau cymunedol ac addoldai ar gyfer pob un ohonynt. Roedd y cymdogaethau'n ddigon mawr i fod yn hunangynhaliol ond yn ddigon bach i sicrhau bod y cyfleusterau o fewn pellter cerdded hwylus i bawb a bod ysbryd cymunedol yn datblygu rhwng y trigolion newydd. Rhoddwyd pwyslais mawr gan y Gorfforaeth ar ddefnyddio ffurfiau adeiladu a dylunio newydd ac arloesol.

Dim ond un elfen o'r Dref Newydd sydd wedi'i rhestru ar hyn o bryd ac nid oes unrhyw ardaloedd cadwraeth yng Nghwmbrân. Fel enghraifft arbennig o gynllunio a phensaernïaeth drefol ar ôl y rhyfel, a oedd yn ceisio cynnig gwell bywyd i'w thrigolion, mae'n bwysig iawn i ni gydnabod a diogelu nodweddion unigryw y dref Gymreig hon.

2 Introduction

2.1 Purpose and Aims of the Study

Cwmbrân, Torfaen, is the only Mark I New Town to be designated in Wales. The purpose of this study is to identify the character of the New Town; to provide an outline history of each neighbourhood, together with an overview of its character, and to highlight aspects of buildings and landscape dating from the New Town development which are both worthy of more detailed research and recording, and of consideration for preservation and conservation. The report is designed to inform a considered approach to planning future development which respects and acknowledges the qualities of the New Town, its historical background and heritage, and its physical environment and context. It is hoped that it will form a basis for further study and is intended to be a starting point for future investigation of, and discussion around, the place of Cwmbrân in the built heritage of Wales.

This study follows a template for urban area characterisation developed by Cadw for describing and recording historic towns in Wales. It is intended to be a development of, and complementary to, Cadw's work in this field that applies a similar descriptive and appraisal approach to the unique instance of Cwmbrân as the only first-generation New Town in Wales.[1]

This study started in 2019 with initial visits to Cwmbrân and the Gwent Record Office, but most of the work on this report has had to take place under the COVID restrictions throughout 2020 and early 2021. Torfaen County Borough has been under a series of national and regional lockdowns during this period, severely impacting the ability to carry out site visits and leading to the closure of Gwent Archives to the public for much of the period of the study. The report should be read in the light of the restrictions under which it was produced.

2.2 Cwmbrân: Location and Etymology

Cwmbrân is in Torfaen Borough County, in the eastern part of the historic county of Monmouthshire. Between 1974 and 1996 the county was known as Gwent.

Figure 1: An aerial view of Cwmbrân looking north from Oakfield.

It sits in the base of the Afon Lwyd valley some 6 miles (11 kilometres) north of Newport and 3 miles (5 kilometres) south of Pontypool, geologically an area of Old Red Sandstone with areas of river gravels and high ground to the north and west rising to c.600 feet (182 metres).

The name of the place means Valley of the Crow (Cwm = Valley, Brân = Crow). The Cwmbrân Development Corporation was keen to link the name to the character of Brân Fendigaid (Bran the Blessed), a giant and king of Britain from *Branwen*, the Second Branch of the Mabinogi, and the Triads (*Trioedd Ynys Prydein*).[2] No place name studies support this.[3]

Figure 2: Location maps of Cwmbrân.

3 Historical Background

3.1 Prehistoric to Post-medieval Background

Cwmbrân is a unique settlement in Wales as the only Mark I designated New Town, and the only one fulfilling the full criteria of a New Town.[4] However, this town was not laid out on a unoccupied landscape, but on one that had undergone centuries of modification.

Nearby evidence has been found of Neolithic activity represented by funerary and ritual sites such as Gaerllwyd Burial Chamber[5] and Bwllfa Cottages Henge;[6] Bronze Age occupation is evidenced by individual cairns and barrow cemeteries, with the possible origins of later defended enclosures such as Ysgryd Fach also of this date.[7] The Iron Age was characterised by the increase of defended enclosures and hillforts such as that to the west of Llantarnam at Malthouse Road, with south-east Wales in the later Iron Age occupied by the Silures.[8]

In the Roman period, following the inception of the Fosse frontier in BCE47 and subsequent Roman conquest of the Silures by AD 75, the only Roman town founded in Wales was situated at Venta Silurium (Caerwent) to the south of Cwmbrân.[9] Self-governance was established there by the Romans on the terms of 'civitas' status. From AD 55 to 60 significant Roman forts were constructed at nearby Gobannium (Abergavenny),[10] Isca (Caerleon)[11] and Burrium (Usk)[12], and a smaller fort was built at Coed y Caerau, east of Caerleon.[13] A substantial 20 hectare marching camp has been found at Penycae, Pontypridd.[14]

In the Medieval period the Lwyd valley was established as an agricultural area of dispersed settlement, with areas of woodland and upland common. The Cistercian Abbey of the Blessed Virgin was founded at Llantarnam in 1179 by Hywel ap Iorwerth, the Welsh lord of Caerleon, with the associated manor of Magna Porta. A daughter abbey of Strata Florida, Ceredigion, this institution flourished until the dissolution of the monasteries began in 1536, the abbey and its estates being sold in 1554.[15] Although the roofless, 11-bay stone abbey barn is the sole surviving element of the pre-Reformation abbey complex of buildings,[16] much remains of

Figure 3: St Michael and All Angels Church, Llantarnam.

the imprint of the abbey's estate layout on the modern landscape, including woodland, watercourses and boundaries within the Cwmbrân New Town area. Two of note are Cefn-mynach Grange, centred on the present-day Pentre-bach Farm, Llantarnam, represented in a series of earthworks denoting a possible moated site and fishponds, and Scybor Cwrt Grange (latterly Court Farm, demolished 1960s) which was the home farm, and can still be denoted by various field names.[17]

The church of St Michael and All Angels has a nave of possible twelfth- or thirteenth-century origin, but largely dates from the fifteenth century when it was used as a chapel by the tenants of Magna Porta.[18]

With the sale of the abbey in 1554, a succession of wealthy landowners acquired the estate beginning with the Morgan family of Caerleon and Newport, who built a mansion on the site around 1588. This mansion may have incorporated parts of the historic fabric of the former abbey. In the early nineteenth century the Llantarnam estates were inherited by Reginald John Blewitt. In 1834-5 Blewitt had the exterior of the 1588 house completely re-enveloped, with a correspondingly extensive remodelling of the interior. This work was carried out by the architect T. H. Wyatt and cost £60,000.[19] In the 1830s many parts of the parkland and gardens surrounding the house were also re-ordered and added to on Blewitt's instructions to include a lodge, formal garden, pond, greenhouses, gazebo, river, orchard, maze, kitchen garden, well, weirs, walled garden, woodland with vista paths, avenue, pavilion, grotto, parterres, conservatory, carriage drive, contrived antiquity, fountain and a pinetum.[20]

The expense of this work rendered Blewitt insolvent and by 1888 Llantarnam Abbey had been purchased by Sir Clifford Cory, Chairman of the Cardiff coal firm Cory Bros. & Co, who carried out further additions. After being used as an US Army base from 1941, it was bought by the Sisters of St Joseph of Annecy in 1946 as their British Provincial headquarters.[21]

Figure 4: Llantarnam Abbey depicted in a 1828 print by Rudolph Ackermann.

3.2 The Impact of the Industrial Revolution

From the sixteenth century, the area became an important centre of iron working, tin plate making and steel making. Iron manufacture in nearby Pontypool is documented as early as 1588 and in 1951 the New Town Plan acknowledged that Cwmbrân was still one of the principal iron and steel manufacturing centres in Monmouthshire. [22]

From the later eighteenth century the construction of the Monmouthshire and the Brecknock and Abergavenny canals, and the building of two railway lines that run north-south down the Lwyd valley in the mid-nineteenth century, developed the industrial and commercial potential of the locality. The Monmouth canal was authorised by an Act of Parliament in June 1792 and constructed by Thomas Dadford to link Pontnewydd to Newport at a cost of £275,000, with a branch section from Crindau to Crumlin Bridge. The main section of the canal opened in 1796, rising 136 m from its lower level with 42 locks in total, 15 of them in the vicinity of what became the New Town, with the Crumlin branch opening in 1799. Associated tramroad links connected the new canal to mining and other industrial sites in the area, including the Blaen-Din Works and Trosnant Furnace. In 1793 the Brecknock and Abergavenny Canal was authorised as a separate venture to link Brecon to the River Usk at Caerleon, but this plan was modified to create a junction at Pont-y-moel, from there sharing the navigation south to Newport. Further tramways serving the collieries were built as part of this work.[23]

The canal network proved successful, with coal and iron traffic rising from 44,528 tons in 1796 to 816,905 tons between 1842 and 1846.[24] However, in 1845 a bill was passed for the development of the Monmouthshire Eastern Valley railway between Newport Docks and Pontypool via Oakfield and Cwmbrân, with a branch line joining this to the Hereford main line in 1878. The development of these main-line railways, including the upgrading of tramways, adversely affected the canals, and they gradually fell into disuse and finally closed. The section from Pont-y-moel to Pontnewydd was infilled and converted into a railway in 1853. The rights to the canal and rail network were sold to the Great Western Railway in 1888, and nationalised in 1948, with sections of the canal continuing in use until the 1930s. A restoration of the northern part of the canal system was eventually carried out in the mid-1990s.

Metal working was fundamental to the industrial growth of the Cwmbrân area. In the nineteenth century two tinplate works were established by George Conway and his son John: the Edlogan works, Pontnewydd, from 1802, and the other at Pontrhydyrun from 1806. In 1873 the Tŷ Newydd Iron and Tinplate company built the Tŷ Newydd, or Redbrook, works, while the Avondale works were built in 1877.

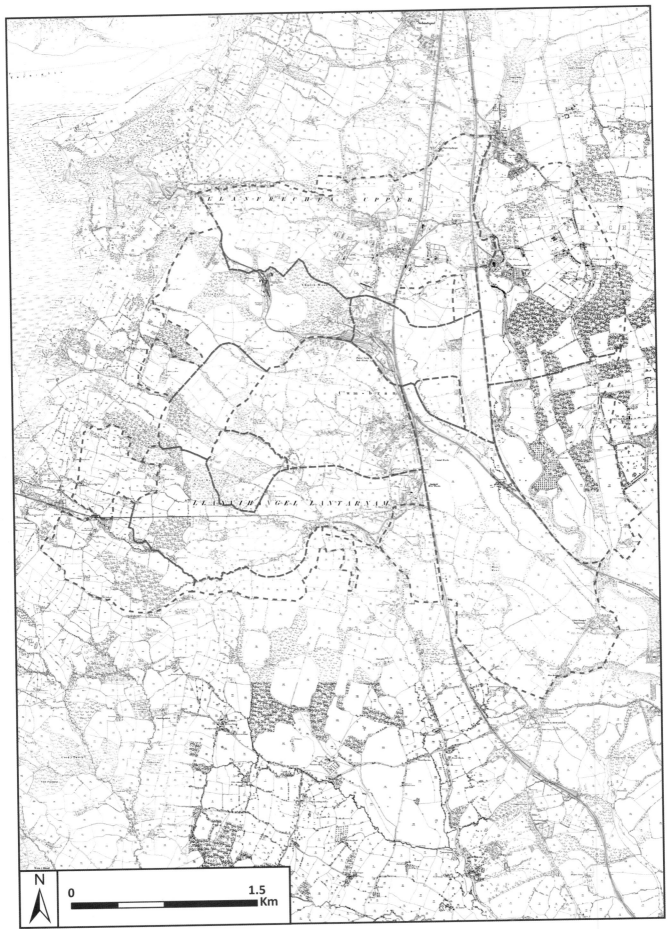

Figure 5: The area later designated for Cwmbrân New Town, 1888, depicted on the 25-inch 1st Edition OS mapping.

In 1847 Reginald James Blewitt established a patent for a method of creating malleable iron and created the Cwmbrân Iron Company. Not only did this lead to the rapid growth of iron working in the area from the mid-nineteenth century, but it was also a catalyst for developing brick making, lime kilns, quarrying, iron ore mining and coal mining in and around the settlements of the Cwmbrân area.

Blewitt's company was joined by the iron works of the Patent Nut & Bolt Company from the 1870s which opened and developed the coal adit at Colomendy Road in 1879, bought in 1902 by Guest, Keen and Nettlefolds. Also developed at Pontnewydd in the later nineteenth century was the Oakfield wire works, bought in 1925 by the Whitehead Iron and Steel company; a vitriol works followed later in 1860, bought by the Cwmbrân Chemical Co. in 1911, which merged into Imperial Chemical Industries in 1926.[25]

The population of the Cwmbrân district rose from around 600 in 1801 to nearly 10,000 by 1891, an increase of more than 16 times.[26] Despite this growth in population and industry, settlement growth was relatively localised with extensive areas of woodland retained and housing development remaining comparatively confined. This characteristic pattern of restricted development continued in the first part of the twentieth century and until the Second World War.

During the 1920s and 1930s the industries of the Cwmbrân area went into sharp decline. In the economic slump of the early 1930s the main colliery closed, together with other large industrial sites that had been major employers. For several years half the insured population available for work in the area were registered as unemployed.[27] Abandoned collieries and clay pits were left as scars on the landscape of the valley.

The Government's response came in the Special Area Acts of 1934-37 that designated 'distressed areas' and set up the Special Areas Reconstruction Association (SARA) to provide financial grants to potential industrial development companies. SARA was instrumental in bringing about the establishment of the Pilkington Factory, Pontypool Road; Cwmbrân Engineering, Grange Road; and the Weston Biscuit Factory, Llantarnam. By the mid-twentieth century, while the remaining older industries of Guest, Keen & Nettlefolds, Whitehead Hill Co. and Avondale Tinplate Co. were still seen as a mainstay of employment, a more diverse range of industrial

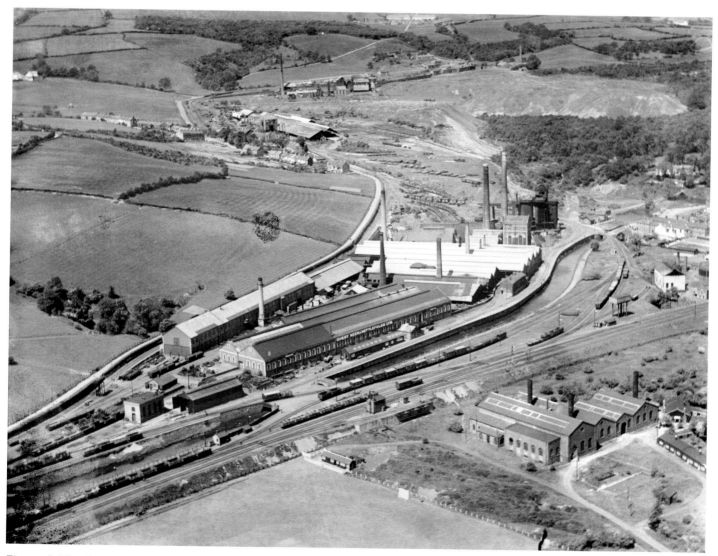

Figure 6: The Guest, Keen & Nettlefolds' Patent Nut and Bolt works, 1930.

development was taking place with companies such as Joseph Lucas and Alfa-Laval Co Ltd also established. Post-war, Girling Ltd became the largest local employer, manufacturing shock absorbers and brakes for the automotive industry.

Figure 7: The Weston Biscuit Factory, Llantarnam, decked out in celebration of the end of World War II in 1945.

By the time the New Town Master Plan was created in 1951, there were 24 factories within the designated area employing over 6,000 people.[28] Around 75 % of jobs were based in metal and engineering industries, while further employment was provided outside the designated area at Panteg Steelworks, British Nylon Spinners and at the Royal Ordnance Factory, Glascoed. Owing to the shortage of housing in the area, the majority of workers travelled more than five miles daily, prompting the Government's view of the need for the New Town.

4 Topography and Landscape

The geology of the Cwmbrân area consists of the Raglan Mudstone formation to the centre and eastern parts of the designated area, overlain along the valley floor by river alluvium deposits that were instrumental in the later brick making industry of the area. To the west Argillaceous rocks and Sandstone dominate, with limestone formations and coal seams exposed in the eastern slopes of Mynydd Maen.[29]

The town sits within the Afon Lwyd Valley, a wide north-south valley running from Pontypool to Usk where the River Lwyd enters the River Usk. The town is centred on the flat valley floor at a height of some 90 m above present sea level (APSL) but was prevented from following a linear formation along the valley by the proximity of Pontypool to the north and Newport to the south. As a result, the town extends east and west, rising to a height of c.230 m APSL to the west on the lower slopes of Mynydd Maen and c.89 m APSL to the east. Both the topography and the desire to retain the discrete nature of the town has prevented expansion of the designation area to any large degree since the winding-up of the Cwmbrân Development Corporation in 1986.

5 The New Town

5.1 The New Town Plan

During the Second World War, thought was given by planners and architects to the reconstruction of Britain's towns and communities after the conflict. In 1944 the Greater London plan drawn up by Sir Leslie Patrick Abercrombie included a proposal for eight New Towns encircling London, providing new and improved housing for up to 500,000 people from inner London boroughs. The following year, the Attlee government appointed Lord Reith as the Chair of a New Town Commission to assess the proposal and in 1946 the New Towns Act was passed.[30]

Working in conjunction with the Distribution of Industry Act of 1945, the investigation for sites for New Towns in Wales focused on two growth areas in the eastern coalfields, central Glamorgan and east Monmouthshire. Owing to the increased growth in factories in Eastern Valley and subsequent levels of commuting, the proposal for a New Town at Cwmbrân was taken to the New Town committee in 1948. Initially the area was considered 'too drab' by the committee, which asked that 'a more attractive site than Cwmbrân-Pontnewydd' be sought. After further campaigning and a Ministerial visit to Eastern Valley ('I find it a good deal more attractive than the committee imagined'), approval was given to proceed.[31]

At that time the combined population of the villages of Pontnewydd, Cwmbrân, Croesyceiliog, Oakfield and Coed Eva was c. 13,000 people, with manufacturing industries employing over 6,000 people.[32] The principal intention was to provide a New Town with good quality housing, schools and a

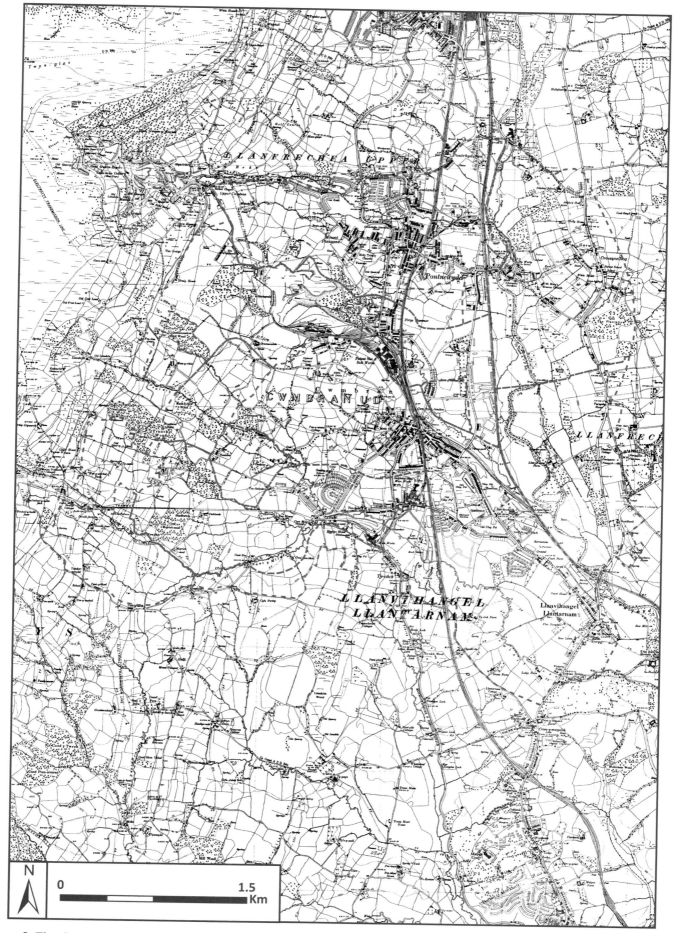

Figure 8: The Cwmbrân area immediately prior to designation, depicted on the 25-inch OS mapping of 1948.

well-designed town centre in the south-east of Wales. This settlement would serve the enlarged population of the area, employed for the most part in existing local industries and businesses that at the time were considered to have a long-term future.

When a public inquiry was held into the proposal on 6 October 1949, the main concern was that the New Town should be located further to the north-east because of its possible impact on Newport.[33] The original site was pursued as it was already well advanced as a concept, and also because it was argued alternative suitable locations would have required the loss of considerably more agricultural land. The Cwmbrân New Town Designation order was formalised on 4 November 1949, confirming the decision to implement and develop a New Town and leading to the establishment the Cwmbrân Development Corporation (CDC) on the twenty-fourth of the same month.[34]

T. H. Huxley Turner was appointed as first Chairman of the CDC, Major General Wynford Rees as General Manager and J.

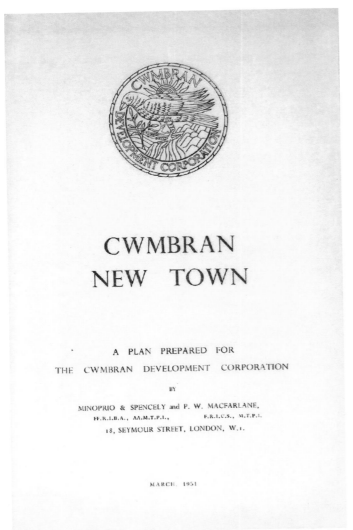

Figure 9: The masterplan for Cwmbrân New Town by Messrs. Minoprio & Spencely & P. W. Macfarlane included the creation of the Cwmbran Development Corporation logo.

C. P. West as Chief Architect.[35] In March 1950 the firm of Minoprio & Spencely & P. W. Macfarlane (MSM) were appointed as planning consultants, largely on the basis that Minoprio had recently completed the Master Plan for the New Town at Crawley.[36]

MSM and the CDC produced an outline plan for the New Town in Cwmbrân by November 1950 with the strategic Master Plan published in March 1951. The plan set out proposals for a central shopping and civic area, surrounded by seven largely residential areas. The zoning of commercial, industrial and residential sectors was dictated by topography and existing industrial activity. The central flat valley bottom would be used for the town centre, industry and recreational areas, while housing would be located on the higher ground. Within these overall guidelines the Master Plan importantly allowed for a measure of flexibility in how future development should proceed. It further recommended where new schools would be required, and how people would travel around, to and from the New Town. Local transport and communications were a particularly fundamental planning issue, with roads, railways and a river dissecting the site and the remains of clay pits and industrial works scarring the landscape.

A second public inquiry on the master Plan was held on 10 July 1951, with 2,000 copies of the Planning Report sold in the local area.[37] Although the Master Plan was not formally approved by the Government until 1952, the first two annual reports from the CDC ending 31 March 1951 and 31 March 1952 showed that substantial work was already underway with CDC staff recruited and offices built. There were later significant modifications to the proposals which were accommodated within the strategic plan.

3,160 acres (1,279 hectares) around the existing villages of Cwmbrân, Pontnewydd and Croesyceiliog were allocated for the designated area. The original target population was 35,000, to be reached over a fifteen-year programme of development. However, by the time the development corporation was wound up in 1988, the planned upper limit of population had been increased first to 45,000 (a revised limit which was reached), and then to 55,000 in 1961.

5.1.1 Architects

Although there were exceptions, successive Chief Architects were responsible for most new residential and public buildings constructed in Cwmbrân. The most prominent exceptions included new school buildings, the responsibility of Monmouthshire County Architects Department, and the Monmouthshire County Hall and County Police Headquarter, both designed by Robert Matthew, Johnson Marshall and Partners. New religious buildings constructed within the New Town were also designed by private architectural practices. The New Town's Chief Architects were J. C. P. West (1950-62), Gordon Redfern (1963-69), J. L. Berbiers (1969-72) and J. L. Russell (1972-82).[38]

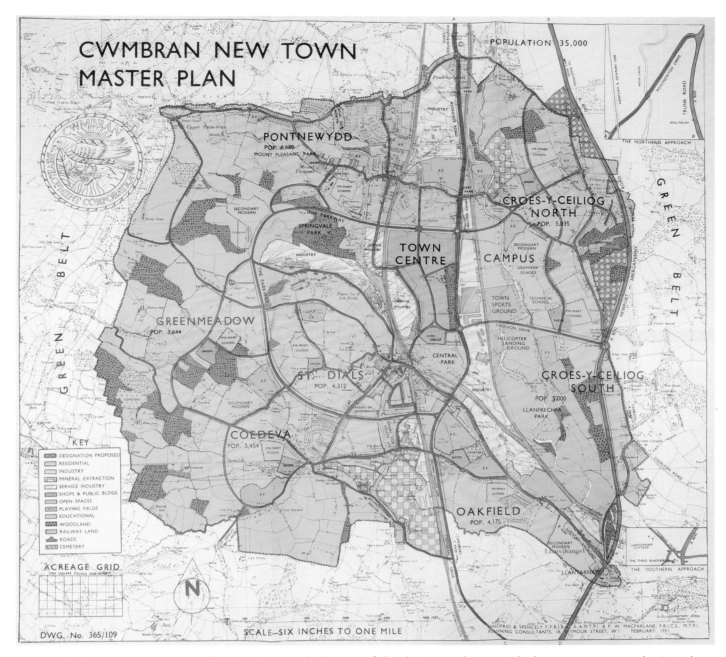

Figure 10: The masterplan map of 1951 showing the layout of the designated area with the town centre and original seven surrounding 'neighbourhoods'.

5.1.2 Communications

The Master Plan dealt with three types of traffic: long-distance travel that would be served by the Newport-Abergavenny trunk road, traffic coming into Cwmbrân from the surrounding area, and traffic within the town.

The plan ensured regional north-south traffic was excluded from residential areas by the diversion of the A4042 trunk road to the east. Northern and southern approaches (Pontnewydd Drive and Cwmbrân Drive, respectively) would link the town with this road, while a link road would go to Caerleon.

Within the town, a network of roads would ensure rapid, safe, and easy movement (for drivers and pedestrians) from one area to another with several new bridges over the river, canal and railway lines linking the east and west parts of the town. The north-south spine of this system was Grange Road, with The Parkway providing the east-west axis. The rising ownership of cars was represented in the acknowledgement of the need for plentiful and well-distributed public car parks.

For those without private transport, a conveniently located central bus station would serve the shopping centre, industrial parks and educational campus.

It was recommended to centralise the four existing railway stations at Llantarnam Junction, Cwmbrân, Upper Pontnewydd and Pontnewydd, seen as inadequately equipped for modern day use, into one central station in the north-east part of the town. British Rail stated that the proposal was unacceptable, and no new station was included in the 1951 Master Plan. A station was finally opened in 1986. It was also recommended that developments in air travel made it sensible to reserve land for a helicopter landing ground.[39]

5.1.3 Industry

One of the chief considerations in the creation of the New Town was the need to reduce time people spent commuting to work in Cwmbrân area by locating appropriate housing close to those industries.

Industry covering 127 acres (51 hectares) of land was divided into three categories of older metal working, brickworks and light industry. The first two were seen as problematic in terms of waste and impact on the landscape, the third as the most significant developing sector of future employment. Larger factories at a further distance, but employing significant numbers of people, were the Panteg steelworks, Pontypool Glassworks, British Nylon Spinners and Glascoed ordnance factory.

The proposed 35,000 population of the New Town was expected to include 16,000 workers – 11,000 in manufacturing and 5,000 in service industries – 14,000 of which already existed. It was decided that should new industries be attracted, competition for male labour would ensue and create a shortage of labour for the required services industries. Therefore, little of the designated area was allocated to industry outside of 43 acres (17 hectares) for expansion needs at existing works.

The largest expansion of industry was planned for the service industries to meet the needs of the town's population, rising from 600 to 5,000 jobs. This included shopping, business, local government, transport, garages, cleansers, bakers and dairies which would be allocated their own sector areas.[40]

5.1.4 Residential

Seven residential areas, grouped around the town centre, were planned to house between 3,600 and 6,700 people each, based on the retention of existing settlements as the nuclei for the new neighbourhoods and the local topography.

Neighbourhoods had several benefits. The modest populations would engender a sense of community in which residents would get to know each other more easily, while being large enough to maintain a neighbourhood centre of shops, bank, libraries and schools that was convenient for people in terms of walking distance. They were also seen as a safe way of managing traffic, particularly for children and the elderly, allowing main routes to pass between rather than through them.

Each neighbourhood was intended to have a variety of housing to suit all ages, family types and incomes. Flats were considered the accommodation least likely to be popular,[41]

with wide-fronted terraced houses being viewed as the most economical and best suited to the undulating contours.[42]

DWELLINGS IN AN AVERAGE NEIGHBOURHOOD OF 5,000 POPULATION.

No. in Household	No. of Dwellings	Percentage of Dwellings	Types of Dwellings	No. of Each Type	Total No. of Persons
1 person	100	7	Flats	60	60
			Houses	20	20
			Bungalows	20	20 — 100
2 „	350	24	Flats	80	160
			Houses	250	500
			Bungalows	20	40 — 700
3 „	390	27	Flats	70	210
			Houses	290	870
			Bungalows	30	90 — 1,170
4 „	280	19.8	Flats	40	160
			Houses	220	880
			Bungalows	20	80 — 1,120
5 „	160	11	Flats	20	100
			Houses	135	675
			Bungalows	5	25 — 800
6 „	84	5.8	Flats	10	60
			Houses	74	444 — 504
7 „	41	2.9	Houses	41	287
8 „	21	1.4	Houses	21	168
9 „	9	.6	Houses	9	81
10 „	7	.5	Houses	7	70
	1,442 dwellings	100			5,000

SUMMARY.

Type	Nos.	Proportion of Dwellings per cent	People Housed	Proportion of Population per cent
Flats	280	20	750	15
Houses	1,067	74	3,995	80
Bungalows	95	6	255	5
	1,442	100	5,000 popn.	100

Figure 11: The list of dwelling allocations by type and occupancy for the neighbourhoods in the 1951 masterplan.

5.1.5 Commercial

The focus of commercial development was the town centre, a 71-acre (29 hectare) strip west of the railway line. The main shopping street would run north-south, utilising the small hill at Little Gelli to provide a conspicuous location for a civic square at its south end. Here it was expected that public buildings could be located in a prominent position and in full view from the southern approaches. The entire shopping area was designed as a fully pedestrianised place, with free and plentiful parking recognised as a prerequisite for modern shopping.

The town centre stood at the apex of a tiered hierarchy of commercial spaces. Each neighbourhood was to be provided with a neighbourhood commercial centre, supported by sub-centres. The centralised location of these would ensure easy access by foot from any part of the neighbourhood, with the number and diversity of commercial buildings (shops, banks, hairdressers, etc.) determined by the designated population of the neighbourhood.[43]

5.1.6 Education and Health

Schools were planned in conjunction with Monmouthshire County Council and designed to be in accordance with latest Ministry of Education requirements.

Primary schools were to be located as close as possible to each neighbourhood centre, ensuring easy accessibility, school drop-offs/pick-ups to be combined with shopping and encouraging the use of school buildings as community centres in evenings and weekends. Four secondary modern schools were to sit on the boundaries of the neighbourhoods they served, while the whole of the Designated Area was to be served by one Technical School and one Grammar School on an educational campus at Croesyceiliog.[44]

Only one health centre was expected to be required, supplemented by maternity and childcare clinics in each of the neighbourhoods.

The number of cemeteries was to be doubled, from two to four, with one of the new sites incorporating a crematorium. [45]

5.1.7 Open Space

From the outset in Minoprio's plan, the provision of public open space throughout the New Town was always an important consideration. Over ten per cent (323 acres/131 hectares) of the designated area were reserved as parkland, with four new parks proposed. Land was specifically recommended for public open space at Llanfrechfa Park, Central Park, in the Garden of Remembrance, at Canalside South, Canalside North, at Mount Pleasant Park and at Springvale Park.

Minoprio also recommended that land be set aside for greenways, cycle tracks and a riverside park, and the redevelopment of canal-side gardens within the New Town.

A clear intention was set out in the forward to the New Town Plan that 'within the framework of this Master Plan it is hoped will be created a happy, friendly and pleasing place which will set a standard of what an industrial town should be.'[46]

More than fifty per cent of the population of the New Town moved to Cwmbrân from other parts of south Wales, in particular from neighbouring industrial valleys. The quality and quantity of open space made available in the planning strategy was almost certainly an important factor in making the New Town an attractive and appealing prospect to those new residents from the outset.[47]

No Green Belt was officially scheduled for the designated area, but the preservation of an open belt of land was consider particularly necessary to the south, where the housing estates of Newport threatened expansion northward, and the north, to contain the industries of Panteg and Griffithstown.

5.2 The Development and Modification of the New Town Plan

The annual report of March 1953 reported that the Master Plan was to be modified 'in light of more detailed knowledge' regarding the topography, landscape and existing built environment.[48] Transport routes were modified owing to British Railways' refusal to consolidate the existing four stations into a new central Cwmbrân station.

By 1960 plans were in progress to raise the target population to 55,000, though approval for this upper limit was only received from the New Towns Commission (NTC) in 1968.[49] In early 1971 the NTC extended an invitation to the Cwmbrân Development Corporation (CDC) to further raise the target population to 75,000, and after commissioning a feasibility study into the potential for growth, a proposal was submitted. A draft order for the extension was published on 10 April 1975, and after a twenty-five-day-long public inquiry during which the plan was supported by both Cwmbrân Town Council and Torfaen Borough Council, approval to the further increased size was given in 1978.[50]

In the run up to the 1974 county restructuring, it was decided that the new Monmouthshire County Hall would be built in Cwmbrân, making it an administrative centre for local government.

5.3 What Was Not Built at Cwmbrân

The original Master Plan proposed a further education college, but this was subsequently never designed or built during the time of the CDC; only now is it under construction, due for completion in June 2020.[51] Similarly plans for a technical school, designed to complement the grammar school and secondary modern school complex, were discarded owing to a national revaluation of secondary education in the 1950s.

A central swimming baths for the town centre was proposed from the outset, with Ministry of Housing and Local Government approval passed in 1964 when the CDC agreed to make a substantial grant to the Cwmbrân Urban District Council towards the building of the pool. Owing to difficulties both with funding and responsibility for maintenance, and the overall development of the Civic Square location, the swimming baths were never built.

There were no plans for a district general hospital to serve the New Town. In 2003 initial proposals were prepared for the redevelopment of Llanfrechfa Grange for the Grange University Hospital, approved in 2017. Currently under construction with Welsh Government funding, when opened in 2022 the hospital is intended to provide 470 beds, emergency, critical care and specialist facilities to serve a catchment area of Monmouthshire and south Powys from a focal location at Cwmbrân.[52]

In 1979 Norman Foster's architectural practice, Foster Associates, designed a major scheme for the southern part of the Town Centre described as the Open House Community Project Centre. A site model, 175 drawings and four reports were produced by the practice as documented in the Norman Foster Foundation archive. This would have been a major addition to the public facilities and spaces in the town centre but was never carried out owing to a lack of funding.[53]

5.4 The End of the New Town Corporation

From 1982 onwards the CDC began to dispose of its assets. Community assets including rented and shared ownership housing was transferred to Torfaen County Borough Council, while in 1985 the Town Centre was sold to City and County Property. On 31 March 1988 Cwmbrân New Town Corporation was formally dissolved, and its residual assets and liabilities transferred to the Commission for the New Towns. Responsibility for the administration and local government of Cwmbrân is now with the County Borough of Torfaen.

6 The Character of Building

6.1 Historic buildings

The 1951 Master Plan identified only a small number of buildings within the New Town area that could 'claim to be called architecture', namely Greenmeadow Farm and barn (seventeenth/eighteenth century) in Greenmeadow; St Michael's Church (fifteenth/sixteenth century) and churchyard cross (Medieval), the Greenhouse Public House (1719), Brook House (early nineteenth century), Abbey Cottages (eighteenth/nineteenth century), Coopers Arms Cottage and Bambrook Cottage (seventeenth/eighteenth century) in Llantarnam; Bethel Chapel (1889) in Upper Cwmbrân; Turnpike House (nineteenth century), two thatched cottages at High Garage and Poultry farm (undated) and Jim Crow Cottage (nineteenth century) in Croesyceiliog; Llan-yr-afon Farm (early seventeenth century) and associated barn in Cwmbrân; Pontnewydd House in Pontnewydd; and Pontrhydyrun Baptist chapel (1836) in Pontrhydyrun.

It was claimed that 'apart from these old buildings… the standard of architecture is generally low' and that existing buildings should be cleared, or if they needed to remain, screened by trees or new buildings.[54]

Figure 13: Jim Crow's Cottage, Croesyceiliog.

Historic buildings overlooked at the time as not being of sufficient architectural interest, the value of which has in several instances been subsequently reassessed (though not all survive), make up a substantially longer list. These include, for instance the sixteenth and seventeenth Cwm Aeron house, Waun-y-pwll house, Llanyrafon House and Farm, and the eighteenth century Llanyrafon Mill in Llanyrafon. and Llanyrafon Farm has since been described as 'the principal survivor from the pre-industrial landscape'.[55]

Similarly, in Llantarnam, we find the sixteenth and seventeenth century Pentre-bach Farm and Tŷ-coch Farmhouse. The former, with its long two-storeyed mid-sixteenth century stone range with a three storey porch, may have been built by the recusant landowner, Edward Morgan (1548-1633) and is Grade II* Listed. In Llanfrechfa, there's

Figure 12: The Greenhouse Public House, Llantarnam.

Llanfrechfa Grange (1848), whereas Cwm-Brân House and gardens (shown on the first to third edition Ordnance Survey (OS) maps, though the gardens structure is not shown on the third edition) and St Gabriel's Church are located within the historic village of Cwm-Brân. Upper Cwmbrân includes the Ebenezer Primitive Methodist Chapel (1840/1865) and Siloam Baptist Chapel (1838/1904), and in Coedeva we find Penywaun Independent Chapel (1819/1907) and Glan y Nant Farmhouse (seventeenth century). Other significant historic buildings include Pont-rhydyryn House (shown on the first to third edition OS maps) in Pontrhydyrun; Holy Trinity Church,

Mount Pleasant Road, Pontnewydd House and gardens (shown on first to third edition OS maps), Elim Independent United Chapel (1844/1867), Mount Pleasant Baptist Chapel (1876/1891), Hope Methodist Church (1866), King's Head hotel and Station Road – all in Pontnewydd; Ebenezer Baptist Chapel (1860) and Gospel Hall (early twentieth century) in St Dials; and, finally, Court Farm (demolished in the 1960s to make way for a new school) in Croesyceiliog.

A full list of buildings within the designated area on the Cadw Listed Buildings Register is included in **Appendix I**.

Figure 14: Llanyrafon House, Llanyrafon, now used as the Llanyrafon Manor Museum.

Figure 15: Llanfrechfa Grange, built as a private mansion in 1848, has been variously used as a Boys' Domestic Training Centre, maternity hospital, and hospital for those with mental illness since 1933.

6.2 Civic Buildings

With the early focus on housing, civic elements of the Master Plan were left until the 1960s. A 1963 scheme for the southern 'Civic Square' included a range of civic buildings, together with a multi-storey car park and a 'Hall of Culture'. Problems with funding a public swimming baths and the 'Hall' by the Cwmbrân Urban District Council (CUDC) meant they failed to materialise, while both the Cwmbrân Development Corporation (CDC) and CUDC ended up using offices built in Gwent House instead of bespoke accommodation.

The only elements of the scheme that were finally built, therefore, were the police station and magistrates' court. Cwmbrân Central Police Station, designed by Monmouth County Architects Department, is a stark building of two storeys constructed of pre-cast concrete panels of graduated heights. The adjacent Magistrates Court, by F. R. Bates, Son & Price, is of similar style and construction, the advancement of panels between window openings giving a slight variation, though has been over-clad and extended to the rear, re-glazed and a porch added to the front entrance. Described as 'uncommunicative cubic blocks' their low height has not provided the visual impact originally expected for this area.[56]

Figure 16: Cwmbrân Central Police Station, Civic Square.

Figure 17: The Magistrates' Court, Civic Square.

The most important cluster of civic buildings was eventually constructed at Croesyceiliog, namely the County Hall, the County Police Headquarters and the Police Training Centre, all of which are now either demolished or under threat.

A new County Hall to replace the Shire Hall in Newport, built in 1889, and a series of other buildings across the county had been under discussion for some time. Three sites in and around Cwmbrân were assessed in 1951, the County Council deciding that at Croesyceiliog was the most suitable though this lay just outside the designated area. A 'County Hall Sites Committee' was recorded as requesting compulsory purchase of land at Llanfrechfa for the hall in 1952, while 1955 saw the County Council returning to discussions with the CDC over the Croesyceiliog site, stating 'the time had come for the preparation of the outline plans and estimates'.[57] Despite this optimistic report, in 1962 the County Council were again assessing possible sites for a new County Hall to accommodate increased staffing in the run up to new legislation.[58] The County Hall at Croesyceiliog was finally built between 1969 and 1977, designed by the private practice of Robert Matthew, Johnson-Marshall and Partners.[59] Accommodating 500 staff, 88 members and with 200 parking spaces, it was unfairly described as 'well-proportioned, straightforward but not particularly memorable'.[60] On opening, it was occupied by the newly-formed Gwent County Council until abolition in 1996, after which it housed the successor Monmouthshire and Torfaen Councils. In 2012 a structural survey identified the need for £30 million worth of repairs to the building, and it was subsequently demolished in 2013.

Figure 18: The Gwent County Hall, Croesyceiliog, opened 1977 and demolished 2013.

With its bands of bronzed glass windows interspersed with dark exposed-aggregate concrete panels, Y-plan and terraced open walkways to the lower council chamber block, this was one of a handful of new county halls built to accommodate the redesignation of the counties in Wales in 1974, surviving examples of which are increasingly rare. Its Modernist design was strikingly different from the same practice's Hillingdon Civic Centre, completed the same year, which through its radical expression in traditional materials and vernacular forms was a landmark in British architecture.

The 1964 Monmouthshire Joint Standing Committee approved a new County Police Headquarters for the 1968/69 police building programme on the site adjoining the County Hall. Costing £225,000, work was underway by 1969 and the building opened in 1975.[61] Also designed by Robert Matthew, Johnson-Marshall & Partners, it is in a similar idiom to County Hall, with alternating horizontal bands of glazing and pre-cast concrete panels, but of a lower scale of two and three storeys. In 2018 a new HQ building was approved for Llantarnam Industrial Park, due for completion in 2021. Forming the first phase of a county-wide review of policing accommodation, the building is designed to introduce 'agile' working and 'digital policing' as well as being environmentally sustainable.[62]

Figure 19: The Gwent Police Headquarters, Croesyceiliog. A new headquarters at Llantarnam Industrial Park is currently under construction, making the future of this building uncertain.

In addition to the County Headquarters, Cwmbrân was home to the Wales and West of England Police Training Centre. This was built at St Dials in 1974, designed by J. L. Russell, and a sizable complex dominated by the main, U-plan building, differing from the County Hall and Headquarters in its use of red brick and zinc cladding.[63] Further ancillary buildings made good use of the same materials with a range of mansard and mono-pitched roofs to add variety, internally accentuated by a range of differently trussed and timber-clad roof structures. The centre included an assembly hall, swimming pool and bar, all with original fittings. The centre was closed in 2005 and demolished in 2015.

6.3 Commercial Buildings

In the early history of the New Town, commercial development took a back seat as, with a reasonable range of shops at Pontnewydd and Cwmbrân already, and the proximity of Pontypool and Newport, the commercial success of an ambitious New Town centre was not assured. The early strategy developed for commercial buildings in the New Town, however, was as cascading facilities to provide different levels and types of services: the town centre, the neighbourhood unit centres and the sub-centres.

In 1951 the Ministry stated that they thought Minoprio had overestimated how large the new shopping centre needed to be considering the facilities available at Pontypool and

Figure 20: Late-nineteenth-century shops in the historic core of Pontnewydd.

Newport. They recommended the number of shops be substantially reduced, taking the overall total for the designated areas from 340 to 250. An initial survey of existing shops within the designated area was carried out by the CDC and completed in 1952. The local Chamber of Commerce and existing traders were both consulted as to the type, size and layout of new shops required within the neighbourhood units. The CDC Estates Officer estimated there were already some eighty units existing and there were various thoughts put forward as to how the remaining 170 should be distributed between the town centre and neighbourhoods, and what provision should be made for expansion.[64]

Early designs focused on the neighbourhood units, with a standard design initially produced for all. J. C. P. West, Chief Architect, recommended that all unit centres were single storey, at most two, as for instance at the Maendy Centre, West Pontnewydd. He declared that a more imposing architecture may 'in such a small and compact scheme… lead to monumentality with a solid and rather crushing effect instead of the intimate and cosy atmosphere we are trying to create', with this scheme instead lifted by the creation of a village green feel through tree planting.[65] Similar schemes were developed across Oakfield, the first to be opened, in early 1954, Croesyceiliog in 1957 and Llanyravon in 1959. Where neighbourhoods were large or had barriers such as roads or railways dividing them, such as at Croesyceiliog, sub-unit

Figure 21: The Unit Centre for the Llanyravon neighbourhood.

Figure 22: The Fairwater Centre, the unit centre for the south-western areas.

centres or individual pantry shops were built to supplement the main unit centres. Regardless of size, each of these centres was based on an existing model of shopping – predominantly carried out by women, who walked to shops daily, often combining the outing with the school run – and failed to foresee the substantial increases in car ownership that were imminent.

For the south-western areas, there was a greater reliance on pantry shops, which were located to allow people to walk to their nearest one within ten minutes. The twelve shops across the area were thus set at a density of 650 people per shop.[66] These were designed to supplement the larger and more architecturally ambitious 'South-Western Areas' unit centre at Fairwater. Constructed between 1963 and 1967, the centre contained eighteen shops as well as a range of other facilities including a health centre and public house. To combat the exposed nature of the site together with the 'high rainfall, mists and variable winds' prevalent in the area, Gordon Redfern designed an enclosed, high-sided space that would physically and mentally shield shoppers during their visits.[67] This protective environment extended to creating a central play area that could be viewed from the shops, allowing a more enjoyable experience for children, and was radically different from previous developments.

The original plans for the Town Centre were also drawn up by J. C. P. West, with the project seen as the main incentive in attracting a good town architect to join the CDC. His design was put forward in 1953 and was predicated on the idea that, in order to compete with Pontypool and Newport, Cwmbrân needed to offer something different. He broke with the traditional 'high street' design that had been assumed by Minoprio, of a single road lined with shops, instead going for a pedestrianised centre that was largely undercover to protect from what he saw as exceedingly high levels of rainfall. This was highly innovative and contemporaneous with designs being implemented at Stevenage and Coventry at this date, but completely different to post-Blitz reconstructions underway at other Welsh towns and cities such as Swansea. Ministry architects labelled it as 'one of the most interesting, if not the most interesting, New Town Centre schemes we have had'.[68] With approval passed in 1955, appointed consultants Hillier, Parker, May & Rowden modified the scheme to such an extent that the Ministry described themselves as 'frankly disappointed' with the now standardised design.[69] The increased revenue got the scheme passed, however, and as building started it was realised that the ability to lay out large car parks would allow the scheme to compete favourably with other towns.

In 1962 West resigned as Chief Architect to be replaced by Gordon Redfern, a younger man with radically different ideas from West. It was under him that plans for the Town Centre were rejuvenated and much of the building work achieved. One of the first buildings designed by Redfern was that for David Evans on Gwent Square in 1964, currently in remarkably unaltered form with its ground floor mosaic portico and first

Figure 23: Architect's sketch by J. C. P. West for the Town Centre.

floor cladding of timber 'fins'.[70] Other notable commercial, if not architectural, developments in the Town Centre were the opening of Kibby's supermarket, Monmouth House, which had claim to being the largest supermarket in Wales at the time, and in 1976 the first Sainsbury's opened in Wales.[71]

Glyndwr House and Gwent House were an attempt to address the CDC's concern regarding the lack of professional 'office' jobs being attracted to Cwmbrân. Glyndwr House opened at the southern end of the shopping centre in 1968 over ground floor shops.[72] Gwent House combined desired offices with the need for a central building in the Town Centre with a non-retail focus. The 'Central Building', as it was initially known, had been the subject of discussion for some time, with the CDC desiring the inclusion of elements such as club, a dance hall and a hotel. Eventually external architects Richard Sheppard, Robson & Partners was commissioned to design a multi-purpose building containing six floors of offices, a public library, a Youth Employment Centre, a multi-purpose conference and exhibition hall, and three floors of restaurants in addition to another fourteen shops.[73] The hotel, for which the CDC had particularly pushed, was abandoned owing to a lack of interest from any investor. The building was formally opened on 18 January 1973, a monumental concrete-framed block that stands in contrast to the lower level rooflines of the rest of the shopping centre.[74] As no other tenants for the offices could be found, the CDC used the majority of the office space themselves, with two floors occupied by Cwmbrân Urban District Council (CUDC).

One of the most successful features of the Town Centre was the ability of the CDC to respond to the first indicators of the growth of car ownership and provide increasing numbers of multi-storey car parks from the early 1960s onwards. Abundant free parking, together with the provision of chain stores such as David Evans, Boots, Woolworths, WoolCo, Marks & Spencer and Sainsbury's throughout the 1970s, meant that Cwmbrân was increasingly popular with shoppers in relation to Pontypool, Newport and further afield.

In the 1980s projects were put forward to 'modernise' the Town Centre, including one to relieve the 'relentlessly flat' skyline and 'stubby towers' with the addition of copper domes and spires at a cost of some £52,000, and provide new

signage for the shops.[75] The funding for this was not forthcoming and in 1985 the Town Centre was sold to Town and Country, a subsidiary of the Ladbroke Group. After the sale, the metal-framed canopies currently in place were added by Hildebrand & Glicker.[76]

A survey of existing provision of public houses was also undertaken. There were attractive nineteenth-century pubs existing at The Greenhouse, Llantarnam and the Upper Cock, Croesyceiliog, which were both modernised and improved. The survey concluded that five new public houses were needed in the initial neighbourhoods, one each at West Pontnewydd, Croesyceiliog and Oakfield and two in Llanyravon.[77] These were all to serve food and some were designed to have separate halls that could be used for community benefit, justifying CDC involvement. All were built and funded direct by brewers, however, and the Upper Cock and Greenhouse were also rebuilt and modernised without the need for public investment. With the expansion to the south-west further public houses were designated. Only one public house, The Moonraker, was built within the Town Centre. The first pub built by the brewers Watney Mann in Wales, it was designed by J H Threaves & Son of Newport in conjunction with Gordon Redfern and opened 1965.

Figure 24: The Crow's Nest Public House, Llanyravon, opened 1964.

6.4 Education

Despite the designation of the New Town and the establishment of the Cwmbrân Development Corporation, Monmouthshire County Council held responsibility for education and the building of new schools within the town. The 1944 Education Act, stipulating secondary education for all, had still to be implemented in the area with no senior school available and only one grammar school at Pontypool. There were several existing Victorian junior schools in the area which, as the designation prompted the provision of new educational facilities, would become redundant in the New

Town. Croesyceiliog Infant School, The Highway (a private nursery) and St Dials School, Oak Street (demolished) were two brick-built school complexes in the Gothic style of the late-nineteenth century. The last was designed by E. A. Landsdowne and opened in 1874 with an adjoining master's house. The similarly built Upper Cwmbrân infant school was reused as 'The Learning Zone' from 2008 to 2011, while the nearby junior school was replaced by a Community Education and Advisory Centre building in the 1970s.

A total of four secondary modern schools were proposed, all located on the boundaries of the neighbourhoods they served: Llantarnam School served Oakfield and part of St Dials, Llanfrechfa, Ponthir and Caerleon; Green Meadow School

Figure 25: Croesyceiliog Infant School, now the Two Counties Nursery.

Figure 26: The Grammar School and Secondary Modern Campus, Croesyceiliog, later combined to form Croesyceiliog Comprehensive School.

served part of St Dials and Coedeva; Springvale School served Pontnewydd, the northern half of Greenmeadow and a third part of St Dials; and Croesyceiliog School served north Croesyceiliog and Llanyravon.

Llantarnam School was the first 'secondary modern', opening in 1955 and designed by the Monmouthshire County Council architects department led by Colin Jones.[78] The complex consisted of a central hall with full-height glazing and long classroom ranges with plentiful lighting provided by bands of continuous glazing set below shallow pitched roofs with deep eaves supported on brick piers. The caramel brickwork, light and airy feel, and the clock tower all became characteristic of the county's style.

In addition to the secondary modern, the campus at Croesyceiliog was designed with two single-sex grammar schools and a technical school. This site was chosen because of its isolation from both railways and industry, and accessibility from several neighbourhoods. However, only a co-ed grammar and the secondary modern were built, later combined to form Croesyceiliog Comprehensive. The grammar school soon excelled itself; on opening in 1959 it was described as one of the best-equipped grammar schools built by any authority in England and Wales since the war and it gained an equally good reputation for its teaching.[79] Designed by assistant County Architect T. E. Moore, it was on the whole consistent with the design of Llantarnam, though the rear classroom ranges were developed with the use of steel framing to form the curtain walls so popular in school design of the 1960s.

Hollybush Secondary School, built 1961, also maintained the county style but Fairwater Comprehensive, built between 1969 and 1971 by the then County Architect Sydney Leyshon, shows a radical change in approach.[80] Of a darker brickwork, only single or two-storeyed and with less expansive glazing, the site feels more inward looking and lacking the airy feeling of the earlier schools. The north-east part of the site was given over to leisure facilities that were designed for community use

Figure 27: Fairwater Comprehensive School, opened 1971, illustrated a radical change in direction in school design by the County Architects Department.

after school hours, both maintaining the CDC's early ideas for the schools to double up as adult education/improvement facilities and the CUDC's strategy of using the schools' sporting facilities to meet the need of leisure opportunities.

The CDC and Monmouthshire County Council had developed the idea of community colleges, in which school buildings could be opened in the evening as 'village colleges' providing adult education from the start. In a step further, separate adult wings were incorporated into the West Pontnewydd Primary and Croesyceiliog secondary modern to facilitate both recreational and educational activities for adults.[81]

The principles of education planning in Cwmbrân were to place new infant and junior schools as close to each neighbourhood centre as possible. This ensured schools would be easily accessible from local homes and the neighbourhood shopping centre, allowing school drop-offs/pick-ups and shopping to be combined, and keeping schools away from larger roads encircling the neighbourhoods. Their prominent locations within local communities would both highlight new architect-designed buildings and encourage use outside school hours for adult education classes and other social uses.

The first new primary school, opened in 1955, was Mount Pleasant Primary School, West Pontnewydd. Again designed by County Architect Colin Jones, the two-storey, double T-plan structure has been described as 'formal' for primary architecture with the caramel brickwork, continuous bands of glazing and copper clad roofing mirroring Llantarnam Secondary.[82] Similarly, it set the tone for light, airy primary school surrounded by open, grassy, grounds. Llanyrafon Primary and Croesyceiliog Junior and Infant, both built in the mid-1950s by Jones, are built in a similar idiom, though increasingly with single-storey classroom ranges and flat roofs. This was further developed at Ysgol Gymraeg, St Dials, between 1960 and 1961, where the complex was entirely single-storey with flat roofs, daylight being provided by clerestory glazing. Jones deviated from his usual material at Oakfield Primary School (now demolished), using corrugated zinc cladding to the low schoolroom ranges in contrast to the brickwork central tower.

Maendy County Primary School, also opened in 1961, was the first to be designed by a private practice, Richards & Trollope.[83] Here the complex can be seen in two distinct parts, one interestingly following the county style established by this date, but incorporating a two-storey, curtain-walled range of a type that was to become dominant in school buildings of the 1960s. Coed Eva Junior and Infant School, destroyed by fire in 2016, also designed by a private practice, Stephen Thomas of Newport between 1964 and 1967, was less ambitious.[84] Woodland Junior and Infant, built between 1975 and 1977, follows the style set by Fairwater Comprehensive; a single-storey complex of darker brick, its courtyard form faces largely in towards its central spaces. By the time the Development Corporation was wound up in March 1988, more than 10,400 new school places had been provided in Cwmbrân.[85]

Figure 28: The Oakfield Primary School, built 1955–57 in the 'county style' created by Colin Jones of the Monmouthshire County Architects Department, but distinguished by the use of zinc cladding.

Figure 29: The Woodlands Road Primary School, 1977, continuing the development in compact design set by Fairwater Comprehensive School.

A college of further education, stipulated in the Master Plan, was not built during the time the New Town corporation was functioning. However, it may eventually be realised in 2020, when building of what is now described by the Local Education Authority as the Torfaen Learning Zone is planned to be completed and opened. This £24 million learning centre, run by Coleg Gwent, is due to deliver the English medium A-level provision for Torfaen. The complex was designed by Boyes Rees Architects (a now defunct Cardiff practice) to meet the specified current standards of 'accessibility and social inclusion'.[86]

6.5 Health

As with other public services, health-care allocation was tiered in the planning of the New Town to allow suitably devolved provision to be made in each of the neighbourhoods. Maternity and child welfare clinics, day nurseries and nursery schools were proposed for each neighbourhood, with a larger town centre health clinic to provide additional services.

The New Town Centre was located only two and a half miles away from the County Hospital sited to the north at Griffithstown, which at the time of designation was being planned to be expanded and upgraded. A new hospital was also to be established at nearby Pontllanfraith. Therefore, it was not expected that Cwmbrân would have a hospital, although the Master Plan earmarked a suitable site at Llanfrechfa Grange should it be required. This site was eventually adopted in 2017, when construction started on the £350 million Grange University Hospital developed by the Aneurin Bevan Health Board. Designed by BDP, this complex is intended to be an exemplar of new health-care delivery, the brief being to allow the facilities to be 'flexible, adaptable and expandable' and designed as far as possible around patient and staff flows. The buildings are also designed to be carefully connected to the environment, exploiting views and the countryside setting for the well-being of both patients and staff.[87]

Figure 30: Croesyceiliog Health Centre, Brynhyfryd Road.

The first health centre in the New Town was located in the Town Centre. Though the site was agreed as early as 1954, sketch plans were not prepared until 1958 and, after the designs were modified several times, building works started in 1959.[88] Neighbourhood clinics were made available at Croesyceiliog, West Pontnewydd, Oakfield and Fairwater between 1960 and 1967, the last also having a doctor's surgery adjacent. These were on the whole single-storey, utilitarian brickwork buildings typified by those still extant at Maendy Square and Brynhyfryd Road.

6.6 Housing

When the New Town was designated, there were already some 3,500 dwellings in the area, 937 of which were local authority houses recently built by Cwmbrân Urban District Council and Pontypool Rural District Council.[89] The remainder were largely nineteenth-century workers houses of brick or stone concentrated in the historic villages of Pontnewydd, Cwmbrân and Oakfield, with a small number of sixteenth to nineteenth century farmhouses and gentry houses.

The designated area was divided into seven residential neighbourhoods – Pontnewydd (including Northville), Croesyceiliog North, Croesyceiliog South (later renamed Llanyravon), Oakfield, St Dials, Coed Eva and Greenmeadow

Figures 31 & 32: Terraced workers' housing, Tŷ Newydd Road, Pontnewydd, and Victoria Street, Oakfield.

– with others developed as the Master Plan was refined and the target population and designated area grew. House building was the main focus for the Cwmbrân Development Corporation (CDC) initially, the need to build large numbers of houses as quickly, and as at a reasonable cost as possible represented in their target to build an average of 500 a year.

Unlike many of the New Towns, which as completely new developments were given a remit of ensuring multi-class communities attracting a cross-section of society, at Cwmbrân it was recognised that the high amount of existing industry and lack of office work made this ideal difficult. With no new industry built, there would be no new management attracted to the area and therefore the housing focused on types the CDC knew would be in demand. Early efforts concentrated on building dwellings that could be let as cheaply as possible to working class families, with only limited amounts of better housing for rent or sale constructed. The CDC faced additional difficulties with the Pontypool Rural and Cwmbrân Urban District Councils (PRDC and CUDC), both of which had been proactive in building local authority housing from the 1930s. Construction of the Clarksville estate at Pontnewydd was in progress when war broke out, while the families of the

Girling-factory war workers were living in pre-fabs built ten years previously; the CUDC was keen to progress with building schemes in relation to both projects. This led to the prospect of CDC and District Council schemes being developed side by side within the designated area. With the CDC having no control over those built by the councils, a working relationship had to be developed quickly. Initially this was somewhat haphazard; the first houses let by the CDC houses were on an inherited CUDC scheme on Yew Tree Terrace, Croesyceiliog, in an area under the authority of the PRDC and adjacent to houses constructed and rented out by them.[90]

The first full CDC housing scheme was at Tŷ Newydd and comprised 40 three-bedroom houses, with a small number of four-bedroom houses and flats. Aware of the need to get a scheme up and running to show that the New Town was underway, and that a chief architect had not yet been appointed, the CDC commissioned Minoprio & Spencely to design the estate.[91] Short terraces of brick-built houses with a coloured cement wash, the scheme was relatively unambitious, similar to nearby local authority estates.

Figure 33: Tŷ Newydd Avenue, the Tŷ Newydd development, Pontnewydd.

With the appointment of J. C. P. West later in 1950, a strategy was implemented that would build 400 in each of the next two years, rising to 750 in the years following. The need to produce houses quickly and cheaply meant that compromises were made, particularly on the 'higher value' schemes at Croesyceiliog, with criticism that the Chief Architect had 'allowed the urgency for housing to override some of his views on aesthetics and preliminary planning'.[92] West's aim to achieve his intimate and cosy atmosphere with these early schemes was also compromised by the rapid increase in car ownership, the importance placed on the integrated landscaping sacrificed to the increasing need for parking provision.

With no local contractors capable of fulfilling the large building contracts, construction work largely fell to national firms such as George Wimpey and John Laing. Wimpey were also able to employ cost-effective methods such as the casting of 'no-fines' concrete house shells, whereas Laing introduced its 'Easiform' system.[93] As both systems depended on the mass building of similar houses, the CDC decided a lack of

variety could instead be surmounted by variations in fenestration, colour finishes and landscaping.

In 1952 a post-war shortage of softwood led Harold Macmillan, Minister of Housing and Local Government, to request an investigation into new building techniques that would reduce the amount of softwood required. The New Towns Committee tasked Cwmbrân, Harlow, Peterlee and Basingstoke to build a series of demonstration houses that tested new methodologies in house building using substitute materials. These were to be available for viewing by, and the experiences of residents reported to, local authorities and other housing building groups. The focus was on using cost-equivalent materials that could be gained from the UK or Commonwealth countries, and included the replacement of softwood joists with pre-stressed concrete and use of hardwood joinery where necessary.

Two terraces of houses were built at Pontnewydd, with two phases being completed: the first group of twelve (six and six) in December 1952, the second phase of eight in May 1953. The first was of brick houses constructed demonstrating different techniques using prestressed beams, earthenware blocks, hardwood, chipboard and bitumen roofing in differing forms. The second terrace of 'New Tradition' houses were of concrete construction (including window frames and skirting board) similarly displaying these different options. Reactions from the tenants were gathered soon after occupation, with the majority relating to the non-traditional layouts of the houses – open staircases, single reception rooms running the depth of the house, storage – rather than the construction details.[94]

As a result of these cost-savings, the housing schemes built through much of the 1950s across Pontnewydd, Croesyceiliog, Llanyravon and Oakfield were on the whole uninspiring, varying only in size and quality of finish with the occasional detailing, such as stone finished porches at Oakfield, distinguishing them from local authority schemes. There were smaller numbers of higher quality houses built for sale or let to management staff, including those working for the CDC. One of the earliest and most successful schemes was Crown Road, Llanyravon. Here, on estates such as Bath Green, the Chief Estate Officer argued that people who would previously oversee the construction of a custom-built house, would now be willing to purchase high-standard properties on small estates.[95] Other schemes proved less successful, particularly where private and rented housing was mixed to create the cross-class communities idealised by the New Town Committee, and by 1953 the CDC was 'finding in common with other New Towns that areas for private development should be for preference be physically separate from areas being developed by the Corporation with standard house types'.[96] As the market for private housing became saturated, developments where land had been included for development by private companies, such as The Plantation, failed to attract investors with the CDC taking on more of this development themselves.

Figure 34: The Cwmbran Development Corporation housing scheme at Green Willows, Oakfield neighbourhood.

Tensions between the CDC and their tenants were caused by the need for the CDC to maintain its accounts in credit, and its rents being consequently higher than those of local authority houses in the designated area. Rent rises during the recession of 1958-59 were particularly unpopular. Despite this, tenants were on the whole impressed with the standards of housing, willing to accept modern developments that came into play such as 'through' living rooms, the omission of fireplaces in the bedrooms, for the quality of fixtures and fittings, and the spacious layouts of the estates. Such properties were a substantial improvement on the nineteenth-century dwellings and pre-war local authority housing and, the CDC argued, the quality of building was vastly superior to that being undertaken by the PRDC and CUDC at the time.

One feature of the early estates that did cause concern relatively quickly was the lack of garages and other parking provision. The rise of car ownership in the 1960s was unforeseen and, when it occurred, space for additional parking was difficult to find.

One early exception from the terraces of these neighbourhoods was Northville, marked to be an intermediary between the town centre and the suburbs and therefore designed to be deliberately more 'urban' in character. With higher-density housing, a greater focus on flats, maisonettes and buildings of up to four storeys, the 71-acre scheme was distinct in style and concept from the rest of the Pontnewydd neighbourhood. Perhaps it is not surprising that the planning permissions for each phase of this scheme were also more fraught with difficulties.[97] By the time a similar scheme to the south of the Town Centre, Southville, was developed in the early 1960s, however, the percentage of flats and maisonettes was even higher. Large blocks of four-storey flats were deliberately placed along St David's road, the main approach road from the south to the Town Centre, as a statement of the architectural impact of the development.[98]

In 1961 the target population was officially raised to 45,000, while in 1962 West resigned as Chief Architect to be replaced by the younger, and more radical, Gordon Redfern. Redfern

Figure 35: The higher-density housing scheme at Northville, immediately north of the Town Centre.

was an advocate of the Radburn planning system, originated in the United States of America to deal with increasing car ownership through segregating the motor car from the pedestrian. This was first and most rigidly implemented at Fairwater, partially designed before Redfern's appointment, and one of the first schemes of the 1960s. A complete break from the layout of earlier estates, this segregated access for vehicles and pedestrians, higher-density housing and layout of courts and cul-de-sacs remained a feature of Redfern's housing throughout his tenure. From July 1962 while planning Fairwater III, Redfern also insisted all housing in the south-western areas of St Dials, Coedeva, Greenmeadow and Fairwater were to meet Parker Morris standards. This increased the quality of housing, but also construction costs with some 'utility' houses subsequently introduced through the removal of some 'optional' internal fittings that tenants could add themselves if required.[99]

In addition to the layout of houses, Redfern radically altered the design of dwellings. Fairwater, Greenmeadow, St Dials and Coedeva neighbourhoods were characterised by innovation and diversity in construction and form, with white rendered exteriors enhanced with pre-fabricated panels in a range of timber and stone materials, large windows to the rear elevations and the use of flat, or shallow mono-pitched roofs.

These designs, possibly inspired by Eric Lyons's Span estates, all gave a greater architectural interest and visual diversity, but the roofs in particular were problematic, with those at Fairwater III (one of the few schemes to be designed by an external architectural practice, Alex Gordon and Partners, (Cardiff, formerly T Alwyn Lloyd & Gordon) requiring remedial treatment for damp within two years.[100] The percentage of flats also increased on these schemes, adding further visual diversity in comparison to the overwhelmingly two-storey landscapes of earlier neighbourhoods, although problems with finding tenants to whom to let these properties re-emerged and numbers were curtailed again in the late 1960s. Two more successful high-rise schemes, and among the more radical, were Monmouth House and The Tower in the Town Centre, which both opened in 1967. The former, along with flats at the north end of the Town Centre, was an attempt to bring more life to the district during the evenings, while the second (for many years the tallest residential building in Wales) acted as a visual marker within the town for locals and visitors alike. Both were designed by Gordon Redfern.

With Coedeva III in 1966 marking the point at which the 45,000 target population would be accommodated, the expansion of the designated area and population target were under discussion from 1965 before a target of 55,000 was

Figure 36: The staggered, flat-roofed terraces of Greenmeadow neighbourhood.

Figure 37: The Tower, Cwmbrân's high-rise residential block which also acted as a marker to the centre of the new town.

agreed in 1968, though the CDC continued to push for 75,000.[101] House building continued to be in the south-western and western areas, although because of the industrial crisis and the reorganisation of Welsh counties in the early 1970s, work on this expansion was slow to get underway, with the focus on completing Coedeva and Greenmeadow. The first new neighbourhood planned was Hollybush, the layout put forward in 1971 with the standard layout for segregation of vehicles and pedestrians. This was reconsidered the following year after the CDC decided that increasing car ownership meant residents wanted direct access to their front doors by car, and a mixer-court layout was adopted providing parking for two cars at each house.[102] This layout was then adopted at all subsequent neighbourhoods. With the replacement of Gordon Redfern as Chief Architect by J. L. Berbiers, with J. L. Russell as his deputy, house design returned to something more traditional – brickwork with hipped tile roofs – though interesting visual variation continued to be implemented through the application of tile hanging or timber to the elevations. At Thornhill, a new split-level design incorporating a first-floor living room was introduced to deal with the increasingly steep topography of some of the new areas.

In 1971 the Right to Buy Act meant that the CDC started selling houses from its rented stock to sitting tenants at discounted rates. Demand was high, though varied according to neighbourhood with the more popular Croesyceiliog and Llanyravon seeing the highest number of enquiries. By the end of 1972, half of the housing stock in the eastern areas was

owner-occupied and by mid-1973 the CDC was complaining of a lack of housing. These sales were rapidly halted by the Labour government of 1974, though restarted after the 1980 Housing Act. During 1980, 227 houses built for rent were sold to sitting tenants, a figure that was surpassed in the first quarter alone of 1981 (266).[103]

Figure 38: The housing at Hollybush I.

South-western neighbourhoods at Hollybush and Thornhill were supplemented in the early 1970s by smaller developments such as Maes-y-Rhiw, with a larger expansion area at Henllys approved in 1977. The expansion area added development to existing neighbourhoods as well as developing new aeras such as Tŷ Canol and Henllys, but all showed the continuation of the traditional forms used at Thornhill, with widespread use of facing brickwork coloured to blend with the surroundings and conventionally pitched roofs.

Increasingly, private development in these areas was undertaken by volume house builders such as Barratt and Wimpey. By 1985 the CDC had built only half of the 2,000 houses it had intended in these areas and with the winding up of the CDC in view, sold the 221 acres (89 hectares) of remaining land to private developers.[104]

In June 1975 the CDC, in association with the Help the Aged Housing Association, started to assess and map its provision of dwellings suitable for older people in Cwmbrân, particularly in terms of sheltered accommodation. Although schemes had been implemented prior to this (such as the George Landsbury home and accompanying flatlets in Croesyceiliog), as a result of this assessment further schemes such as The Beeches sheltered housing development, Wesley Street, was opened two years later by the Borough of Torfaen. One of the most innovative and successful schemes was at Edlogan Way, where older persons' dwellings were integrated with thoughtfully-designed bungalows for disabled tenants. In May 1979 a county-wide conference on provision for the elderly was hosted at County Hall, as a result of which a working party was established in March 1980.[105]

Figure 39: The Taliesin sheltered housing scheme, 1985, by MacCormac Jamieson and Prichard.

One of the last schemes which stood out was Taliesin, Forgeside, designed by London-based practice MacCormac Jamieson and Prichard, and completed in 1985. Built as a UK Housekeepers Association scheme in conjunction with the CDC, it provided fifty-eight flatlets and a warden's house arranged in a series of open-ended courtyards of increasing height from rear to front. This sensitively planned housing, which respects the privacy of residents, gives good pedestrian connections between the dwellings and offers panoramic views out over the surrounding landscape, has been considered a successful smaller reworking of Ralph Erskine's Byker wall, Newcastle, albeit on a much smaller scale.

By the time the CDC was wound up in 1986, it had built some 10,133 dwellings, 3,970 of which had been sold. The remainder were transferred to Torfaen County Borough Council in 1986.[106]

6.7 Industrial Buildings

The industrial history of Cwmbrân up to the designation of the New Town has been covered in the historical background (pp. 8-11). Little survives from the heavy industry of the nineteenth- and early-twentieth century, with later development of Cwmbrân having replaced much of his earlier industrial landscape.

Llanyrafon Mill may originate in the fourteenth century, but the earliest surviving documentation is from 1632. The current structure is largely eighteenth or nineteenth century, in which form the mill operated until bought by the Cwmbrân Development Corporation (CDC) in 1951. The interior machinery and fittings were destroyed in a fire in 1971, but the external cast iron waterwheel survives.[107]

Figure 40: Llanyravon Mill, an eighteenth-/nineteenth-century structure on the site of a earlier mill.

An early nineteenth-century lime kiln is preserved at Tŷ Coch, Two Locks, associated with limestone quarries at Henllys. Operational until 1880, its remains were consolidated and conserved in the late twentieth century and are listed Grade II.[108] Some structures at the Conwy works at Pontrhydyrun survive in a derelict state, but nothing survives from other large industrial works. The GKN Cwmbrân Nut and Bolt Works have made way for the late twentieth-century Cwmbrân Retail Park; the Vitriol works have been overbuilt by the Oldbury Road Industrial Estate; and the Oakfield Wire Works has been redeveloped as the Tŷ Coch Industrial Estate.

While sections of the canal within the town centre were infilled, large stretches through Pontnewydd, Two Locks and Tŷ Coch survive. At Tŷ Coch two aqueducts carry the Monmouthshire Canal over the Dowlais Brook.[109] South of the town, four hump-back, rubblestone canal bridges can be found at Tredegar Lock, Shop Lock, Rachels Lock and Top Lock.[110] All these associated structures are Grade II listed. There are no physical remains of the tramroads, though many lines are fossilized within later footpath systems.

Initially the CDC was prohibited from allowing new industry to establish in Cwmbrân in order to protect the labour levels. An exception seems to have been CWS Bakeries, which commenced building in 1954.[111] Existing industries were encouraged to expand however, GKN, British Nylon Spinners and Alfa Laval all extending their complexes. Perhaps the most significant building was that for the Girling Engineering School in Grange Road, built 1958-1959 and designed by Clifford Tee & Gale.[112] Part of this complex has been incorporated into the current Meritor Inc site with part demolished. The same architectural practice completed the new offices for Saunders Valve Company, also Grange Road, c.1961, now also demolished.[113] Although heavy industry continued to be discouraged through the 1960s, the Board of Trade relaxed terms to allow development of service industry and the establishment of the Avondale Industrial Estate in 1963 facilitated the building of a number of factories and workshops.[114] The CDC's strategy was to build advance units for easy occupation by prospective employers and the success of this policy was borne out as both Avondale and Forgehammer substantially increased levels of light industry. A particularly notable complex of ten unit factories of 2,000 sq. ft. (156 sq. m.) were built 1963-1964 at the Avondale Estate, designed by Newport architects, Powell and Alport.[115] Built of pale brickwork, the units were aesthetically lifted by a series of advanced, mono-pitched roofed, bays but have since been demolished.

Figure 41: The Girling Engineering School, Grange Road, designed by Clifford Tee & Gale.

Discussions around the increase in Cwmbrân's target population in the later 1960s included an allocation of a further 100 acres (40 hectares) for new industry. This caused tension between the CDC and The Board of Trade which wanted no part of the designated area to impinge on the South Wales Special Development Area boundary that had been cemented in 1966 to assist the South Wales Valley, with the Ministry of Labour reiterating that new industry was not to be encouraged. Uncertainty continued through the end of the 1960s and concern was increased by the closure of GKN in 1971.

Figure 42: Examples of the 'Advance Factories' built by the CDC at the Springvale Industrial Estate.

In a change of policy, the CDC bought the GKN site and extended its strategy of pre-allocation building to larger factory units, designed to attract larger manufacturing companies, at the Springvale Industrial Estate established on part of the site. Designed by J. L. Russell, a CDC style of dark green corrugated metal buildings with saw-tooth roofs was established. The Somerset Street Estate was approved in 1975, though the Ty Coch Estate was initially blocked. The CDC increased efforts to advertise Cwmbrân as an industrial destination, including touring six American cities in 1976 to promote investment.[116] The town's locational advantage, increased by the building of the M4 and Severn Bridge, aided their work with investment from Alfa-Laval, GEC-Marconi, Renishaw, Hoffman Engineering Co. and Nimbus Records marking Cwmbrân as 'an oasis of employment in the desert of the Eastern valley'.[117] The Alfa-Laval factory (Now Festive Productions) by Keith Mainstone of the Percy Thomas Partnership and GEC-Marconi (now offices for the South Wales Ambulance Service) by Russell after leaving the CDC, both at Tŷ Coch, are of particular note.[118]

Figure 43: The former GEC-Marconi building, the Tŷ Coch Estate.

After securing orders for large factories from Girling and Ferranti in 1978, the CDC argued that more land was desperately needed for industrial development and it requested land at Llantarnam, previously earmarked for UWIST, be approved for development. This lay outside the designated area, but as unemployment increased owing to job cuts in the steel industry, a 53-acre development was agreed. Llantarnam Industrial Park Phase I consisted of smaller units, the first occupied in June 1981. Owing to concerns that the CDC was replicating work carried out elsewhere by the Welsh Development Agency, subsequent efforts focused on producing more expensive, but sophisticated units to attract high technology industries.[119] Raglan House was approved in February 1983 and, providing a series of small tech units, was immediately successful in attracting companies. With further units provided from 1984, the park now comprises a group of well-designed tech buildings, including Tŷ Gwent and Brecon House, set amongst well-designed and attractive landscaping.

Figure 44: Brecon House, Llantarnam Business Park, one of the units which marked Cwmbrân's development as a destination for high-tech industry.

As the CDC's existence drew to an end, it worked to ensure future economic success. A survey was carried out into the needs of future employers, and recommendations were provided for refurbishing older estates. It continued to develop units at Springvale, Court Road, Tŷ Coch and Llantarnam until all estates were handed over to the Welsh Development Agency in October 1987.

6.8 Public and Recreational Buildings

The 'Central Building' was to be one of the key attractions of Cwmbrân Town Centre located on Gwent Square, though early in the planning stages it was unclear quite what facilities this building should provide. Initially the CDC was advised not to try anything 'too serious' but something to liven up the town centre after shopping hours, and in the difficulty of deciding the nature of the building and how it would be funded, the scheme was put on hold. Negotiations around the functions and design of this building restarted with the appointment of Gordon Redfern as Chief Architect in 1962, the CDC, CUDC and Monmouthshire County Council all with different priorities. While need for a town library was identified, the County Council argued that other parts of the county were

more in need, and while a central town hotel was desirable no willing developer could be found. By 1967 agreement was made on two developments: the central building with offices, shops, library, public house, meeting rooms and exhibition halls, and a conference hall and theatre. Gwent House was completed between 1971 and 72, the central library occupying the first floor, and a series of three pubs catering for a range of tastes and ages.[120]

The CDC was initially keen to have a cinema as part of the Town Centre, but by 1969 stated it had abandoned hope of trying to find developers interested in providing one. In 1971 agreement was made for the development of a supermarket, over which would be built a three-screen cinema 'of the latest design' that could also be used for other entertainments such as bingo and as a social club, with a car park below. At the south-eastern corner of the Town Centre the Scene 123 Cinema opened in November 1972 fulfilling a long-awaited recreational need. Although changing hands, the interior of the cinema is said to remain unaltered, being possibly the only UK cinema with a downward mirror periscope projection system serviced from a large projection room directly above the cinemas still in place.[121] The cinema closed in 2013, having been superseded by the larger, more modern cinema on Glyndŵr Road.

Figures 45 & 46: The Scene 123 Cinema, now closed, and The Congress Theatre, over-clad in the early 1980s with the addition of the figures of 'Dai' and 'Myfanwy'.

The Town Centre recreational complex was completed with the opening of the Congress Theatre, also in 1972, a Brutalist-style building that was contemporaneous with the development of other post-war theatres across Wales, including Theatr y Werin, Aberystwyth (1970-1972) and Theatr Ardudwy, Harlech (1973).[122] The concrete façade was later rendered and adorned with the current 'Dai and Myfanwy'.

At a community level, recreational activities were becoming an issue as, by the mid-sixties, Cwmbrân's demography was dominated by families with older children who were becoming discontented with the lack of social and recreational facilities. The adult educational evening classes and community colleges were becoming an outdated concept, unappealing to the younger generation, and keeping these younger people entertained was a particular problem.[123] In 1964 a report prepared on social facilities in Cwmbrân noted that religious attendance, and therefore the community activity associated with church and chapel, was declining, community colleges were catering for only a small section of the residents and few of the community associations who had attempted to provide social activities within the neighbourhoods had had any long-lasting success.[124]

Much of the recreational strategy had focused on parks, playing fields and other sporting activities. A public swimming baths had long been part of the plans for the Civic Group at the south end of the Town Centre. However, because of the ongoing negotiations between the Cwmbrân Development Corporation (CDC) and Cwmbrân Urban District Council (CUDC) around funding and who would take long-term responsibility for the pool, plans for the facility languished. In 1966 the CUDC stated their policy was to instead provide swimming facilities to the public by opening up the sports facilities of the various secondary schools.[125] A U-turn in 1967 led to them requesting Redfern to design the facility for them, but further problems with finding funding vetoed the plans in 1969.[126] Public swimming facilities were finally provided as part of the successful Cwmbrân Stadium and Sports Centre of 1967-73. The grandstand, the raked seating raised on a ground floor brick building and sheltered by a sloped roof and glazed panels to either end, overlooks international-standard athletics track and playing fields that include home ground of Cwmbrân Football Club. To the rear the sports centre, designed by Dale Owen of the pre-eminent Percy Thomas Partnership, contained a swimming pool, sauna, sports hall and squash courts all opened in 1974.[127]

A number of community halls were provided within neighbourhoods at the request of the tenants, the first built between 1961 and 1962 at Pontnewydd as a result of lobbying by the tenant's association. Further halls followed at Greenmeadow, Fairwater and Coedeva, and are among some of the more architecturally diverse community buildings in Cwmbrân. A higher level of community recreational facilities was provided at the Woodland Road Social centre opened in 1973. This was carried out by Pontypool Rural District Council with funding from the CDC, and comprised a concert hall, changing rooms and terrace overlooking tennis courts, a bowling green and playing field. [128]

In May 1964 Llantarnam Grange farmhouse was restored to provide a combined centre for clubs and societies to use and arts centre. The old gardens were incorporated into the scheme and the whole was seen as a way of incorporating Cwmbrân's history into the area.

Figure 47: Cwmbrân Stadium, Oakfield, *c.*1960.

6.9 Religious Buildings

Lying within the monastic manor of Magna Porta and Llantarnam Abbey, the only surviving Medieval religious building is St Michael's and All Angels, Llantarnam. The earliest parts of this church date from the twelfth and thirteenth centuries, represented in the fabric of the nave, with some relevant documentation found in the Valor Ecclesiasticus of 1535.[129] The church has undergone several expansions and alterations, including a major overhaul in Tudor styling, presumably dating from its re-designation as a parish church after the dissolution of Llantarnam Abbey in 1536. A programme of Victorian restoration was carried out by E. A. Lansdowne in 1869-70.[130]

The parishes of Llanfrechfa and Llantarnam were well served by the Incorporated Church Building Society (ICBS) in the nineteenth century. The ICBS had been established as part of the Church Building Act in 1818, passed in response to the particularly poor provision of Anglican churches in newly industrialised areas, and the corresponding growth of the Nonconformist denominations. The ICBS managed grants of up to £20,000, which were made to cover all or part of a new building project, though the average amount donated was only usually between £100 and £1,000.[131]

In the Cwmbrân area, grants were provided towards the new churches of Holy Trinity, Pontnewydd, as a new parish church, and St Gabriel at Llantarnam. Holy Trinity, Mount Pleasant Road (1857-60) was designed by the practice of Prichard and Seddon.[132] The ICBS was specific in advocating that Gothic architecture was to be used for all funded churches, and the design here is an interpretation of the Decorated Gothic style with characteristic polychromatic stonework and decorated detailing that is more authentically Medieval than many Victorian churches of a similar date. The church has been described as having 'quirky individuality and scholarly reference'.[133] In 1887-90 a further ICBS grant was provided to enlarge this church, with E. M. Bruce Vaughan designing the added north aisle.

St Gabriel, Old Cwmbrân, is a later foundation constructed for the most part in stages between 1907 and 1915. The grant for this church was allocated in 1904, possibly in response to the Nonconformist 'Great Revival' of the same year, and the chancel and south chapel were built in 1907-08.[134] The first two bays of the nave were constructed in 1914-15 after which work ceased because of the war, and the building was not completed until the 1950s in the time of the Development Corporation. Designed by F. R. Kempson, the Decorated Gothic style continued to be used in finishing the building with the original plan adhered to.[135]

Re-establishment of the Catholic faith in the area came about in the late eighteenth, early nineteenth century, boosted by the Irish immigrants who came to work in the various industries. This growth led to the founding of a mission in 1864 by Rev. Elzear Torreggiani, the Franciscan mission priest at Pontypool. Mass was conducted at first in a bakery off Spring Street, then the Forge and Hammer Hotel. Eventually a plot of land was leased and an iron church seating 250 built at a cost of £180. Dedicated to Our Lady of the Angels the iron chapel was replaced by a stone building opened in May 1883, designed by M. Andre of Horsham and built by William Jones & Son Newport. The first resident priest was attached in 1908 and in 1928 a parish hall was constructed adjacent to the church.[136]

The earliest Nonconformist cause, and chapel, in the area is the Penywaun Independent Chapel. Meetings of the cause took place from the late seventeenth century though, unusually, the first chapel was not built until 1819, meetings to this point taking place in houses or other secular buildings.[137] The chapel is built in the early vernacular, lateral-fronted, style common from the Act of Toleration, 1689, to the early nineteenth century. These chapels, wider than they were deep, were designed to allow people to hear the preacher in a central pulpit, worship focusing on the aural 'Word' than the visual ritualism of the established church. The only other chapel surviving in this style is Ebenezer Primitive Methodist chapel built in 1840 and extended in 1865 to provide a gallery.

Figures 48 & 49: St Gabriel's Church, Pontnewydd, and Pontrhydyrun Baptist Chapel, Croesyceiliog.

Bethel Independent Chapel, built in 1837, is a square, hipped-roof chapel. This was a development away from the simple vernacular buildings of the early Nonconformists, moving towards something that was more recognisably non-domestic and was built in relatively small numbers before falling out of fashion. Its tall, round-headed windows light a gallery that easily increased the seating capacity.[138]

Elim Congregational Chapel was started as a daughter chapel of Penywaun in 1844 serving the village of Cwmbrân and is more typical of the simple gable-fronted chapel of the date.[139] Using simple elements of classical styling, including round-headed windows, a moulded stringcourse to the pediment and a particularly fine Greek revival doorcase, the chapel marks itself more confidently as a Nonconformist place of worship.

The first Baptist cause was established at Pontrhydyrun in 1802 by George Conway of the Pontrhydyrun tinplate works. The first chapel was built in 1816, but rebuilt on the current, grander scale in 1836. Costing £2,000, this is an exemplar of the Classical style favoured by all the Nonconformist denominations in Wales through to the second half of the nineteenth century, and for many beyond that, the Gothic style being too associated with the Church of England and Catholic churches. The interior has been altered a number of times throughout the nineteenth century, the gallery, pews and internal baptistry all replaced and heating, chandelier lighting and organ inserted. Despite Grade II* listing, the windows have been replaced in uPVC in the late twentieth century.[140]

There are a number of chapels dating from the 1840s through to the remainder of the nineteenth century. Further Baptist causes included Siloam, founded in 1838, Ebenezer built in 1860, Mount Pleasant Chapel built in 1876 and altered in 1891 and Richmond Road Chapel built in 1882.[141] The Wesleyan Methodist built their first chapel, Hope, in 1866 and the Wesley Street chapel in 1868, while the Primitive Methodists founded Ebenezer in 1840, rebuilt in 1865, and Hope in 1866.[142] All of these chapels are of the gable-fronted form and built using a simple Classical style involving the use of round arch windows of varying proportions. While some do include a slightly higher level of detailing, such as the pediment arch in the façade of Hope Wesleyan Methodist Chapel, the lack of any grander chapels in a fuller Classical style, or Gothic in the later nineteenth century is unusual, particularly in an industrial area, and is indicative of the fact that although the area was becoming increasingly industrialised in the later century, the settlement remained small. The vast majority are rendered or of stone with brick dressings, again perhaps unusual considering the local brick industry. Ebenezer Independent Chapel, 1899, is the only red brick chapel, using yellow brick for the dressings, and is designed using a vernacular style.[143]

The early twentieth century saw the building of a small number of new chapels including Bethania Congregational Chapel and Pontnewydd Gospel Hall, both in 1900.[144] The building of the first Calvinistic Methodist chapel, Trinity, does not appear to have been until 1905 which is unusual for the dominant denomination in Wales.[145] Almost certainly built owing to the 1904-05 Revival, it is again a relatively simple, gable-fronted building.

Within the designated area, the Cwmbrân Development Corporation (CDC) designated that sites for religious buildings would be sold at one-quarter of residential value, with all denominations of all faiths treated equally.[146] A Church Site Committee was formed in 1951 with representatives of the Roman Catholic and Nonconformist denominations, a second committee dealing with the Church in Wales established in the late 1960s. The committees administered the policies, ensuring that sites allocated were both appropriate to the needs of the applying congregation and in relation to existing congregations, avoiding, or dealing with, tensions between new and existing causes. An example of potential tensions rose in 1964, when the Minister of the Pontrhydyrun Baptist Church complained that the CDC had failed to follow due process in consulting the Religious Sites Committee over the allocation of sites for two new causes, a 'Mormon Temple' for the Church of Latter Day Saints (LDS) at Croesyceiliog and an Assemblies of God (AoG) Hall.[147] In permitting the siting of the LDS church some 200 yards from his existing Baptist church, he claimed that the CDC was allowing the 'piling up' of religious sites and failing to protect the interests of local congregations.[148] Technically the new Temple was some three yards outside the boundary of the designated area, the CDC therefore stating it had no jurisdiction over the planning application other than having been passed it as a matter of courtesy.

Dissatisfaction also arose between the CDC and denominations over the development of sites after allocation. In response to a New Town report carried out by the Evangelical Alliance in 1971, providing recommendations for Development Corporations in dealing with faith groups, the CDC voiced its frustrations regarding sites allocated to church groups that subsequently lay undeveloped for many years.[149] This included sites for an Anglican church at Fairwater and a Catholic site at Fairhill, both of which had become overgrown in the intervening years.[150] Interest from other groups was initially high; the site for the AoG was discussed between 1958 and 1964, when it was agreed to sell land at the junction of Henllys Way and Belle Vue Avenue.[151] An application for a building on the site was received in this year and in 1970 the site was described as 'defined' for the AoG.[152] A site was also requested for a Jehovah's Witness Hall at Forge Hammer, the site of which next to Woodside House was considered unsuitable. It was decided to look for a more suitable site in the south-western areas, where, in 1965, an application from the Monmouthshire English Baptist Association was submitted for a new chapel.[153] None of these buildings appears to have been progressed.

A small number of new religious buildings were built within the New Town. The Wesleyan Methodist circuit was the most proactive building both the Fairhill Methodist church (later designated a shared church with the Church in Wales) and Llanyrafon Methodist Church.

A request for a site for a new Methodist church in Llanyravon was received in 1955, when the Presbyterian church was also considering the neighbourhood for a new building, and meetings were held in houses or other buildings from 1957. Designs for the Llanyravon Church were submitted in May 1959 by architect W. H. Cripps, Oxford and contractors Messrs Taveners, Newport, though comments by the planning committee that the church should be made more dominant than the Sunday School and that a steeple may be preferable to a tower led to revised designs being submitted in September 1959. The modified plans were subsequently deemed by the Planning Committee to be less attractive, however, and the original plans approved. The stone laying ceremony took place on 24 September 1960, with the church opening the following September. The cost was £22,245, with £6,000 donated by the Rank Benevolent fund, £1,000 by the Methodist chapel department and £15,000 from sales of chapels at Abersychan and Pontypool.[154]

Figure 50: The programme for the opening of Llanyravon Methodist Church, 1961.

Fairhill Methodist Church was built in 1964-65 in the northern part of the Fairwater neighbourhood. This replaced the Wesley Street Chapel at Oakfield, which was both in poor repair and due to be demolished for road widening by the CDC, the change in location reflecting the need to serve the new populations in the western and south-western districts. The site was donated by the CDC with the proviso of retaining as much of the woodland as possible outside of the building footprint.[155] By 1967, when the then Minister, Rev. R Bamford, left his post to be replaced by only a supernumerary, he described himself as the only Christian minister covering the 10,000 population of the area and church as having a very strong Sunday School.[156] Both of brick, the Llanyravon chapel is more architecturally ambitious, but the exaggerated, though simple, gable roofline of the Fairhill chapel with its simple cross makes an equally bold visual focal point within its neighbourhood.

In September 1964 the CDC received an enquiry from the Church of the Latter Day Saints about use of The Grange for

Figure 51: Fairhill Methodist Church, Fairwater.

services. Presumably this was a temporary measure, as a site for a new LDS church had already been assigned by this date as outlined in the complaint from the Minister of the Pontrhydyrun Baptist Church.[157] The denomination uses set

Figure 52: The Church of Jesus Christ of Latter Day Saints, Croesyceiliog.

designs based on congregation size and type, a typology that has evolved throughout the twentieth- and early twenty-first century.[158] The example of Cwmbrân is one found across Wales and England during the 1950s and 1960s with similar examples in Wales from Rhyl and Rhiwbina.

With the continuance in growth of Catholic worshippers in the 1950s, in particular with a number of Polish settlers, a second mass centre was founded in Pontnewydd Community Hall. St David's Church was built on Avondale Road, opened in July 1961, and designed by F. R. Bates & Son of Newport and Cardiff. Built just before the Second Vatican Council (Vatican II), the interior layout is traditional but 'shows the influence of Basil Spence's design for Coventry Cathedral, then undergoing construction' and is since unaltered.[159] Our Lady of the Angels underwent internal reordering and was extended in 1972. This included a day chapel by Thomas Price of F. R. Bates, Son & Price, to all extent diocesan architects by this time.[160]

Fig 53: The pre-Vatican II interior of St David's Roman Catholic Church, Pontnewydd.

The Salvation Army Corps had been in Cwmbrân since 1883, meeting first in premises of Victoria Street and, from 1928, a building in Wesley Street. Looking to upgrade its premises, an application was made and a site reserved on Victoria Street/Grange Road in 1968.[161] The Corps instead decided to renovate its existing building in 1977-78, before completely building its current hall on the same site in 1994.

6.10 Transport Buildings and Structures

A railway line was built from Newport to Blaenavon in the 1850s running up the west bank of the river, with a second line, the Eastern Valley Line, from Newport to the Midlands and north in the 1870s. The two were joined by a short branch line. The area, before designation, was served by four existing railway stations: Llantarnam Junction, Cwmbrân, Upper Pontnewydd and Pontnewydd. The initial Cwmbrân station and Upper Pontnewydd stations were constructed by the Monmouthshire Railway and Canal Company, opening in 1852, though Cwmbrân station was superseded by a new

station the Great Western Railway built adjacent in 1880 on purchase of the company. Llantarnam and Lower Pontnewydd stations were both constructed by the Pontypool, Caerleon and Newport Railway, opening in December 1874. All were subsequently run by Great Western Railway before Lower Pontnewydd closed to passenger services in June 1958 and the others in April 1965. Goods services remained running at Lower Pontnewydd and Cwmbrân until May 1965, at Llantarnam until September 1963 and Upper Pontnewydd until April 1969.[162]

From this point Cwmbrân was served by the Pontypool and New Inn station to the north of Cwmbrân. The Central Cwmbrân station, lobbied for by the CDC at the designation of the New Town, finally opened in May 1986.

The canal by the time of the New Town was derelict, though legally still open for navigation. Despite Minoprio arguing it could provide an attractive walk through from Pontnewydd to Oakfield, the idea of recreational boating was not discussed, and the central section was removed entirely.

An improved road network was considered fundamental by the CDC to the success of the New Town. However, road building, as with schools, remained under the remit of Monmouthshire County Council, complicating the planning of new infrastructure. The seven neighbourhoods were to be linked by a ring road, 'The Parkway', with a series of roads radiating out from the town centre. The approach roads were also to be improved and realigned; the existing road from Cwmbrân to Pontnewydd was to be widened and improved, while a new Pontnewydd Drive to the north would go to the main trunk road, and Cwmbrân drive to the south.

Early focus was on building roads that would provide access to, and facilitate the building of, the neighbourhoods, those at West Pontnewydd, Llanyravon and Croesyceiliog built first through the early and mid-1950s. These were then joined to the Town Centre through routes such as Edlogan Way and Maendy Way, where work on St David's Road was completed by 1959. Llanfrechfa Way, linking Llanyravon to the Town Centre, was completed in 1961 with Henllys Way following in 1964. By 1966, all the main estate roads required for the initial neighbourhoods were completed.[163] Work was restarted after the expansion agreement, with concentration of those such as Greenforge Way, Thornhill Way and Hollybush Way throughout the 1970s,[164] and then the Henllys Expansion Area from 1982.[165]

The town centre traffic system was redesigned in 1963-64 to provide a one-way system, designed to create a safer and more efficient flow of traffic. This was carried out in conjunction with data from the Road Research Laboratory and, opened in December 1964, looked forward to estimated numbers of road users fourteen to sixteen years in the future.[166] Free parking within the centre was seen as a key factor in driving the commercial success of the town, provided through the creation of multi-storey car parks to the southern corners of the Town Centre and increasing underground car

Figure 54: The roundabout junction of Edlogan Way, a radial road from the eastern neighbourhoods, and Caradog Road, forming part of the town centre ring road, with St Davids Road, one of the main north-south thoroughfares.

parking to the blocks such as 8 and 9 completed in 1967.[167]

The diversion of Croesyceiliog with a new and improved stretch of the A4042 was completed in 1965. The southern approach road proved more problematic; work on the Llantarnam diversion and improvement for Cwmbrân Drive as the main southern approach road started in 1957-58 but by 1959 had been 'delayed'. Design work restarted in 1973-74, but commencement of ground works continued to be delayed, and by 1976 Phase II (linking the Town Centre northwards to the A4042) once again dropped off Gwent County Council's five-year Transport Policies and Programme Report.[168] Phase I was revised and downgraded to a single-carriageway road by 1979, and Stage 1 was finally opened on 11 March 1983.[169] Stage 2, making the final link between the Town Centre and the M4 to the south, was completed in November 1985.[170] Phase II was the subject of a public inquiry in 1983, stage 1 opening in May 1987, and the final stage in March 1988.[171] When the final CDC report was published in 1988, some 106.24 kilometres of road had been built within the designated area.[172]

Further tensions arose between the Cwmbrân Development Corporation, the Pontypool Rural District Council and the Cwmbrân Urban District Council regarding street names. The District Councils had generally chosen English names for new roads, such as Cocker Avenue and Clark Avenue, but from the beginning the CDC decided to adopt an approach of using Welsh-language names. The first scheme at Tŷ Newydd included Tŷ Newydd Road and Tŷ Newydd Close, but as naming continued into roads at West Pontnewydd and Croesyceiliog the District Councils suggested names be curtailed to those 'more pronounceable'.[173]

Figure 55: The central Bus Station, Gwent Square, dated between 1964 and 1971.

The central Bus Station and interchange, designed to sit in the north-east corner of the Town Centre as a large open area that would allow circular through access for buses and plenty of open space for pedestrians, opened in December 1964. The station was provided with eight stops, each furnished with a Mellor modular bus stop, all now removed and replaced with continuous canopies. However, owing to the fact that bus operators were not willing to circle the Town Centre once a one-way system traffic system had been implemented, a sub-station for northbound buses was also opened in General Rees Square in 1970.[174]

6.11 Open Spaces and Public Art

Open spaces in the form of retained pre-New Town landscape and newly created green areas were a vital part of the planning of Cwmbrân.

A study of the monastic landscape of Llantarnam Abbey and the manor of Porta Magna has been undertaken by Edward Proctor, assessing the potential survival of pre-Reformation landscapes in the current landscape.[175] Established in 1179 as a daughter abbey to Strata Florida, Ceredigion, Llantarnam Abbey was founded within a landscape that was already agriculturally productive. The exact extent and location of all the lands are unclear, but the *Taxatio Ecclesiastica* of 1291 suggest the abbey's heartlands were focused on the western floodplain of the Afon Lwyd with granges extending across to the uplands of Mynydd Maen.[176] The grange of Scybor Cwrt (centred around Court Farm) is mentioned in this document, its arable farming providing the abbeys second most valuable source of crop production.[177]

Ministers' Accounts of 1536-37 describe the Gelli-las Grange, formed by the low-lying alder woods of the Afon Lwyd floodplain, with a grange farm the Post-medieval successor to which Proctor suggests was remodelled as Llantarnam Grange (now Llantarnam Arts Centre). Proctor also equates 150 tithe-free acres extending along the wide plain of the Afon Lwyd on the tithe map of 1846 as the remains of the Gelli-las Grange, this area now largely built over by Cwmbrân, apart from the river meads next to the Afon Lwyd now used as playing fields. The grange of Scybor Cwrt lay to the south of Gelli-las, while the possible St Dials chapel is mooted as the centre of a third grange.[178]

The fullest record, describing the *meres* of Magna Porta, dates from 1634 and showed the manor estates of this date covered a similar range of topographies to the monastic lands. The majority of field systems existing prior to the designation of the New Town, however, come from remodelling of the landscape in the seventeenth and eighteenth centuries with increasing enclosure of wood-pasture and meadowlands.[179]

John Leland described Llantarnam as 'still standing in a wood' with the country of 'Base Venteland' around also 'welle plenished with woodes'.[180] The Scybor Cwrt grange is recorded as having a 30 acre coppice woodland variously named Le Therweis, Cae Thuren and Court Wood.[181] Court Wood is

depicted on Ordnance Survey (OS) mapping until the mid-twentieth century, after which it was over built by the Greenwillows area of Oakfield. Tranch Wood is also of proven early origin, recorded within the Ministers' Accounts of 1536-37. Coed Cored, West Pontnewydd and Maes-Mawr, Oakfield, both of which have been built over, and partially extant examples of woodland at Coed-waun-Fyr, Maes-y-Rhiw, Craig-Fawr in Thornhill and Mayrick-moel Wood in Coed Eva, are also suggested by Proctor as surviving abbey coppice woodland, supplemented by increased coppiced woods dating from the nineteenth century.[182]

The CDC was keen to retain woodlands in particular where possible, recognising their aesthetic and recreational value within the townscape. This varied from the small scale, such as the design of Oakfield shopping unit around the retention of a group of 'large fine trees' to the willingness to spend extra

Figure 56: The tithe map of the parish of Llanvihangel Llantarnam in the County of Monmouth, 1846.

money at Fairwater centre to create a car park within, and retaining, the attractive birch wood, and the retention of substantial areas of Greenmeadow and Graig Fawr woods as recreational space. Springvale Park was created from 57 acres (23 hectares) of Church Wood and reclaimed industrial ground to the east and west with green space also retained at the heart of old Cwmbrân in the northern half of St Dials, retaining field patterns that date back to the first edition OS map of 1881 at least and included the site of the possible St Dials chapel. The south-western area of this green space, including the site of the possible chapel is currently undergoing development for a housing estate.

In addition to the retained environment, a number of new parks were created with some 323 acres (131 hectares) set aside in the Master Plan for this purpose. Perhaps the most ambitious park, described by locals as 'an oasis in the middle of town' was the Crow Valley Central Recreation Ground created at Llanfrechfa.[183] Covering 145 acres (57 hectares) of flat ground, the park contains a boating lake at its south end, a five-acre area of water now maintained with a soft landscaped habitat for aquatic and marginal panting, and surrounded by densely planted trees. Tea rooms separate the boating lake from a series of silting ponds, which, though with hard landscaped edges, are among CDC planted trees and provide a substantial habitat for wildlife. Adjacent to these is a small children's play area. The natural planting is maintained northwards along the Afon Lwyd, the remainder of the park given over to various sports recreation grounds including the Llanyrafon Golf Course and South Field Community Sports Facility.

Other green spaces include reclaimed industrial areas, particularly areas of clay extraction. One example is the sports stadium and its associated recreation ground, extending south to the Oakfield Road Cemetery, allotments and park. Canal-side parks were designed in the early planning of the New Town to reclaim the land either side of the canal sections in the north and south of the town; a redevelopment of the canal side with green spaces and trees to the north of the Town Centre was proposed to create a 'delightful' walk from the Town Centre to the northern green belt. A similar development was planned to the south from Commercial Street to Llandowlais Street.[184] Ultimately only Mount Pleasant Park used the canal, based on an existing recreation ground.

In addition to school, local and town playing fields, all of which had land set aside for them, the 1951 Master Plan also

Figure 57: Cwmbrân Park, the boating lake with tearooms and playground beyond.

considered that playgrounds and parks were essential and within its remit. As well as the 54 acres (22 hectares) assigned for the town sports centre, playing fields and industry specific fields, neighbourhood playing fields and playgrounds were assigned at 3.5 acres (104 hectares) per 1,000 of population. Even in the most urban areas, Northville and Southville, it was ensured that adequate playgrounds and 'todlots' were available.

Outside of the official recreational areas and dedicated green spaces, the CDC's emphasis on landscaping and planting within each neighbourhood was maintained. Tree planting along the major roads through to the planting and maintenance of public forecourts at Northville meant that by the time the Development Corporation was wound up in March 1988 a total of 40,557 trees and 699,097 shrubs had been planted in the New Town.[185]

The most significant landscaped areas are within the Town Centre, an outstanding example being the Water Gardens in Monmouth Square. Built between 1968 and 1969, the Water Gardens are designed as a series of built and planted elements that bring together a variety of textures, movement and sounds. A series of descending terraces, planted with a range of shrubs and trees, lead to a shallow pool, the whole contained by revetted walls of board-marked concrete. The rear wall is highly decorative, the concrete moulded with abstract motifs and inset with glass, designed as a backdrop for water to cascade down. Fed by an upper, starker, water feature dominated by an artwork of Pilkington glass, its bold architectural idiom is in context with the sculptured and textured concrete cladding panels that are such a distinctive feature of the detached lift-shaft at Monmouth House. These panels are by the post-war sculptor and designer William Mitchell (1925-2020), one of only two sculptural examples by him in Wales and the only one extant.[186] Well known for his large-scale murals and other public art for both private companies and public bodies, these are predominantly in concrete, as Monmouth House, or glass reinforced concrete and feature heavily moulded, abstract surfaces.

Nearby Monmouth Walk is the location of a drinking fountain comprised of the bronze statue 'Mother and Child' of 1982 by Polly Hope (1933-2013) and Theo Crosby (1925-94). Theo Crosby was an architect and sculptor, part of the Pentagram practice and architect for the reconstructed Globe Theatre among other things; Polly Hope a sculptor, painter, writer and designer who also worked on the Globe reconstruction. The statue repeats their design of a drinking fountain constructed in Hyde Park the previous year marking the 'Year of the Child'. Hope was also responsible for 'Flora and Fauna', a 1983 mural at the Strand branch of Sainsbury's (1979) and for 'Dai and Myfanwy', a polychromatic pairing of man and woman in 'traditional' Welsh dress who work on barometric pressure. These decorate the façade of the Congress Theatre, dating from is refurbishment and rendering in 1982, and stand either side of a clock overlooking Gwent Square.[187]

Gwent Square is the second landscaped space within the Town Centre, to the north of Monmouth Square. Bound by Gwent House, the Congress Theatre, the Town Library and David Evans department store, it is at the heart of the urban landscape of Cwmbrân and has been a focus of schemes to create an identity for the town. Gwent House, a set of offices built from 1969 to 1973, is adorned by three murals depicting phases from the history of Monmouthshire/Gwent: Iron Age,

Figure 58: The Water Gardens with Monmouth House behind, Monmouth Square.

Figure 59: 'Family Group' by David Horn, relocated from its original town centre location and painted white from its original black finish.

Figure 60: Gwent Square murals by Henry Collins and Joyce Pallot, 1974.

Roman, Medieval and Industrial. In the archive of the CDC they are attributed to the artist Henry Collins, but they are likely to have been created jointly with his wife Joyce Pallot.[188] Married in 1938, they worked on over sixty commissions from 1948, their popularity boosted by the mural designed for the Sea and Ships Pavilion at the 1951 Festival of Britain.[189] The 1974 Cwmbrân murals are particularly lovely examples of the moulded concrete works depicting scenes of a cultural and industrial past that typified their work, and are currently the only examples attributed in Wales.

The bandstand was built as part of the original design, signalling the intention of this area to be used for public gatherings and events beyond a purely retail use, and therefore seen as supporting the social function of Gwent House. The red brickwork of the pillars blend into the brick accenting within the hard landscaping of the square. Original paving with bold geometric designs has largely been replaced, but the raised level of the east side with its softening tree planting has been retained.

'Family Group' was also commissioned for the Town Centre, originally located within the spiral ramp at The Parade. Created by the artist David Horn, it was commissioned in 1965 by the Cwmbrân Arts Trust to represent the building, and the coming together of the new communities of Cwmbrân. It was painted white (from its original black finish) and relocated to the Llantarnam Arts Centre in 2001.[190]

7 Central and Local Areas

7.1 The Town Centre

7.1.1 Background

The site chosen for the Town Centre was 71 acres (29 hectares) of largely flat ground to the middle of the designated area. Its previous use for agriculture (the only existing development being on Coronation Road), along with its topography and central location between, and accessibility from, the seven new neighbourhoods, made it a perfect site for the commercial and civic hub of the new town.

While the initial Master Plan contained no detailed layout for the Town Centre, it did specify minimal requirements for a settlement of this size. It also stipulated that to be successful the centre, at least in terms of its commercial aspect, had to provide facilities or opportunities that could not already be found at Newport or Pontypool.

The Master Plan proposed a basic configuration: the prominence of Gelli Hill at the south end of the area was identified as suitable for the Civic Square, with public buildings sited around a terrace overlooking the proposed Central Park.

A corresponding square was to be located at the northern end of the new Town Centre, creating a north-south axis for the main shopping street between the two, giving all shops the benefit of receiving some sunshine throughout the day for most of the year.[191]

The first detailed proposal was drawn up in 1952-53 by then Chief Architect J. C. P. West and was submitted for approval in 1955.[192] Much was made of the fact that this was to be a new generation of shopping centre, completely pedestrianised, with all-weather canopies and excellent bus and parking facilities. This was unusual for a British Town Centre at the time and claimed by Ministry architects to be 'one of the most interesting, if not the most interesting, New Town Centre schemes we have had'.[193] (see Fig. 23) The Cwmbran Development Corporation (CDC) was keen to ensure good press coverage for this plan and advertising for the new centre included a public competition to name streets within the area.[194]

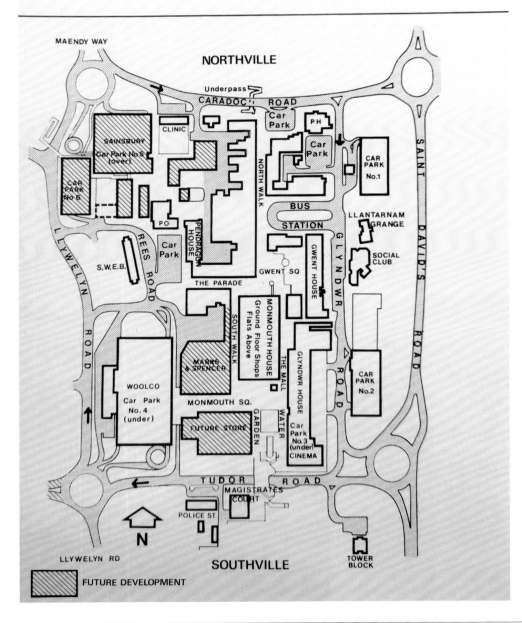

Figure 61: Town Centre plan from *Cwmbran: Garden City of Wales*, 1978.

The plan for the Town Centre was approved in 1956-57, though with extensive modifications, which West claimed 'would not produce a Town Centre as visually interesting or so exciting to walk about as the first scheme', though increased profits of 10% were expected as a result.[195] Work was slow to start on the building phase, with priority given to the neighbourhood housing and centres. Much consideration was given to how the centre linked with adjacent neighbourhoods by both car and on foot, and the first works were on the circular road system, pedestrian links to Northville and a new road bridge carrying Maendy Way over the railway line, ensuring infrastructure to access the site was in place before commercial development started.

Early development, between 1956 and 1960, focused on the northern part of the Town Centre, with the General Post Office (GPO) on the north side of General Rees Square to be the first building constructed in 1956, subsequently opened in November 1959. By the end of 1958 and early in 1959 preparations were underway on the first set of 18 shops at North Walk/Caradoc Road where the first Town Centre trader opened for business in December 1959.[196] A further 22 shops and two banks followed at North Walk and to the north side of the bus station, followed by work on The Parade and General Rees Square. The building of the GPO was followed by the construction of the South Wales Electricity Board Headquarters in 1960 and a health clinic.[197]

Figure 62: The north side of General Rees Square, including the central Post Office.

By 1960 thought was being given both to the civic buildings that would form a group around the southern square, and to other public buildings including a library, town hall and swimming pool. By early 1964 a scheme had been produced along these lines including council offices, a police station, magistrates court, swimming pool and a high-rise block of flats grouped around the Civic Square.

Revised plans were submitted for the Town Centre in 1963-64 to expand the area, bringing in a strip of land west of Llewelyn

Road, and to alter the road system to a one-way circular route going clockwise.[198] In September 1964 the first department store was completed and opened, along with the first multi-storey car park, bus station and 40 more shops in December, which together with The Moonraker Pub which had been opened by Watney Mann in March 1965, all signalled that Cwmbrân was well and truly open for business.

A next major landmark was reached with the opening of the £728,834 Monmouth House by Sir James Callaghan in 1967 featuring luxury flats as well as further shops, and the completion of the 22-storey tower block, a structure which also incorporated the boiler house and flue for the Town Centre heating system. Kibby's Supermarket, on the south side, was one of, if not the, largest in Wales at the time.[199]

The following year Glyndwr House, providing spacious offices and ground floor shops, opened at the south end of the shopping centre, while Gwent House (otherwise known as The Central Building) opened in 1972 after many years of discussion over its desired function.[200] In the end this provided six floors of offices, a central library with 36,000 books, a Youth Employment Centre, a multi-purpose conference and exhibition hall, and three floors of restaurants (one of which, 'the Sign of the Steer', was licenced), in addition to another 14 shops.[201] This development was particularly seen as providing the heart to the Town Centre, a situation that was strengthened by the addition of the Congress Theatre in October 1972 and a bandstand, completing Gwent Square. The theatre complemented the three-screen cinema and bingo hall opened at the southern end of the centre in 1971. The technology utilised was unique in having all three screens fitted with a downward mirror periscope projection system, possibly the only cinema to still be using this system on its closure in 2013.[202]

Parking was considered particularly important to the success of the Town Centre, with a further multi-storey car park being opened in December 1965, and two underground car parks completed in 1967.

Public art was from the beginning considered an integral part of the Town Centre. The lift tower to Monmouth House for example was clad with an abstract concrete design by the sculptor William Mitchell, and Gwent House incorporated three substantial murals by Henry Collins across its elevation to Gwent Square. In addition to the buildings themselves and the commissioning of public art for the Town Centre, standard designs were created to promote consistency in street furniture and there was extensive planting of shrubs, trees and flowers. The first piece of free-standing public art to be added to a public area was 'Family group' by David Horn, unveiled on 23 September 1965,[203] said to represent the strains of forming a new community.[204]

On its opening on 25 July 1969, the 'impressive fountain, water falls [sic] and planted area' that formed the sunken landscaped garden to the south of Monmouth House attracted numerous favourable comments from residents and

The Woolco store completed in October 1975 ▲

▼ Congress Theatre and Bandstand

Figure 63: The Woolco Store and the Congress Theatre in its original incarnation, from *Cwmbran: Garden City of Wales*, 1978.

visitors' alike.[205] Plans had been submitted in early 1966, and constructed by Truscon throughout late 1968 and early 1969 at a cost of £29,825.[206]

The addition of public works of art to the Town Centre environment continued. Under the space frame roof in Monmouth Walk was placed the bronze fountain 'Mother and Child' constructed in 1982 to the design of Theo Crosby (1925-94) and his professional partner and wife Polly Hope (1933-2013).[207]

By the mid-1970s the success of the shopping facilities provided in the Town Centre meant that further land was required to allow expansion. Tudor Road was realigned to provide a suitable site in the south-west corner of the Town Centre for a major new development. The largest element of

this development was the Woolco store which opened in October 1975 with an adjacent 875-space car park.[208]

Also in the 1970s, two 'firsts for Wales' occurred in the history of Cwmbrân's New Town. These were the first of the new 'job supermarkets' in Wales that opened in October 1973 and allowed people to browse from 500 to 600 possible job cards at any given time, and secondly Wales's first Sainsbury's supermarket, which opened in November 1976.

While plans for the sale of the Town Centre after the eventual winding up of the CDC were being discussed as early as 1979, large scale developments continued in the later 1970s and early 1980s. Monmouth Square continued to be developed with further shops added including a flagship Marks & Spencer store, and The Strand, which was built between December

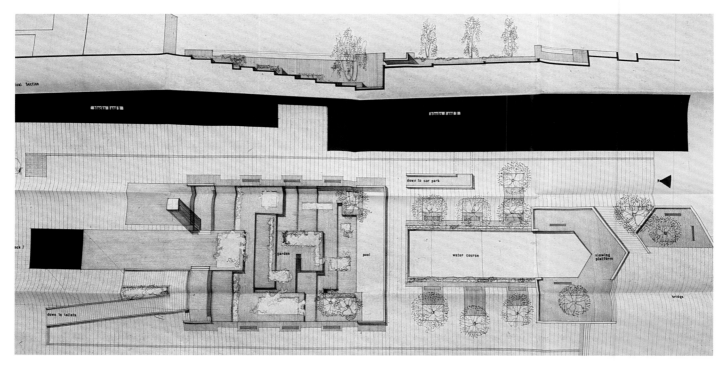

Figure 64: Plans and sectional drawing for the Water Gardens, Monmouth Square, by CDC Chief Architect Gordon Redfern, 1966.

1978 and the end of 1981. Increasingly, however, the focus in Town Centre development was on small scale improvements such as the provision of canopies and lighting and the negotiation of infill schemes with private developers.

As part of this, an initiative was proposed by the Cwmbrân Arts Trust in 1982 to enhance the aspect and appearance of the Town Centre, and therefore its value. This built on the scheme that was then underway to re-front the Congress Theatre with the addition of the clock, figures and chimes that would 'bring a new and colourful element to the Square'. Further work suggested to complement this included redevelopment of the column, adding a statue of Bran to the plinth to create a landmark monument 'comparable to Nelson's Column' and the construction of a steel structure encasing The Tower, fitted with 4,000 computer-controlled lights programmed to run in infinite patterns. Enhancement of the 'relentlessly flat' rooflines was suggested through the addition of copper domes and spires.[209] One scheme that was taken forward from these proposals was the blue and white tile mural, again by Polly Hope, in General Rees Square.

In contrast to the Town Centre, the Civic Centre was problematic in its development. The scheme proposed in 1963, when development of this area had 'become urgent' consisted of a swimming baths, council offices, new police station and magistrates court, and multi-storey car park in addition to The Tower.[210] The multi-storey car park was eventually incorporated underground, while the site of the public swimming pool desired by the CDC failed to find approval or funding from the Cwmbrân Urban District Council (CUDC), as did a 'Hall of Culture' proposed by the CUDC in 1963 at the south end of the area, but seen as an

unnecessary addition to the facilities at Gwent House. A hotel and shopping complex, designed by Powell Alport & Partners immediately west of the Water Gardens, and the municipal offices, designed by the same firm to form the southern boundary of the Civic Square also both failed to find funding.[211] The Police Station and Magistrates Court were built between 1963 and 1964 on a slightly amended plan, and together with the Water Gardens form the only original elements of the Civic Square.

One major new development proposed that reflected the struggling economy of the late 1970s, rising unemployment and the decline of traditional industries was the 'Open House' project, a scheme drawn up by Foster Associates in 1978. This was described at the time as the 'response by a local community to economic and technological developments which will increasingly change the way we live'. Developed by the Cwmbrân Children's Trust, the Community Projects Centre and LSD Leisure and Recreation with Foster Architects, the purpose of the project was to develop a leisure scheme, creating over 100 jobs as well as a profit-making income that could be used to financially support community schemes throughout the region, highlighting 'what ordinary people can do – especially the young – to face an unpredictable future with more confidence and skill'.[212]

The proposal included a community enterprises centre and a leisure complex, the main attraction of which was to be an international size ice-skating rink with the capacity for 1,200 skaters over weekend evenings and seating for 5,000. To be built in conjunction with shops, restaurants, exhibition space and a discotheque, it was seen not only as a facility with regional appeal, but also as something that would bring 'glamour to the mundane … add a touch of magic to everyday life'. The proposal also sought to fulfil the potential of the 'Civic Square' space south of the water gardens, which had still not been developed at that time. Unfortunately, despite considerable efforts of the part of the CDC throughout 1979 and 1980, the scheme was eventually not commissioned for implementation after a financial assessment declared it unviable in the economic context of the early 1980s.

In 1985 the Town Centre was sold to City and County Property.[213] Development and growth continued, with a central railway station finally being achieved in 1986. In the 1990s the centre was expanded into land to the west of Llewelyn Road, when the Lockgate Retail Park was built.

Most recently, by 2019, planning proposals were developed for a revitalisation of Gwent Square and the Civic Square. These schemes include the re-facing of the Congress Theatre and recladding of House of Fraser and the infilling of the Water Gardens to create a café piazza.[214] Land to the south of Morrisons Supermarket, previously in industrial use, is now the location of the in-progress further education college.

7.1.2 Character of Area

The Town Centre buildings all date to the post-war New Town, with no earlier buildings incorporated. The core of the Town Centre as built is characterised by a series of north-south pedestrianised shopping streets: North Walk, South Walk and The Mall. A two-storied shopping element is present in The Parade, set at 90 degrees off The Mall, while further commercial properties line Gwent Square Bus Station and form part of Gwent Square. All of these elements retain the basic structures as built in 1959, although substantial late-

twentieth- and early twenty-first-century alterations have taken place in terms of glazing materials, signage and street furniture that have heavily obscured the clean lines of the original modernist design. In particular, The Parade has lost its cobbled paving, gallery railings, the majority of shop fronts and its open nature (with the addition of a canopy), the original scheme facilitating the incorporation of planting boxes around the gallery level, adding what was a vibrant level of greenness to the modernist space.

Completed incrementally, these shops show a reasonable continuity of form, design and height from Caradoc Road to Monmouth Square, to ensure an overall harmony, with variations in roof level and materials providing diversity and visual interest. The northern section, onto Caradoc Road, was defined by the use of brickwork in the North Walk shops (now rendered and painted), with strongly horizontal sets of large-paned, aluminium-glazed glazing to the first floors. Concrete canopies at first floor and roof level, which accentuated the strongly horizontal lines, have sadly been lost.

Gwent Square Bus Station is lined by shops that continue the use of brickwork to a smaller degree, but which are dominated by the use of curtain-walled facades. There is a pleasing diversity with the continuation of horizontal focus to the north side of the station, accentuated by continuous glazing and panelling to the first floor, originally strengthened by a full-length canopy defining the separation between ground and first-floor levels, in conjunction with grey marble slab cladding. This contrasts with the vertically accentuated frontage of 12-16 Gwent Square facing down the length of the bus concourse, the four-storey structure highlighted with the use of a light aluminium-framed facade with alternating sections of glazing and panelling. The strong lines of both schemes have had their impact reduced by the replacement

Figure 65: The Town Centre looking south from Caradoc Road.

of much of the glazing frames with uPVC and the addition of later bus shelters and canopies that interrupt the original sightlines.

In Gwent Square, the large House of Fraser store (originally David Evans) marks the centre of the shopping area. Its original, dark, vertical timber cladding gives it a strikingly modernist character for the time being (a planning application is currently in the application stage to replace this). To the south of this, the shopping development in South Walk, The Parade and Monmouth Square is characterised by two-storey structures of pre-cast concrete and aggregate panels, with thin, horizontal lines of glazing at first-floor level connecting the design scheme to the northern section of the complex. These were originally aluminium framed, but the majority have been replaced with thicker uPVC that detracts from the lightness of form displayed in earlier photographs.

There are few original elements that survive at shop level, with the only features being small sections of mosaic tiling to corner pillars and spaces between shop fronts. General Rees Square is perhaps one of the most contrasting areas of original and modern, with generally well-preserved curtain-walled facades to the eastern and northern sides (although aluminium framing has been replaced by uPVC). To the south, complete redevelopment has taken place with 'Cwmbrân Shopping' including the flagship Primark store, while the site of the first Sainsbury's in Wales now houses a modern Asda of nondescript design.

The main architectural statements in terms of height and design are provided by the non-commercial buildings that are integrated throughout the Town Centre. Gwent Square is particularly characterised by a mixture of shops and public buildings with the main character of the square coming from the range of public buildings that sit to three sides.

The original strongly Brutalist form of the Congress Theatre has been replaced by substantial later rendering and cladding, together with the addition of two figures, 'Dai' and 'Myfanwy' whose representation of a rural Welsh idyll are perhaps incongruous within the context of the new town. Gwent House, providing office space on the east side of the square, has survived better and with its heavy roughcast concrete construction of eight storeys provides a visual anchor to the middle of the Town Centre. The long stretch of continuous lines of glazing and imprinted concrete to each floor are broken by the vertical lines of the lift shafts and stairways of board-shuttered concrete. A particular feature of this building is the set of three moulded-concrete murals by Henry Collins depicting the Roman, Medieval and industrial history of the area.

Further vertical forms are provided through the inclusion of residential blocks. The 22-storey residential tower, designed by Redfern's team as 'a campanile... to serve as a landmark to travellers' in 1965 and built between 1965 and 1967, stands at the south-east corner of the Town Centre in complete

Figure 66. Gwent House, opened 1972 and bordering the east side of Gwent Square, in contrast to the two-storey library.

Figure 67: Monmouth House, opened 1967, is remarkable for the William Mitchell sculptures to the external lift shaft.

contrast to the surrounding built environment. Consciously planned as a dramatic visual marker of the Town Centre's location, this tower contained 81 flats and was for many years one of the tallest residential buildings in Wales. At its lower levels it contained (and concealed) the boiler and flue for the Town Centre's principal district heating system. In recent years the tower has been over-clad.

The seven-storey Monmouth House forms one side of Monmouth square. Again, the emphasis is on vertical lines, with perpendicular pairs of windows alternating with pilasters of smooth concrete, an open corner tower containing a spiral fire stair, and most impressively an external lift shaft attached to the block by covered walkways. This is decorated with fine cast-concrete murals by William Mitchell, with alternating bands of hemispherical reliefs and board-shuttered concrete, the latter denoting the position of the short link-corridors from the lifts into the main block. The concrete used for the construction of Monmouth House is a warm, cream coloured material with Cornish granite aggregate, but apart from the lift tower, has been externally over-clad. The building plan is asymmetrical, a central well offset to allow for a variety of shop depths and therefore sizes to the lower floors, the upper

storeys housing 56 maisonettes. Both shops and flats are served by underground parking.

The car parking for the Town Centre is at the corners of the site and access to them was adapted to suit the sloping ground levels. Unfortunately, when Gordon Redfern was the Chief Architect, the original intention in the scheme design to provide covered routes for pedestrians was not carried out as constructed. These were only added later in 1986, as a not entirely satisfactory and evident afterthought. Similarly, the Civic Square planned at the south end of the Town Centre was never realised. The Gwent police station and Cwmbrân magistrates' law courts are the sole elements of this scheme, standing to the south of the Town Centre beyond a pedestrian bridge.

In addition to the buildings themselves, the design schemes included hard surfaces and street furniture. Resurfacing has taken place across the shopping centre, including the cobbled sett surface in The Parade and the geometrically patterned, polychrome paving to Gwent Square. Original street furniture survives in the form of the distinctive round, concrete planters, some with incorporated timber seating.

Figure 68: The south end of the shopping centre in 1998, with the combination of original building and street furniture, with later shop fronts and the giant protective canopy, added 1986 by Hildebrand & Glicker.

There are three planned open spaces within the centre: the bus station, Gwent Square and Monmouth Square. The bus station is a well-planned space providing ample room for a one-way bus system, with green space to the centre and now-mature trees, but cleared of further original planting. The original provision of Abacus bus shelters has been replaced with continuous canopied shelters, which, together with a proliferation of signage and other street furniture, has given the space a more cluttered feeling.

Gwent Square is an important and pivotal space in the middle of the Town Centre, with some of the most important commercial and public properties facing onto it. Mainly hard paved with replacement paving and brickwork, a small number of mature trees in the south-east corner provide the only soft planting. The bandstand, just off centre, provides an important focal point to the space.

Monmouth Square houses the most distinctive feature in the form of the Water Gardens. The design focused on the elements of texture and movement, with water being the vital constituent, and comprises a series of water features of differing types, a variety of hard surfaces and carefully chosen planting.[215] At the north end is a sunken terraced garden with a variety of planting, including trees providing height and shade. The retaining walls to the east, west and south are constructed of vertical concrete slabs, the southern retaining wall incorporating an advanced section over which water slides to form a 10-feet (3 m) fall into a pool below. The surface of this section is moulded in abstract geometric designs and embedded with patterns of Pilkington glass. The waterfall is fed from a 'canal' to the south, which used to consist of a horizontal water jet into a rectangular pool again containing large pieces of Pilkington glass (Pilkington opened a factory in Cwmbrân in 1975). Designed to exploit water movement in a variety of ways, ranging from gentle trickling to active agitation, unfortunately the water features are no longer working. These gardens are both unique in Wales as a designed Town Centre garden of this period, and provide important green space that, owing to its sunken nature, allow for a removal from the bustle of shopping activity.

Figure 69: Gwent Square incorporating the original bandstand, hard landscaping and trees, as photographed in the late 1960s. The landmarked column has been removed and plans have been approved for the removal of the bandstand and re-landscaping of this area. Plans have been approved for external refurbishment, including the replacement of the original vertical cladding, of David Evans's store (later House of Fraser).

Figures 70 & 71: The upper fountain and pool, and lower sunken garden of the Water Gardens.

Finally, the artwork 'Family Group' has been removed from the Town Centre and relocated outside the Llantarnam Arts Centre.

7.2 Pontnewydd

7.2.1 Background and Development

Pontnewydd neighbourhood covered 315 acres (127 hectares) to the north of the Town Centre. Falling topographically from 130 metres above sea level in the north-west to 61 metres in the south-east, it was sub-divided into three smaller areas by the canal and Eastern Valleys railway line.

The neighbourhood established in the Master Plan was named after the existing village of Pontnewydd that, at the time, had a population of 4,220. In the nineteenth century this was a twin-focused village centred around Commercial Street (originally High Street), Chapel Street and Richmond Road to the west and around Pontnewydd House, Conwy Terrace, Afon Terrace and Somerset Road to the east, the latter grouped around the Avondale and Edlogan tinplate works. To the immediate south-east of the Edlogan works, Pont-newydd House had associated gardens and orchards; far more extensive gardens and parkland were found at Cwm-brân Gardens to the north-west of Pontnewydd village, with Cwm-brân House at Five Locks. Facilities included Holy Trinity Church, with adjacent parsonage, graveyard and school (Boys & Girls) to the west of Pontnewydd, a Baptist chapel and the two railway stations.[216]

The village of Pontnewydd had grown slowly through the first half of the twentieth century, with an extension north along Lowlands Road to Charles Street, south along Chapel Street past Stanley Place and westwards to Mount Pleasant. To the east the newly constructed Tŷ Newydd Road led to the newly developed Tŷ Newydd Tinplate works.[217] The White Rose Cinema, opened in 1914, and the Public Hall joined the growing facilities.[218] In the immediate post-war period development was focused around Lowlands, Five Locks and extending west along Cross Roads and Upper Cwmbrân Road, including 80 to 90 new council houses. This included the development of much of Cwmbrân Gardens for housing.[219]

As many services were already in place by 1951, this was the first neighbourhood in Cwmbrân identified for residential expansion by the CDC. The first compulsory purchase order issued in the new town was for land at Tŷ Newydd, West Pontnewydd and Station Road.[220] A total of 900 dwellings were planned, with Maendy Road as the main access road to connect the neighbourhood with the Town Centre.

The first development built as a Cwmbrân Development Corporation (CDC) housing scheme was Tŷ Newydd (Tŷ Newydd Avenue, Lowlands), which consisted of five acres (two hectares) containing 48 houses, six flats and 10 garages designed by Minoprio and Spencely. The importance of trees, hedges, grass verges and footpaths within this first scheme was emphasised by the architects, though the CDC requested an immediate amendment that the scheme should achieve a higher density. Eventually, approval was given to build 54 three-bedroom houses, four four-bedroomed houses and five two-storey blocks containing 10 two-person flats. One block

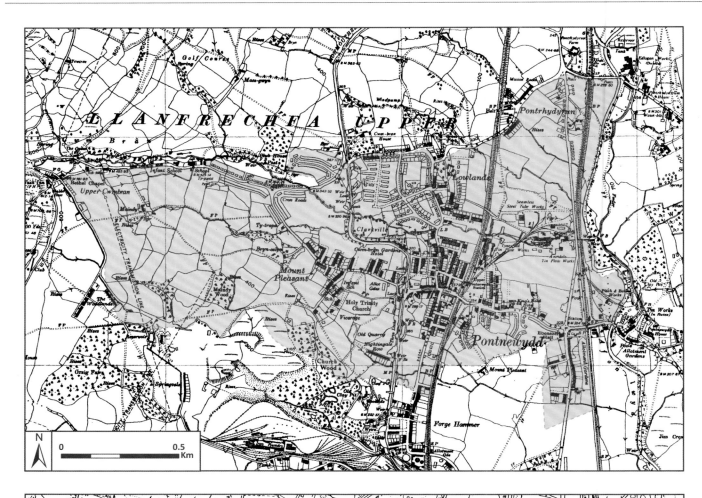

Figure 72: The area of Pontnewydd depicted on the OS mapping of 1948 and 1972.

was eventually relocated within the layout, from Middle Green to Pontrhydyrun Road, owing to its proximity to the railway line and the potential for noise disturbance.[221] The design of the houses closely followed the Housing Manual.[222] They were built in common brickwork, with pale colour renders and slate roofs, internally laid out with a living room and parlour, the latter with open fireplaces.

Figure 73: CDC housing on Maendy Way, Pontnewydd West, 1954.

A larger scheme for 300 new houses was developed shortly afterwards for this neighbourhood at West Pontnewydd, so named to distinguish it from the original village. A hundred and ninety-three of these dwellings were to be of the 'no fines' concrete shell construction system developed and patented by Wimpey in order to reduce costs, and further pressure by the Welsh Board of Health to decrease unit prices even further resulted in a number of modifications including the removal of the fireplace surrounds and clothes posts. The mix of dwellings consisted of 62 two-bedroom houses, 119 three-bedroom houses and 12 four-bedroom houses indicating the expected increase of family occupancy requirements. By early 1953, 294 dwellings had been occupied, with another 190 under construction. These were nearly all two-storey houses and by that time thought was being given to including in the next scheme of 162 dwellings a 'pleasing variation' by introducing three- and four-storey blocks of flats. Celyn Court, completed in 1955, was one such block, located towards the centre of Pontnewydd. The additional height of these taller blocks, alongside the buildings of the neighbourhood unit on Heol y Pwca, also provided a visual marker in the new geography of the area.[223]

In December 1952 and January 1953 two phases of terraced houses demonstrating different building methodologies for the reduction of softwood in residential properties were constructed at Bryn Celyn Place. Built on the instructions of the Minister of Housing and Local Government, they used a series of substitute materials, forms and plans that allowed experimentation with the use of concrete, hardwood and chipboard at a time when softwood , as an imported material, was at a premium. Similar 'Demonstration Houses' were built at Harlow and Peterlee New Towns and all were opened to

local authorities and other housing developers to assess the costs and residents' experiences of these properties.[224]

Figure 74: The second phase of Demonstration Houses at Maendy Wood Rise, 1953.

As the 1950s progressed, the planning and construction of the Pontnewydd Unit Centre began to be implemented with the first eight shops completed in early 1955.[225] It was recognised by both tenants and the CDC that the centre would need to provide social and recreational amenities as well as further commercial facilities. A children's play area was completed in early 1957 and the Yew Tree public house opened in December 1959 containing a bowling alley that proved a particularly popular local attraction.[226]

Figure 75: The Pontnewydd Unit Centre, Maendy Square, 1955.

By March 1957 the CUDC had completed the scheme on the western edge of the area, and by 1959 the CDC housing scheme for Pontnewydd was complete with subsequent development being largely the infilling of previously vacant sites. From 1964 the CDC returned to established sites to carry out improvement works, such as landscaping, planting and improving playgrounds, and also to supplement parking arrangements that were considered out of date and services such as the additional health clinic in west Pontnewydd.

A Catholic mass centre was founded in Pontnewydd Community Hall to accommodate the growing numbers of worshippers in the town in the late 1950s, boosted by Polish immigrants to work in industry. This was followed by the construction of St David's Church, Avondale Road, opened in July 1961 and designed by F. R. Bates & Son of Newport and Cardiff.[227]

On 16 July 1955 the Pontnewydd Primary School opened on Church Road/Bryn Celyn Road, the first new school opened in Cwmbrân.[228] The school quickly set the pattern of utilising its facilities for adult education classes outside of the school day and this, together with the tenants' hall opening in the early 1960s, was seen to contribute significantly in encouraging the societies and clubs that would bring the neighbourhood together. This was supplemented by St David's Roman Catholic Junior and Infants school, opened on Avondale Road on 14 March 1968.

Pontnewydd also included the large Avondale Industrial Estate, where 33 acres (13 hectares) was set aside in 1959-60 for the development of advance workshops and factories for light industry around the Avondale and Ty Newydd Tinplate Works.[229] This allocation was increased following the demolition of the Avondale Tinplate Works and associated hostel in 1963-64. Early developments in local industries here included the CWS bakery, a steel fabrication shop and a soft drinks distribution depot located within the mix of new factories and workshop units (5,000 square feet (465 sq. m) in total). Purpose-built factories were also developed on the site including the new Atlas Copco factory of 1967. The advance factories and workshops proved to be very popular resulting in the scheme being expanded to larger (26,000 square feet (2,415 sq. m)) premises and then copied across other industrial estates in Cwmbrân.

By the 2011 census the ward of Pontnewydd contained a population of 6,305.[230]

7.2.2 Character of Area

The historic settlement of Pontnewydd, forming the core of the neighbourhood, is characterised by a dense mixture of single-fronted terraced housing and semi-detached and detached town villas of late Victorian and Edwardian design. Though the settlement only developed from the later nineteenth century onwards, its piecemeal growth until the designation of the New Town means there is little cohesion to the earlier buildings resulting in a diverse mixture of forms and styles. The predominant building materials used are red brick or a narrow-coursed stone, frequently with yellow brick or ashlar stone dressings. The various gradations in housing status across this area are indicated by the inclusion of bay windows, the use of polychrome and moulded decoration within the brickwork, terracotta or ashlar dressings and the provision of small front gardens to take the front doorway from the pavement. There has been substantial replacement of original windows in the later twentieth century for uPVC double glazing and frequent application of render or pebble-dashing to the exteriors.

The historic shopping centre is focused around the intersection of Commercial Street, New Street and Chapel Street. This mix of commercial premises sits within a narrow system of partly one-way roads with little parking. Shop fronts are largely later twentieth century/early twenty-first century replacements or substantially modernised, with large plate glass windows within wooden or uPVC framing and modern signage, with domestic accommodation to the first floor. Notable frontages of more interest include 6 Commercial Street, a late nineteenth-century former bank with simple moulded architraves to the door and window openings; 16 Commercial Street, the Odd Fellows Arms public house; and 10 Chapel Street, which retains a substantial amount of the original architrave and tiling to entrance, though with later alterations.

Figure 76: Commercial Street, the historic high street of Pontnewydd village.

Interspersed with the commercial and residential properties are the late-nineteenth-century facades of Hope Methodist Chapel and Richmond Road Methodist Church. Both are gable-fronted chapels of stone construction with brick dressings, and are relatively plain in style for their date. The Edwardian police station, also located on Richmond Road, has been demolished and replaced by flats.

The historic elements of Lowlands and Mount Pleasant, both developed between 1889 and 1914, show a much greater uniformity of terraced and semi-detached stone housing. Holy Trinity Church, dating from the 1850s and originally in open countryside, sits as an early survivor opposite the turn-of-the-century terraces of Church Road.

Outside of these three historic cores, the character changes substantially to one dominated by post-war housing development. Inter-war and immediate post-war local authority housing at Clarksville in the Lowlands area of Five Locks Road, Clark Avenue, Parc Avenue and Maesgwyn, are typical semi-detached houses of the period, rendered or pebble-dashed with largely replacement windows, porches and boundary walls and fences. The CDC estates that form the most substantial part of the neighbourhood mirror these with sinuous estate roads and short terraces or semi-detached pairs of houses. Tŷ Newydd – with its variety of short terraces, link-detached and semi-detached houses in almost wholly white rendered forms, set in an open, well-planted environment – is reminiscent of the early garden villages. Further west and south-west, the predominance of terraces increases, the estates dominated by rows of uniform brick or rendered housing with various degrees of personalisation added by private owners in recent years. The open layout of wide roads, front gardens and 'greens' is retained. A level of architectural diversity is created through the inclusion of key buildings such as the four-storey Celyn Court and the Pen-y-parc retirement housing scheme of 1976 with its use of steeply pitched and mono-pitched roofs. A 1960s scheme of flat-roofed housing can be found at Tŷ Box Close. Later housing is generally in the form of infill schemes, or small estates on the fringes of the neighbourhoods, and is typified by semi-detached or brick estate housing with little distinguishing character.

The commercial centre at Maendy Square, typical of the single-storey unit centres, retains a range of shops, though these now focus on providing local services rather than day-to-day shopping requirements. This centre also retains its health centre and tenants' meeting hall but the public house, The Yew Tree, is closed and boarded up. Industrial development is confined to the eastern edge of the neighbourhood at the defined Avondale Industrial and Business Park.

Figures 77 & 78: The first CDC housing scheme on Tŷ Newydd Avenue and Celyn Court, Heol y Pwca, West Pontnewydd.

Within the denser housing of the historic cores there is little open green space, but the post-war housing estates emphasise provision of both front and rear gardens. The housing frontages generally face on to wide pavements, some retaining grassed verges separating the path from the carriageway. Open greens and squares are a regular feature, with tree planting carried out by the CDC. Cwmbrân Drive, running north-south through the neighbourhood, is lined with a dense planting of trees allowing properties on either side to be screened.

Larger green spaces are provided through the provision of parks and recreation grounds. Pontnewydd Park is the largest green area, fringing the line of the Monmouth canal; sitting at the heart of the neighbourhood it has not been encroached upon, providing important open and wooded recreational space. Other prominent areas of green open space in Pontnewydd include the churchyard areas adjacent to Holy Trinity Church and the extant woodland areas of Church Wood adjoining Maendy Way north of the Springvale estate. Allotments, highly sought after by tenants in the early years of the New Town, survive at the northern end of Ty Newydd Road, and are still well used.

7.3 Northville and Southville

7.3.1 Background

Northville was developed as a defined residential area within the Pontnewydd neighbourhood situated immediately to the north of the Town Centre. The 71-acre site was designed to be distinctly different from previous housing estates, providing a higher-density, more 'urban' backdrop to the Town Centre; consequently, there was more controversy around the design and planning stages than many of the other estates. Planned from early 1953, when the land was purchased for £12,000, the area was to provide 450 corporation houses with a further 150 flats and maisonettes. With all houses in long terraces, a density of 17 houses to the acre could be achieved.

The original submission was for an initial scheme of 210 dwellings and 25 garages which was approved in October the same year.[231] While the board and the ministry were both impressed by the novelty and low cost of such a scheme, the Cwmbrân Urban District Council (CUDC) objected to the lack of private gardens and what they perceived as unattractive nature of the designs. The second phase of 135 houses and 29 garages in 1954 also had difficulty with approval because of ongoing tensions between the Cwmbrân Development Corporation (CDC) and the Ministry over what were seen as inappropriate rent levels, while the submission for the third and final section of eight houses and 21 maisonettes for the central portion of the site in June 1957 was met with concern about the play area and the closeness of the flats.[232]

The dwellings focused on a series or a mix of two-, three- and four-storey buildings laid out among a series of small enclosed courts and squares and pedestrian ways, with a main north-

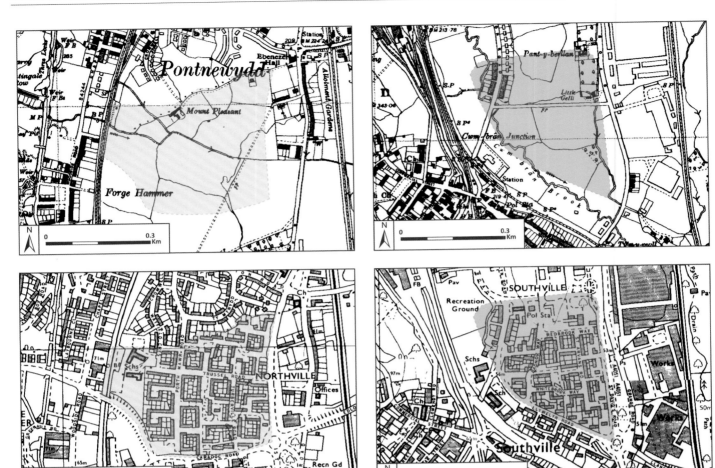

Figure 79. The areas of Northville and Southville depicted on the OS mapping of 1948 and 1972.

south way linking directly to the Town Centre via an underpass. The scheme was completed by 1960, by which time some of the earlier flats were already experiencing problems with damp penetration. One of the solutions provided was the construction of roofs over the external stairs and landings to stop water entering through the porches and coal bunkers. A lack of drying areas was also highlighted, solved by the provision of drying courts.[233]

The combination of two- to four-storey dwellings was seen as providing both architectural variety and creating a visual link

between the Town Centre and more suburban neighbourhoods. While the open spaces were much smaller, great consideration was given to paving to create play areas and a dense and varied planting scheme within the public forecourts, the responsibility for which as public spaces was retained by CDC. The scheme of enclosing these, together with the expansive planting schemes agreed in 1956, cost some £20 per house.[234]

The Maendy County Primary School was built on the western edge of the scheme between 1960 and 1961 designed by

Figure 80: Maendy County Primary School, Southville.

Richards & Trollope, the first in the New Town to be devised by a private practice.[235] The design combined the 'county style' as set by the Monmouthshire County Council Architect, and a range of curtain-walled construction that was repeated in later schools across the town.

Southville was developed as part of the 1962 expansion plan. It was at the opposite end of the Town Centre to Northville, a similar development with a slightly lower density of 16 dwellings to the acre, but a higher percentage of flats: 24% of the dwellings were one- or two-bedroomed flats.[236] Some 25 acres (10 hectares), the ground sloped down from north to south with a ridge of higher ground running through the centre. It was close to the proposed civic centre and college of further education and adjacent to the planned central park; the 'urban' layout was designed to blend this section of the Town Centre with the suburban neighbourhoods to the south and south-west.

The first submission of 310 houses, 83 flats and 83 garages was approved in August 1957.[237] The layout was of houses grouped around 'safe and quiet' culs-de-sac, the majority two-storey but with five blocks of three-storey flats interspersed along St David's Road. A central north-south spine road and footpath provided direct access to the southern Town Centre, and educational facilities were to be provided by primary schools at Maendy and St Dials.

The higher density of housing meant that open space was limited. This was justified by the CDC on the basis that the Town Centre and Llanyrafon were both within close walking distance. However, both a central playground for the children of the neighbourhood, and a series of grassed areas within the culs-de-sac, were deemed essential by the CUDC. Open

forecourts were maintained by the CDC as at Northville, and particular attention was paid to the planting of various climbing plants that could screen and soften the fencing and screen walling provided.

Tenders were invited for the first phase of 135 houses and 23 garages was in September 1958, with the second scheme of 178 dwellings and 49 garages following in 1959.[238] By this date the CUDC had requested a small site to construct a series of older people's bungalows, reducing the overall number of CDC dwellings for the neighbourhood.

In 1960 thoughts turned to the three-storey flats along St David's Road. To increase the architectural and visual impact of these, the Chief Architect heightened the blocks to four storeys, while the materials chosen were designed to bring together the two previous phases of building, namely brick built houses by Bryant's and no-fines house by Wimpey. As 'high-rise' dwellings, the flats qualified for an additional subsidy provided at £8 per dwelling.[239] Constructed by Modern Building (Newport), variations in the brick colouring were also intended to add to the visual diversity. Each block had an adjoining small building provided storage and laundry facilities. Despite being well-appointed, the CDC recorded that on completion it was difficult to find tenants willing to take the flats or maisonettes. It was decided to widen the search from the waiting list to offer them directly to workers in the Spencer Works.[240]

In 1964 Brookfields Infants and Junior School opened on the western edge of Southville.[241] This was closed and merged with Hollybush Primary school to form Nant Celyn School in 2010.[242]

Figure 81: A general view over Southville from the west c.1960.

7.3.2 Character of Area

The Northville and Southville estates are unusual in being almost entirely of one date and design concept. Formed on land with no pre-existing buildings, there is also little in the way of later building schemes other than alterations to individual properties. At Northville the character is one of repeating terraces set in straight lines and at right angles, forming a dense network of roads and courts best understood from aerial views. The terraces are made up of two-storey dwellings at their most simple; brick frontages punctuated by a doorway and three windows with no extraneous ornamentation. The roof lines are kept extremely shallow, placing further emphasis on the facades. While doors and windows have been replaced in uPVC, the external additions and alterations are minimal, largely retaining the uniform nature of the area. Where front gardens were provided, the original brick walling survives to a great degree, those shallower forecourts originally left open now largely enclosed with a variety of later walling and fencing.

These repeated lines are punctuated by blocks of three-storey flats at Plas Craig and along Pontnewydd walk, the facades of which display strong horizontal lines of glazing, more prominent than that used in the housing, and open walkways to each floor on one elevation of each lock. The provision of balconies breaks up the otherwise flat facade of the opposing elevations. Parking is provided through the use of small parking courts or on-road.

Figures 82 & 83: Northville from the air showing the density and pattern of housing layout, and four-storey flats at Plas Craig.

At Southville a slightly higher level of architectural diversity is displayed, the topography encouraging some terraces to be stepped, both vertically and along the horizontal plane, allowing the line of facades to be broken. Where straight terraces are used, wider use of porches acts to provide visual breaking points to the otherwise flat elevations. There is also a wider range of materials displayed, with a more diverse application of render, rough-casting and the use of timber panels as at Whitebrook Way.

Height is provided through the five blocks of flats laid out at right angles to St David's Road. In contrast to those at Northville, the windows are small, increasing to the living areas, with access provided via an internal stairway. Originally a contrast of red brick and hung tiles, the flats were re-clad *c*. 2017.

Figure 84: The four-storey blocks arranged along St David's Road, with The Tower to the distance marking the southern edge of the Town Centre.

Within Northville, all houses and maisonettes are provided with rear gardens and varying sizes of front gardens or forecourts; these make up the vast majority of the open space within the area. The main through-roads, Porth Mawr Road and Trussel Road, have a limited amount of grass and tree planting, the narrower width of other roads having pavements only. There are limited but extant areas of open grassed areas at Llandaff Green, Plas Ebbw and along Pontnewydd walk, the north-south route to the Town Centre, but the extensive public planting schemes described by the CDC within the public spaces, including rose bushes and shrubs, no longer exist.

7.4 Croesyceiliog

7.4.1 Background

Croesyceiliog was identified in the New Town plan as a long narrow area to the east of the Cwmbrân Branch railway. Advanced as one design proposal with 'Croesyceiliog South' (Llanyravon) covering 750 acres (304 hectares), and with an overall target population of 10,000, the CDC's intention here was to create two neighbourhoods, each with its own distinct centre. The land in these neighbourhoods slope gently from around 107m above sea level in the east down to about 46m

above sea level towards the river and both areas were considered as providing particularly attractive sites for new housing.[243]

The neighbourhood of 'Croesyceiliog North' expanded on the existing village of Croesyceiliog. This small settlement had, in the nineteenth century, comprised two public houses, the Upper Cock and Lower Cock, a smithy, a post office and boys' and girls' school interspersed with a small amount of housing, which in the early nineteenth century was focused along The Highway and Garw, developing along Woodland road in the later nineteenth century.[244] To the west was Pont-newydd house, with its extensive grounds and garden, adjacent to which developed the Pontnewydd Tinworks, the owner of which was instrumental in Pontrhydyrun Baptist chapel founded in 1817. In the south part of the neighbourhood were two extensive areas of woodlands, Jim Crow's Wood and The Plantation, with the remainder of the area in agricultural use.[245] By the early twentieth century the tin works were marked as 'in ruins' and Pitch and Benzal works were developed to the north-west. St Mary's Mission Church was opened in 1903 to supplement the All Saints Church, Llanfrechfa.[246] In the inter- and post-war periods, the Pontypool Rural District Council (PRDC) started a scheme of local authority housing development along Black Road and south of Croesyceiliog, including Ashford Close which started to encroach on The Plantation woodland.[247] The CDC subsequently encouraged PRDC to refrain from further planned building work in the area after the designation of the New Town in order to prevent any impact on its own plans.[248]

The scope of early housing development across north and south Croesyceiliog was constrained by a difficulty in improving the water supply in the area, with existing services being only adequate to provide for a total of 300 new homes. Despite this, the development of the neighbourhood was seen as a priority for CDC owing to the lack of previous development and the beauty of the area. Works started with a small infill development of 14 houses at Garw in October 1951, with the first full scheme for 300 dwellings approved in 1952.[249] An initial contract for 88 houses started in mid-1952, the scheme also including a number of plots for private developers. A full development plan for Croesyceiliog North was submitted in 1953, alongside an outline planning application for Croesyceiliog South, and by 1956 555 houses were occupied with the final contracts for Section V let to complete the intended house building. By early 1959 all housing within the initial plans was completed. One drawback of this 'attractive' neighbourhood was the fact that its eastern boundary was formed by the busy A4042 Newport to Pontypool road, but the layouts ensured that no houses fronted on to this. Despite this, and the fact that the houses themselves were of the same traditional form and materials as those used at West Pontnewydd, houses were quickly sought after by tenants.

A 1957 study indicated that parking provision in the housing schemes built up to that time had been underestimated and

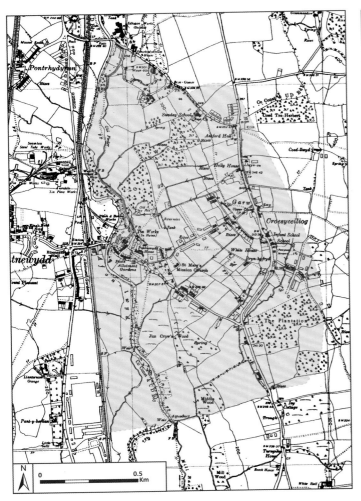

Figure 85: The area of Croesyceiliog depicted on the OS mapping of 1948 and 1971–72.

that 66 garages were required to supplement the parking provided in the neighbourhoods. This was achieved by using a site previously reserved for private development.[250]

In 1959 a further area of 14 acres (six hectares) was reserved for 'The Plantation' in Croesyceiliog North, a development of 74 houses and 36 flats and maisonettes completed between 1964 and 1966. A further 28 plots were assigned for development by private developers. It was hoped that this

shared development of houses, maisonettes and flats in a landscaped area would produce a more interesting and varied design in comparison to other estates planned across the town at the time.[251]

After this date, the majority of the further housing schemes in Croesyceiliog were on small, infill sites, such as at Bryn Gomer, where a site for seven privately developed houses was made available in 1960, and the early 1970s Highway scheme of 14

Figures 86 & 87: CDC housing on Chepstow Rise and Whitehouse Road, Croesyceiliog, undated.

houses. In 1976 a scheme of 54 one- and two-bedroom flats were built at Bronllys Way in the grounds of the former Pont-newydd House, still with a number of planted features and small number of cottages that were retained and improved.[252] At the same date 'sensitive' restoration and improvements were also carried out on a terrace of nineteenth-century cottages at Garw Row, described as having 'no individual merit, yet as a group possessed character and charm and were of great interest as typical workers' housing of their time'.[253]

A final, larger housing scheme was carried out at Edlogan Way in the late 1970s. This was facilitated by the closure of the Gwent Pipe Works, freeing up land for 174 dwellings.[254] Designed by the Chief Architect in collaboration with Torfaen County Borough Council, the scheme included innovative bungalows specifically designed to allow disabled tenants to live within, and reintegrate with, the community, the importance of which was recognised by an official opening by the Secretary of State for Wales in October 1979.[255]

A 1981 Report on the Condition of Rented Houses in Croesyceiliog identified problems with properties on Woodland Road and Chepstow Drive. These included roofing problems in both houses, where the weight of the clay roof tiles were overstressing the roof timbers, and flats where wind action on aluminium roofs was causing leakage. The report also highlighted the need to improve heating systems across all dwellings in the area.[256]

The Croesyceiliog North neighbourhood unit centre was planned from 1953 at Edlogan Square to contain six shops, a public house and a meeting hall, with construction starting in 1956. In 1957 a development of three- and four-storey flats was underway to add 'architectural interest' to the complex.[257] On completion of the centre in 1958 it was proposed to add a further two shops, with sites reserved for social buildings and future development. Owing to the extended nature of the neighbourhood a sub-unit centre was proposed on the recommendation of the Ministry of Housing and Local Government for the south-eastern fringe of the area. This scheme included a further four shops and was finished in 1955.[258] In 1963 the Six-in-Hand public house opened and in 1977 a further two shops were built for the Highway scheme in Croesyceiliog.

In the early 1950s a new complex of Croesyceiliog infant and junior schools at North Road, was planned and built by 1956 designed by Colin Jones of the Monmouthshire County Council Architect Department.[259] The 240-place infant school was built first in 1953. Although this was originally intended to supplement the existing Victorian infant school on the Highway, by the time it was opened the old school was no longer being used for educational purposes. The junior school commenced building in 1955, also opening in 1956.

A large new educational campus was also proposed in the early stages of the new town Master Plan to sit between the two neighbourhoods of Croesyceiliog North and Croesyceiliog South. It was initially planned to accommodate a grammar school, technical school and secondary modern school. The secondary modern element was opened in autumn 1957 and was soon reported as being well used for social and cultural purposes outside of school hours.[260] The grammar school was next completed, taking its first influx of pupils in the autumn of 1959. Both were again designed by Colin Jones, assisted by job architect T. E. Moore.[261] In 1971 the two schools were

Figure 88: The Croesyceiliog Sub-Unit Centre on North Road, undated.

amalgamated into Croesyceiliog Comprehensive School, with extension work taking place in 1974.[262]

In 1961 a small health clinic was built to serve Croesyceiliog and the 'George Lansbury Old Peoples Home' was opened by Monmouthshire County Council in 1967, supplemented the following year by a group of 23 flatlets for older people built by Pontypool Rural District Council and designed by Gordon Redfern.

In 1951 Monmouthshire County Council, in searching for a site for a new county hall, decided that it should be built in Croesyceiliog. After some years of indecision and negotiation (see section 5.2) designs for the new building were finally produced by the private practice of Robert Matthew, Johnson-Marshall and Partners in 1965. Building took place between 1969 and 1977, and when opened the County Hall accommodated over 500 people.[263] It was occupied by the newly-formed Gwent County Council until 1996, and then Monmouthshire and Torfaen Councils until its demolition in 2013.

By 1964 a site for a new 'Mormon Temple' had been assigned on the northern edge of Croesyceiliog, its proximity to the Baptist Chapel causing some tensions with the Minister there.[264] The site was technically outside the designated area and, while passed by the CDC's Churches Committee for courtesy's sake, fell under the jurisdiction of Monmouthshire County Council.[265] The church was built in the late 1960s to the central designs of the denomination.

7.4.2 Character of Area

Croesyceiliog is a large neighbourhood in the north-east corner of Cwmbrân and forms a discrete unit bounded to the west by the railway line, to the east by the A4042, by open countryside to the north and the complex of recreational grounds and schools to the south. The topography alters from the flat, low-lying valley bottom of the western half of the neighbourhood to gently sloping in the east.

Pre-New Town development survives in a number of small, scattered buildings concentrated around the historic settlement of Croesyceiliog. These include the Victorian school, now re-purposed as a nursery, and the refurbished Upper Cock public house both on The Highway. Pontrhydyrun Baptist Chapel is a particularly fine surviving example of an early-nineteenth-century nonconformist place of worship, reflected in its Grade II* listing.

A range of Post-medieval housing survives. Early rural vernacular is represented by Holly House marked on the tithe mapping as a cottage and so possibly extended and improved in the latter half of the nineteenth century, being depicted on the tithe mapping of 1842.[266] Jim Crow cottage is an early nineteenth-century dwelling built in the picturesque gothic style, through its name associated with Jim Crow's Wood depicted on historic OS mapping to the south-west.[267] Much of

the housing is nineteenth century and early twentieth-century workers' housing ranging from brick and stone terraces such as Yew Tree Terrace and Bryn Eglwys to the refurbished stone cottages at The Garw. The later-developed Woodland Road displays a range of late nineteenth- and early twentieth-century houses of higher status including the detached villa at 78 Woodland Road and the two terraces at 25-29 and 30-42 Woodland Road, which display good use of polychromatic and moulded decorative brickwork.

Figures 89 & 90: Woodland Road & Ashford Close.

Inter-war housing is limited to a small development of 10 bungalows and two semi-detached houses on the corner of Chapel Lane and Newport Road. These are characterised by Arts and Crafts influences, the splayed gables, bow windows and arched porches giving the bungalows a cottage feel, while the pair of semi-detached houses on the corner have a more marked 'Tudorbethan' style with the use of applied timber-framing to low-sitting gables that rise the height of the first floor and attic. While these houses are well maintained in their original form, many of the bungalows have undergone modifications with some wholly rebuilt. Post-war local authority house building undertaken by Pontypool Rural District Council along Bryn Eglwys and Ashford Close followed the existing pattern of linear, roadside development.

Housing from the period of development by the Cwmbrân Development Corporation (CDC) makes up the majority of building within the neighbourhood, and the period of development and the mix of CDC and private building has led to a diverse range of forms and styles. The early CDC development, as at Pontnewydd, followed the traditional form

Figure 91 & 92: CDC terraced housing at Cwrt Glas and Fairoak Lane.

Figure 93 & 94: Pettingale Road and Plantation Drive.

used by local authority housing in regular plot sizes as short terraces and semi-detached pairs in either brick or render dominate the central and western areas of the neighbourhood between The Highway and Edlogan Way. Diversity is limited to various porch treatments and the staggering and off-setting of some terraces to relieve the longer terraces where the terrain allows, while streetscapes are broken up by the use of an irregular road pattern partially based on pre-existing field boundaries. Houses are provided with front gardens or courts and rear gardens, many front gardens converted to driveways to combat the lack of off-street parking, and set within a landscape of open courts and greens. In the north-west corner of the neighbourhood the naturally steeper topography either side of Caerwent Road is enhanced by the inclusion of four pairs of three- or four-storey blocks of flats. Early examples are characterised by the use of natural stone to the gable walls and open balconies, later infill blocks grey rendered and flat roofed.

Along the eastern side of the neighbourhood housing becomes more varied. While still predominantly two-storey housing, the mixture of hipped and gabled and terraced, semi-detached and detached forms increases within the same streetscape, with a wider range of materials including dark brown to yellow brickwork and timber panels incorporated. Larger semi-detached housing, with generous gardens such as that on Pettingale Road represents the type of higher rent housing developed by the CDC in this neighbourhood. This diversity is supplemented by the mixture of privately developed, and in some cases architecturally designed, properties in an area that was considered more attractive and therefore desirable for private housing. Further south, The Plantation estate is formed largely of larger, detached houses and dormer bungalows, distinct from the rest of the neighbourhood in its extensive use of hung scalloped tiles to the elevations.

Both the Edlogan Square and North Road unit centres comprise single-storey, brick-built units initially designed to replicate a row of high street shops, but now modified and combined to form larger stores, which have been modernised and replaced the original frontages. The Six in Hand, located at the Edlogan site, has its original exterior but has been closed since 2018 and is currently awaiting a new use. The pair of 'pantry' shops on Pettingale Road are still in use by independent retailers, maintaining their original form with external stairs to first floor flats.

The adjacent junior and infant schools on North Road have been combined to form the Croesyceiliog primary school, but the buildings have been externally maintained as built in the 1950s' 'county style' of largely single-storey yellow-brick ranges. The complex of grammar and secondary modern schools at the southern boundary of the neighbourhood contrasted this in their use of large, four-storey, curtain-walled ranges with extensive aluminium-framed glazing. Demolished and rebuilt between 2017 and 2019, the new school buildings reference the form and style of their predecessors.

Figures 95 & 96: Edlogan Square Unit Centre with the Six in Hand Public House & Croesyceiliog Primary School, formerly the Infant and Junior Schools.

After demolition in 2013, the site of the former County Hall is currently unoccupied and awaiting development.

There are a number of religious buildings of varying date throughout the neighbourhood. Pontrhydyrun Baptist Chapel, dating to a 1836 rebuild, is a Grade-II-listed example of the transformation of nonconformist places of worship to more prominent gable-fronted buildings using recognised elements of Classical architecture in the first half of the nineteenth century. Its particularly fine exterior and early internal gallery are representative of its funding by the owner of the Pontrhydyrun Tinplate works. St Mary's Church, opened in 1903, is constructed of red brickwork in the more 'recognisably religious' Gothic style though veering more towards later Perpendicular than Early English and without transepts. The only church established during the New Town development is the Church of Jesus Christ of Latter Day Saints on Newport Road. Its asymmetrical design of yellow brick with diamond-panelled motif running up to the apex line of the folded roof that shelters the whole structure, and detached 'spire', is one of a series of set patterns provided by the central church to congregations wishing to build a place of worship with similar examples found worldwide.

The neighbourhood retains substantial areas of planned open land for either formal or informal recreation. The cricket and

rugby club is set within the heart of the neighbourhood, adjacent to a large informal green around which the historic village of Croesyceiliog was focused. Smaller courts and green remain scattered throughout the estates, but there are no equipped children's playgrounds. More substantial recreational ground exists along the Afon Lwyd and the western boundary and in the extensive playing fields bounding Llanyrafon to the south. There are surviving ribbons and small areas of Garw Woods woven along Edlogan Way and to the west.

7.5 Llanyravon ('Croesyceiliog South')

7.5.1 Background

The southern neighbourhood of 'Croesyceiliog South' (extended and renamed Llanyravon in 1954) included Llanyravon Farm, a seventeenth-century gentry house in origin, and Llanyravon Mill. Built in the late eighteenth century, though possibly on a site of a fourteenth-century predecessor, this was located on a mill race branching off the Afon Lwyd. The historic site of Llanfrechfa Grange (containing Llanfrechfa Manor) and its associated gardens and grounds lay just outside the boundary to the east. Throughout the nineteenth and first half of the twentieth century there were substantial areas of woodland including Mill Wood and Bath Wood, with the area remaining predominantly in agricultural use up to the designation of the New Town.[268]

Crown Road was identified as the most attractive and visible site in the neighbourhood, commanding 'magnificent views across to the valley to the west and south-west with Mynydd Maen and Mynydd Henllys creating an exceedingly dramatic background feature' and with Caerleon Road providing 'magnificent trees forming a beautiful background and skyline'.[269] It was therefore selected by the CDC as the location for building comparatively higher value rental properties and houses for sale, together with a mix of privately developed properties, ensuring that the existing nature of the area was retained. As such it was one of the first areas to be developed in the two neighbourhoods and, by 1951, 168 traditionally built houses were planned here by the Chief Architect with, in contrast to developments in Pontnewydd, a third of them designated as private housing. Considerable thought was given to the range of house plans developed in relation to the family groupings (children, in-laws, elderly parents) that would use them and the finishes and amenities were designed to be of higher quality than elsewhere. Construction started in 1954, but the scheme was revised owing to concerns about recuperation of the higher cost of building; the original cost per house including road and land value was in the region of £490. A revised layout included the reduction of road and footpath costs by providing footpath-only access to some properties and the use of minimum frontages, smaller plots with higher density of buildings and a greater sale to rent ratio.[270] The initial scheme was completed by 1955 and applications for

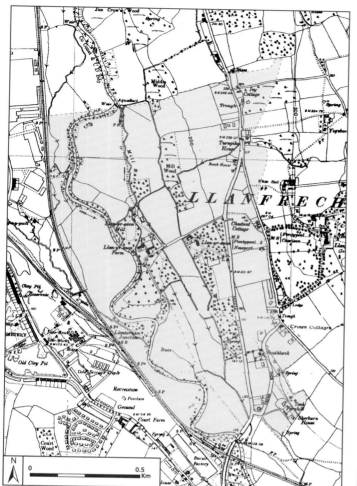

Figure 97: The area of Llanyravon depicted on the OS mapping of 1948 and 1971–72.

purchase were quickly being received.[271] A further infilling scheme was completed in 1960.

Figure 98: The style of higher value housing built by the CDC on Crown Road and Crown Rise, undated.

The scope of early housing development across Croesyceiliog was otherwise constrained by a difficulty in improving the water supply in the area, a situation that was improved in Croesyceiliog South from 1953. An outline planning application for the neighbourhood was submitted in 1953, by

which time it was renamed Llanyravon after the farm and mill. This scheme increased the proposed population for the area from the original Master Plan with the expanded Llanyravon housing schemes I to VII being approved for completion up to 1961, alongside the Llanyravon unit centre (Scheme IV). The first contract at Llanyravon I for 289 traditional style houses started in October 1956 and on 4 June 1959 Llanyravon was the location for the opening of the CDC's 3,000th house.[272] As at Crown Road, the percentage of higher-rental and private houses developed was greater than in any other neighbourhood; for instance Phase VI had 19 plots and Phase VII 43 plots for private sale; in 1960 a plot on Caerleon Road was made available for entirely private development.[273] Further housing development largely consisted of infill schemes from the mid-1960s with developments such as the Grey Waters flats in 1973-74.

The main Llanyravon unit centre of eight shops and 12 flats was approved in 1957 and built through 1958, opening in January 1959. At this point it was also decided to build a single shop serving the occupants of Crown Road, who were separated from the main unit centre by the trunk road.[274] Three further shops were added to the unit centre in 1963-64, together with The Crow's Nest public house.

Figure 99: The Llanyravon Unit Centre, flanked by blocks of three-storey flats to augment the sense of a neighbourhood centre.

In 1953 both the Welsh Presbyterian Church and the Methodist Church requested sites for new chapels in Llanyravon. A site for the Methodist church, church hall and Sunday school on Llanyravon Way was let in 1958, during which time services were being held in the builders' canteen. The Presbyterians, by 1959, had had second thoughts about proceeding with their church, the site for which was in the unit centre, and the Methodists were instead asked to take over the site left vacant there as the CDC were keen to maintain the cluster of buildings in the neighbourhood centre. Despite this, the Methodists decided to keep the site on Llanyrafon Way, which was both larger and more prominent, and more convenient for members living in Croesyceiliog. The foundation stone was laid in 1960 and the chapel opened in 1961.[275]

Llanyravon Infant & Junior School opened in 1957, again designed by Colin Jones of Monmouthshire Architects department.[276] A social centre was requested for the neighbourhood by the Pontypool Rural District Council and designed by the Chief Architect, this opened next to Llanyravon Mill in 1973. At this date both the mill and Llanyravon Farm were in the ownership of the CDC and were subsequently transferred to the Torfaen Museum Trust to be restored and opened to the public. Llanyravon House, which was converted to The Stirrup Club in the 1960s, was demolished to make way for The Commodore Hotel in 1973. Built by a private developer, the hotel closed in 2011 and has since been demolished and replaced by housing.

A defining feature of Llanyravon was the provision of the substantial open space defined in the 1951 Master Plan as Llanfrechfa Park. 149 acres (60 hectares) of land, deemed suitable for a wide range of recreational purposes owing to its level topography and attractiveness, was reserved for this. At the northern end, the plan optimistically included a helicopter landing ground, which 'developments in the transport of passengers and goods' suggested may become essential, as well as being 'the only type of air service for which the designated area appears to be suitable'.[277] In 1971 Cwmbrân Urban District Council developed the four-acre boating lake towards the southern end of the park, aided by £30,000 towards costs by the CDC.[278]

7.5.2 Character of Building in Llanyravon

Llanyrafon is an extended neighbourhood on a north-south orientation and mainly occupies the flatter ground of the river valley, the Afon Lwyd running down the western boundary, rising to eastwards of Turnpike Road. Pre-New Town assets comprise the listed Llanyravon Farm and Llanyravon Mill, both of rubble stone with slate roofs and restored, though the mill race powering the latter has been infilled and built over by a

Figures 100, 101 and 102: CDC housing at Narberth Crescent, Beaumaris Drive and The Alders.

series of detached and semi-detached inter-war housing on Caerleon Road.

Development is otherwise characterised by the CDC development of the 1950s, housing again dominated by the traditional forms found at Pontnewydd and Croesyceiliog and similar to those of local authority schemes. The northern section of the neighbourhood is formed around the circular route made up of Caernarfon Crescent and Liswerry Drive, which provides easy access around the estates, and through the centre of which Llanyravon Way forms north and south access points. Within this area the layout is a loosely random pattern of roads, terraces and pairs of houses that form a variety of streets, courts and culs-de-sac that limits and varies the viewpoints along the streets, avoiding long vistas of uniform housing. This is maintained to a lesser degree further south as the developed area narrows between Llanfrechfa Way and Turnpike Road.

The majority of housing consists of two-storey properties, varied by the use of porch types – which have been heavily modified and added to in consequence of private ownership – and materials, including brickwork, render, local stone, tile hanging and timber boarding. Dispersed within the estates are two-storey maisonettes, distinguishable from the housing only though the presence of external stairs and first-floor balconies. Towards the southern end of the neighbourhood, particularly exhibited along The Alders and Friars Drive, the housing becomes less dense consisting of large detached houses and bungalows. These have a particularly rich mixture of brick colours, terracotta tiling and timber treatments.

All properties are provided with front and rear gardens, with a range of on-road and pedestrian access in the western section of the neighbourhood. The use of culs-de-sac and courts, grassed areas of pedestrian access and the provision of larger grassed areas designed to be used for playgrounds and greens are complemented by retention of mature woodland the CDC tree planted to roads and open areas.

East of the A4042 Turnpike Road the area of Crown Road and Crown Rise displays higher quality housing, mainly laid out along north-south roads that maximise the views for the maximum number of houses. The CDC housing uses a greater mixture of forms and rooflines, including the use of shallow-pitch and mono-pitch roofs that aided the retention of people's views, with attention to decorative detail and finish. Crown Road, on the other hand, exhibits a greater emphasis on houses built through private development and individually architecturally designed, leading to one of the most organically developed streetscapes within Cwmbrân. A number of these properties are of particularly fine design and merit further investigation.

The provision of flats is limited, those within the original design consisting of three-storey blocks flanking the unit shopping centre on Llanfrechfa Way. These visually mark the 'centre' of the neighbourhood and provide impact along the main approach road from the south, though their presence is

Figures 103 and 104: Examples of privately developed houses on Crown Road and Brynrhedyn Road.

softened by the use of local stone to the gabled ends. This is in contrast to the later flats at Grey Waters, a starker and more angular block in grey render. The unit centre is the most successful, and the most original surviving within Cwmbrân. A neat L-shaped complex of 11 shops set under a pantile roof rising from a wide, protective canopy the unit is still fully occupied by a diverse and useful range of local shops and services. The adjacent Crow's Nest public house is one of the most visually interesting and attractive in the New Town with its multifaceted roof line with slate grey tiles and mellow stone and timber panelling.

Later development includes a small housing estate developed at Twm Barlem View and Tudor Woods. One prominent recent building is Palm Grove from 1999, a large, detached property externally designed in an architecturally correct International Modernist style on Brynrhedyn Road.

The natural attractiveness of the area has been maintained with the high level of open ground retained for recreational and aesthetic purposes. Bath Wood was retained in its entirety within the original landscaping, though this has been

encroached upon by recent residential development, while a smaller section of Mill Wood was incorporated into the landscape of the northern part of Llanyravon. Most notable is Llanyravon Park with its range of natural, landscaped and recreation parkland providing the most important area for recreation within the town, the lake in particular providing important habitat for wildlife.

7.6 Oakfield

7.6.1 Background

The Oakfield neighbourhood was a triangular wedge comprising 156 acres (23 hectares) between the Eastern Valleys and Cwmbrân Branch railway lines, lying south of the Town Centre.[279]

This neighbourhood included the historic and rural village of Llantarnam at its southern extremity, including St Michael and All Angels Church, Brook House and the Green House public house. At the north end was the existing village of Oakfield based along Llan-Dowlais street, comprising houses, shops and chapels, and part of the old village of Cwmbrân, centred around Ventor, Victoria and Merthyr Roads. This northern area was a focus for industry by the end of the nineteenth century, including Star Brick and Tile Works, the Oakfield Wire works and the Vitriol Works, and included a number of clay pits and brick and tile works. By contrast, the southern area was agricultural, dominated by farms such as Court Farm and Ty-Coch farm.[280] Small areas of nineteenth-century housing along Oakfield Road and Llantarnam Road continued to spread through the early twentieth century with substantial expansion of the clay pits in the northern area.[281]

Post-war development was already in progress by the Cwmbrân Urban District Council (CUDC) when the New Town was established, with housing being developed along Llantarnam Road by the Llantarnam Housing Society and war-time housing estates of 50 prefabs built to the south of Oakfield Road, and another at Court Farm, built to house workers in the nearby factories.[282] The CUDC was keen to start on a building programme to replace these and provide further local authority housing, while the design and planning of the Llantarnam Comprehensive School by the Monmouthshire County Council architects department was also underway in 1950 (this school was eventually demolished in 2016). All these developments, along with a residual industrial landscape containing considerable areas of old clay pits and brickworks and an old cemetery site, made this neighbourhood comparatively difficult for the CDC to develop.

Alongside the necessary infilling of the clay pits, the first CDC housing scheme in this neighbourhood was started in 1952 and comprised 16.5 acres (7 hectares) with 167 houses and 28 garages, these first houses being Wimpey 'no-fines' concrete construction.[283] A neighbourhood centre of six single-storey shops at Croeswen Road was planned largely around the decision to retain a group of 'large fine trees'

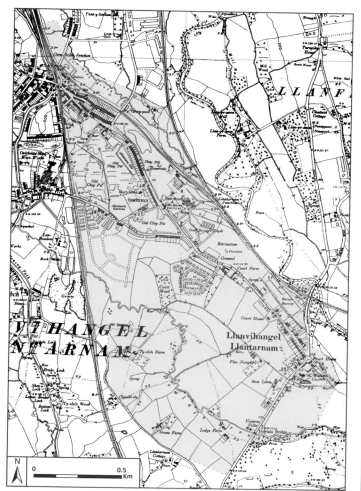

Figure 105: The area of Oakfield depicted on the OS mapping of 1948 and 1983–84.

some of which still stand.[284] The centre was the first to open in Cwmbrân, the ceremony taking place in March 1954 by Lord Raglan, lord lieutenant, and was a test bed for establishing a letting policy that was both financially beneficial for the CDC and fair to existing businesses. Its success was rapid as the centre quickly established itself as a focal point of the neighbourhood. Sketch plans for a public house to complete the centre were submitted in 1958, with building of The Oakfield Inn completed in 1961. Improvements were made to the shopping unit in 1965 to bring it up to the standard of

subsequent centres in other neighbourhoods, including the provision of additional car parking and improved landscaping.[285]

In 1954 the Llantarnam Secondary school opened, the first in the designated area and setting a 'county style' followed by County Architect Colin Jones over the next decade. By 1957 the Oakfield Primary School opened adjacent to the unit centre, creating a level of architectural diversity and 'enliving the area'.[286] While this followed the form of county style,

Figure 106: The CDC housing scheme at Ash Green, undated.

Figure 107. The Oakfield neighbourhood Unit Centre, Croeswen Road, 1954.

Jones diversified in his use of building materials with the use of zinc cladding to the elevations. Both schools have been demolished in recent years, the Oakfield Primary site under residential development in 2020 and Llantarnam Secondary rebuilt as the Llantarnam Community Primary School in 2016.

By the late 1950s the majority of the housing was complete. The CUDC approached the CDC in 1971 to aid redevelopment of the Arcon site at the north end of Fields Road, having redeveloped that at Crown Farm in 1963. As a result, 32 local authority dwellings were completed by the CDC between 1974 and 1977 on behalf of Monmouthshire County Council.

Cwmbrân Stadium was built between 1963 and 1964, consisting of a grandstand incorporating a gymnasium, changing rooms, and café and overlooking playing field, football pitch and running track. This was extended by the CUDC in 1973-74 to include two sports halls housing a 25-metre swimming pool, sauna and two squash courts, the halls designed by Dale Owen of the renowned Percy Thomas Partnership.[287] The running track was upgraded to a tartan track of international standard, the CDC contributing £20,000 towards this and the sports halls.[288]

In the early 1970s the CDC turned its thoughts to the building of 'Cwmbrân Drive', the southern approach road laid out in the 1951 plan as running along the western edge of Oakfield adjacent to the Eastern Valleys Line, but which had not been achieved. Owing to extended discussions about the form this road should take and how it should be funded, construction did not finally start until 1981, reaching Henllys Ways by early 1983.[289]

In the early 1970s the University of Wales, Institute of Science and Technology (UWIST) was searching for a site to establish a new centre. Its first choice was a site at Llantarnam, just outside the designated area of Oakfield, in 1972. This scheme was not realised, and in 1978 the CDC instead designated the land for industrial development, allowances being made to extend the boundary owing to increasing unemployment levels. The first phase of the Llantarnam Industrial Park Phase was completed mid-1981, after which focus switched to developing the area as a park for the tech-industry (see Section 5.7). Raglan House was approved in February 1983 as the first development, with further units including Ty Gwent and Brecon House from 1984.[290] In 1984 work started on the 'luxury' Parkway Hotel and conference centre to complement the business park, the 46-bedroom hotel opening in July 1985.[291] The final phase of CDC development took place in 1987-88 with the completion of Tintern House and Afon House, at which time the development and planning permission for a fourth phase was sold to the Welsh Development Agency.[292]

7.6.2 Character of Area

The Oakfield neighbourhood sits on the low-lying, flat valley floor of the Lwyd Valley, situated on the western side of the River Lwyd. The presence of alluvial deposits, together with the topography, made it suitable for agriculture and the increasing industrial development and its associated settlements from the nineteenth century, and the area was designated for a mixture of residential and industrial development by the CDC. The neighbourhood has a number of clearly delineated areas of defined development type, more marked than many of the other neighbourhoods in Cwmbrân.

Pre-New Town development is focused in at the northern and southern extremes of the neighbourhood, where it encompassed the villages of Llantarnam and Cwm-brân. Llantarnam was tightly focused around the Medieval parish church of St Michael and All Angels. This stone parish church of mainly fifteenth- and sixteenth-century, late perpendicular and Tudor detailing, sits within a large graveyard with mature trees to its boundaries reflecting it rural origins within the Magna Porta estate. The surrounding village was small, with few pre-designation properties accompanying the church. Brook House and The Greenhouse Inn are the two most significant of these, recognised by their Grade II Listing. Situated either side of the church, the large detached house is Georgian in external character with a white lime render and slate tile roof, the inn of whitewashed rubble stone. These contrast with the more regimented line of detached and semi-detached Edwardian villas along Llantarnam Road to the

Figure 108 and 109: Historic Llantarnam village: Victoria Street and Llantarnam Gardens.

north of this group. Despite the village's incorporation within the designated area, the open nature of the settlement survives with large areas of green space in the form of the churchyard and gardens. Housing development around the village core has taken place only relatively recently, comprising a series of small cul-de-sac estates using a varied range of 'mock' historical elements ranging through 'Tudorbethan', Georgian and Victorian with differing levels of success.

The industrialisation of the area in the nineteenth century is represented by contemporaneous associated settlement. The most significant area of this is the portion of Cwm-brân village integrated within the northern end of the neighbourhood. Focused around Ventnor Road and Victoria Place, it extends southwards along the northernmost stretch of Llantarnam Road (originally Cemetery Road). Here the nature of the housing is largely of narrow fronted terraced and semi-detached Victorian and Edwardian properties built between 1881 and 1916. The narrow plots are extended in length, the houses giving way to long rear gardens uncurbed by back-to-back development. Narrow-fronted terraces with street frontages, exemplified on Ventnor Street and the northern end of Victoria Street, have subtle variations in design regarding dressings, the use of bay windows and recessed porches, though there are high levels of modernisation to many of the facades, with high instances of late-twentieth-century rendering and ubiquitous replacement of windows with uPVC frames. Further south on Victoria Road the mixture of brick and stone-built terraced houses dating to the last decade of the nineteenth century are of higher in quality. These dwellings have small front gardens creating off-street entrances, bay windows in some instances rising to two storeys and the use of decorative moulded brickwork. This is mirrored in the contemporary housing along the western side of Llantarnam Road. Of note are the small number of semi-detached properties on Ventnor Road orientated with the facades facing away from the road. While this would have provided street access to the kitchen entrance, the facades facing away from the narrow lane, the lack of road or footpath to access the front entrance makes the layout unusual.

Notable civic buildings include Ross House, originally the offices of the CUDC and Monmouthshire County Council Library, a fine turn-of-the-century brick building in Baroque style, and the former police station of similar date, again of red brick with yellow brick dressings, now in use as The Council House.

Outside of these historic cores and the joining thoroughfare of Llantarnam Road, the neighbourhood is principally characterised by New Town development. This is segregated into distinct zones of industrial, residential and open space that reflects work required during the early years of the CDC to reclaim previous industrial areas and the extension of the Designated Area within the life of the CDC.

Residential development is primarily within an east-west swathe south of Heol Oakfield and extending from the A4051

to Llantarnam Road, its southern boundary reflecting the original edge of the Designated Area. This was developed on flat agricultural land with little to affect or inspire the nature of development. These CDC-developed estates are characterised by the short terraces or semi-detached pairs of traditional two-storey housing, predominantly rendered or pebble-dashed with tiled roofs. The majority have been externally modernised, but one example remains unaltered at 43 South Road. This rare survival displays the original aluminium framed glazing, half-light door and render. Subtle variations in design exist throughout the estate in the treatment of porches and render. Interspersed within the terraces are maisonettes, largely identical in form, and the few discrete groups of bungalows follow a similar pattern. The dwellings are laid out along curving estate roads, small courts and culs-de-sac that help to add some visual interest to the largely identical housing, the terraces allowing a density of building that ensured large open spaces and greens, in addition to front and rear gardens. The CDC planting of trees in some of these open spaces, mirrors the dense treelines that are visible to the southern and northern horizon, where the residential area is bounded by mature woodland and parkland, helping to enclose the estate, restricting views and creating a sense of locale.

Figure 110: 43 South Road, a rare CDC-built house surviving without exterior alterations.

Figure 111: A CDC sheltered housing scheme on The Highway, fronting onto an open green.

Llantarnam Road and Heol Oakfield, the main two thoroughfares within the neighbourhood, provide a greater level of built diversity, a mixture of nineteenth-century, inter-war, CDC and recently built housing that provides a visual variety of materials and form. East of Llantarnam Road, Grayson Way through to Poplar Place is a 2010 estate development, the densely developed red and yellow brick houses designed with a limited palette of Victorian inspired motifs.

Commercial development outside of the historic core of old Cwm-bran village is provided by the neighbourhood centre at Croeswen. The single-storey, staggered shopping units with their low-pitched gables and muted colour palette are architecturally discreet, the site marked by the continued retention of mature trees. The units retain their original form, though with replacement glazing. Opposite, the Oakfield Arms, although two-storey, replicates the style and form of the surrounding housing, distinguished by signage rather than architecture.

The neighbourhood contains three distinct areas of light industrial land use in the form of Court Road Industrial Estate, Oldbury Road Industrial Estate and Llantarnam Industrial Park. Court Road and Oldbury Road Estates are both located in the northern section of the neighbourhood, developed on reclaimed industrial and extractive land. Both are relatively low-density developments, consisting of single-storey brick and corrugated steel-clad workshops and small factories as characterised by the advanced factories built by the CDC. The low-pitched roofs, landscaping and planting of trees ensures these are visually unobtrusive within the neighbourhood.

Figure 112. The Oakfield Unit Centre, Croeswen, today retains its impressive trees though the shop units have not fared so well.

Llantarnam Industrial Park occupies a substantial portion at the southern end of the neighbourhood, occupying the expansion land outside of the original designated area. This estate is also comprised partly of light industrial and engineering factories, ranging from blocks standardised brick and corrugated steel-clad, CDC-built manufacturing units at

the north end of Llantarnam Park Way to more architecturally facaded units such at Usk House. Interspersed are higher quality tech-industry units: the best grouping of which is Tintern House, Brecon House, Raglen House and Ty Afon in the north-eastern corner of the estate. Built throughout the 1980s, these display a variety of materials and designs that mirror the advent of a new type of industry to the town. They are mirrored by the early twenty-first century development of The Pavilions, housing a range of software and chemical engineering companies. The Parkway Hotel, situated on Ty Coch Lane, represents the national and international nature of the companies located on the park. The units sit within spacious grounds, with substantial areas of attractively planted landscaping across the park including swathes of trees that soften the sometimes-stark nature of the built environment. This is particularly evident at the entrance to the business park at Newport Road, where development of the Dolwais Brook has created an attractive naturalised habitat.

Figure 113: Tŷ Gwent.

The centre of the neighbourhood, immediately south of Old Cwmbrân, contains a large area of open recreational ground bounded by Henllys Way, Oakfield Road and Llantarnam Road. Comprising the stadium field and track, playing fields, parkland and Oakfield Cemetery, the whole provides an attractively planted and open area in the heart of the neighbourhood.

7.7 Fairwater

7.7.1 Historical Background

The Fairwater neighbourhood was developed from 1961 to 1974 in the south-western part of Cwmbrân, developing out of the Coedeva neighbourhood in 1959 when indecision on the raising of the New Town population made full development of Coedeva impossible. Coedeva III was instead developed as Fairwater. Designed to house a population of 2,000, this scheme brought the CDC to its target population of 35,000.

The area was one of historic woodland including parts of Maes-y-rhiw Wood to the north, Coed Waun-fyr to the

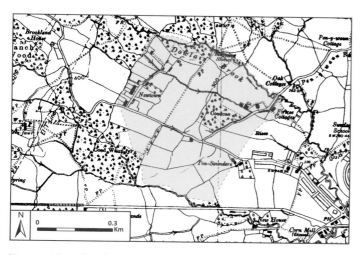
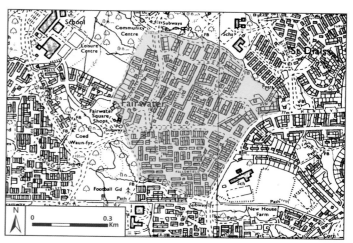

Figure 114. The Fairwater area depicted on the OS mapping of 1948 and 1984.

south-west and Coedcae in the south-east. Maes-y-rhiw and Coed Waun-fyr have been recorded as historic abbey coppice woodland and smaller sections of these survive on a reduced scale, but Coedcae has been completely overbuilt. The remainder of the area was agricultural with a small cluster of nineteenth-century houses at Newtown (later Fairwater Avenue, now Fairwater Close).[293] Apart from the gradual reduction in size of the Coedcae woodland, there was no real development of the area throughout the first half of the twentieth century.[294]

Development was split into Fairwater I (369 dwellings), Fairwater II (60 dwellings), Fairwater III(a) (89 dwellings) and Fairwater III(b) (224 dwellings).[295] This was the first neighbourhood to be designed on the principles of Radburn planning adopted from housing schemes in the USA, separating vehicular and foot traffic to create higher levels of safety for pedestrians, and designing housing layouts based around culs-de-sac. This was illustrated by the designs produced for Fairwater III by Alex Gordon of Alex Gordon and Partners, Cardiff, in 1962, modified with input from Gordon Redfern. This was named as the Fairhill Estate.

This scheme provided a housing layout avoiding long terraces, instead arranging the houses in clustered groups around a repeating pattern of culs-de-sac. The housing blocks were

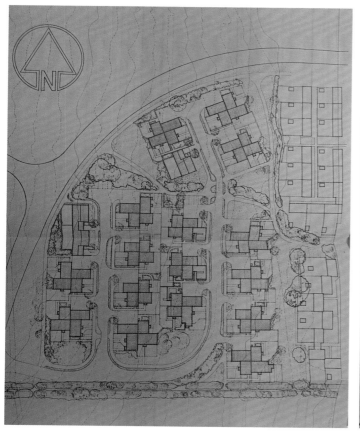
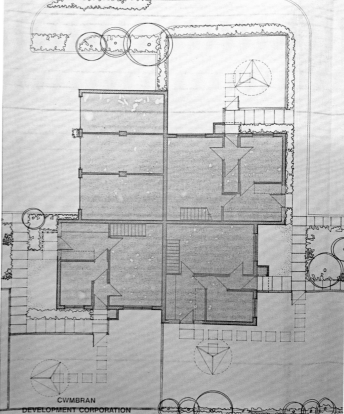

Figure 115: The estate layout for the Fairwater 4 scheme, together with detail of the cluster group approach.

deliberately orientated to try and make the most of natural daylight while single-aspect layouts provided more private gardens than in previous layouts. Separate road and footpath networks ensured that children, mothers with prams and older people could walk to schools or shops without crossing, or walking immediately alongside, a road but it was also ensured that, for convenience, no house was more than 150 feet (46 m) from a road. The scheme consisted of a mixture of three- and four-bedroom houses together with a 'bachelor's mews flat', originally designed as six-storey blocks but reduced to three storeys on request of the CDC.[296]

Along with the other Fairwater schemes, and in contrast to previous neighbourhoods, all dwellings conformed to the Parker Morris standards, complying with the recommendations in the report 'Homes for Today and Tomorrow'. Many were designed with either flat or shallow mono-pitched roofs, and some with the use of timber panels to the external elevations, in an attempt to break away from the traditional form associated with the inter-war local authority housing. However, Fairwater III, in particular, saw problems with damp ingress through flat roofs, with remedial work needed a couple of years later.[297]

The first 369 dwellings were completed by 1966, with a mixture for rent and for private sale. By 1968 concerns were raised by the CDC that more than half of the 40 houses put on the market had failed to sell, with potential buyers being unwilling to purchase a private home situated among rented properties. This prompted a change in direction for future planning, the CDC stating that future properties for sale should be built in discrete schemes on the edge of developments. A seven-acre development of 34 houses by a private developer begun in 1969 led to the houses being sold as quickly as they could be built, proving that this policy worked.

Smaller housing schemes continued to be built in the neighbourhood through the early 1970s, including a development of 12 two-person flats at Ty'n-y-Coed, 10 pensioner bungalows on Ty Gwyn Road for Torfaen CBC and a 36-bedroom 'old people's home' built on behalf of Gwent County Council.

In 1982 the Expansion Area led to the Fairwater IV scheme of 62 dwellings.[298] To the west of the original Fairwater (Coedeva III) development, the scheme was bounded to the north and west by the expansion of Fairwater Way, and to the south by the pedestrian route linking Fairwater to Henllys village. Again, it had a number of landscape assets with mature hedgerows lining the southern and eastern boundaries and a small brook running though the site, and it was decided to retain these within the landscaping as far as possible. The topographical and access constrictions of the site led to a change of approach away from the 'mixer-court' designs that had been hitherto popular in later schemes at Thornhill and Hollybush. Instead a 'cluster unit' layout was used, containing a higher percentage of smaller dwellings

than usual for the CDC, with some 48 per cent being one- or two-bedroom houses, flats or bungalows, including specific provision for 'disabled persons' bungalows. This move to smaller dwellings was a direct response to recommendations of both the CDC's Commercial Director and the Welsh Office Circular 42/75, though this also led to the houses being built 10 per cent below Parker Morris standards on a 'value for money' basis, the CDC looking to eventually sell the properties to tenants.[299] Parking was provided at 115 per cent with 100 per cent garaging in groups of three or four. The final residential scheme was carried out in 1985; Fairwater Close provided nine mixed-type dwellings.

The Fairwater Unit Centre, planned in 1963-64, was to be the main centre for the south-western areas of the New Town.[300] Originally planned for the junction of Henllys Way and Fairwater Way, it was moved further west to bring to the geographical centre of the south-western areas after expansion had been agreed. The west side of this new site was bounded by an attractive birch wood, which Redfern decided to retain, incorporating areas of informal and irregularly placed car parking among the trees despite the extra expense this incurred. The centre was designed to include 18 shops, public lavatories, a medical practice and a health clinic, a combined public house and community centre, an Anglican church and a petrol filling station, and was laid out on the segregation of vehicles/pedestrians principle.[301] Space was left in the layout for four additional shops should they be required at a later date. Four different shops types (1/10, A, B and C) were provided on increasing floor footage for facilities ranging from barbers to grocery shop, all with storage to the first floor and eight with a two-bedroom maisonette. 15 van garages were provided for the use of traders, along with 26 reserved parking spaces and 60 free parking spaces.[302]

Owing to the prominent, elevated position and the 'high rainfall, mists and variable winds' prevalent in the area, it was decided to create an enclosed space that would protect shoppers from inclement weather both physically and psychologically. The natural changes in level of the topography were enhanced by the fact that buildings on the south-west side were extended higher, the upper stories used as the maisonettes, the whole creating a highly visible focal point for the neighbourhood. The shopping experience was further enhanced by the provision of more generous canopies to the shop fronts than at other centres to further protect shoppers, and the fact that the plan created a safe central area, away from traffic and visible from all shops, for use as a children's play area. Owing to the desire to create an architectural statement with this enclosed 'ring' of shops, the plan for the individual units was hexagonal, something that created considerable discussion between the Chief Architect and Estates Officer. The latter's concern that the shape would cause inefficiencies in floor-space usage, added to the cost of fitting out and create an additional number of blank 'dead' walls, was overridden by Redfern.[303]

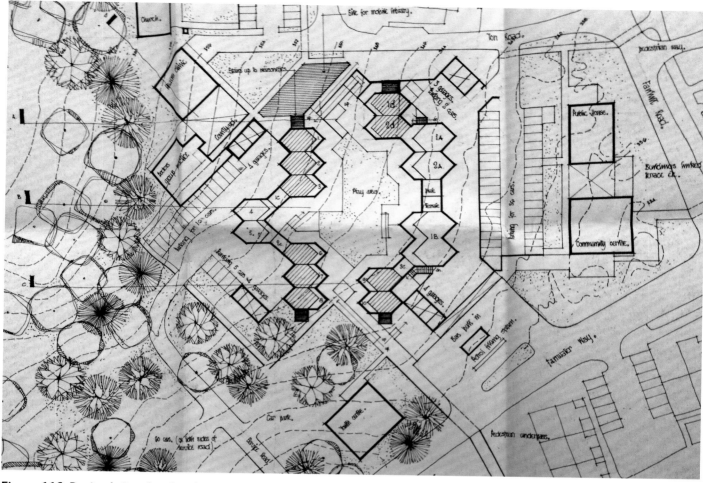

Figure 116. Revised site plan for the Fairwater shopping centre, January 1964.

Ove Arup & Partners was appointed as the structural engineer in April 1964, with construction work undertaken by Gee, Walker & Slater, a firm already undertaking work on many of the Fairwater, St Dials and Greenmeadow housing developments as well as the Ringland shopping centre, Newport.[304] The schemes was estimated at a cost of £214,106.[305]

Building was severely delayed by the exceptional winter weather of 1963-64 and tenders for tenancy of the first six shops were not advertised until January 1965 for expected occupancy in March 1967. By summer 1966 a butcher, baker, chemist, grocer and newsagents had taken leases, and the remaining units advertised on a 14-year lease to commence January 1967. The majority of the units came fully fitted out by the CDC, with finishings as required by the various trades; the General Post Office, for instance was requested to be fitted with telephone booth, posting box, stamp machine and half-glazed panel for advertising services. One exception was the bank, which Lloyds requested as a shell only to ensure fitting out to company standards.

The Health Clinic and Medical Group Practice were built in association with the centre and designed by Redfern, though constructed separately by H. T. Watkins (Newbridge) at a cost of £23,718.[306] Designed with three consulting rooms on the ground floor, the first floor being a separate unit reserved by a dental practice, the centre opened in 1967.[307]

The unit centre was opened 12 September 1967, shared with the opening of Monmouth House, both undertaken by Rt. Hon. James Callaghan, M.P. A scathing article written the following month by architectural critic Ian Nairn dismissed the design as a 'kind of in-turned medieval village … an oasis of picturesqueness in a desert of statistical units' designed for, rather than with, the inhabitants and therefore destined for commercial failure.[308]

At this point all buildings other than the public house, meeting hall and filling station had been built. The joint public house/community centre was a vital part of the centre, providing a social hub at the centre of the new neighbourhood. This joint provision was intended to make the community facilities more attractive to an 'increasingly sophisticated public' who, it was considered, were increasingly less inclined to prepare for, and clear up after, community social events and instead wanted professionals on hand. However, in order to ensure that non-drinkers, including young people, could still comfortably use the premises it was considered imperative that separate entrances and the appearance of distinctiveness was maintained.[309] Ansell Ind Coope (Allied Breweries) agreed to take on the lease and Fairwater House opened in July 1969.

The large function suite with its separate entrance immediately proved extremely popular.[310]

The opportunity for a church building had, by 1963, been taken up by the Methodist Church. The Chief Estates Officer expressed concern that both the building plot and car park originally allocated for this facility were too small and a larger plot was found at the Fairhill Estate. Built in 1964-65 to replace its historic site on Wesley Street, St Dials, this formed a functional and flexible complex but marked by the gabled roof that rises to some twice the height of the building for visibility within the neighbourhood. In 1971 the Methodist Church agreed to share the building with the Church in Wales, the first time such a shared arrangement was made in Wales.[311]

Work on the Fairwater Junior and Infant School at Blenheim Road started in 1963, completed in 1965.[312] While the need for a secondary school was recognised as urgent, a site was not acquired until 1969 and building was not completed until 1972.[313] Designed by Monmouthshire County Council architect Sydney Leyshon, successor to Colin Jones, it was built in a radically different style from the earlier schools being far more inward looking in its form. The school was provisioned with extensive recreational facilities including a swimming pool and in 1974 the CUDC allocated £150,000 to upgrade the sporting facilities to meet the standards required for public use as a leisure centre, mirroring the successful dual use of other schools in the town. This included the additional provision of social areas and restaurant, floodlighting and two squash courts.[314]

7.7.2 Character of Area

Fairwater is a small neighbourhood, having been created from land originally allocated to Greenmeadow, St Dials and Coedeva. The only surviving pre-New Town housing in the Fairwater area is at Fairwater Close, a terrace of late nineteenth-century cottages, initially marked Fairwater Cottages in 1881 and by 1899 Newton.[315] This stone terrace is made up of narrow frontages, originally of two-up, two-down properties, and is now largely rendered with the addition of porches, rear extensions and uPVC windows.

The character of the area is overwhelmingly defined by the concentrated period of development by the CDC between 1961 and 1974, with limited amounts of later redevelopment. This is dominated by the terraces and courts of two-storey housing. North of Fairwater Way the housing is traditional, following closely the forms and materiality set in the earlier estates such as Pontnewydd and Oakfield, though laid out on pedestrianised principles, with courts and terraces of houses facing onto grassed walkways or central greens and parking bays and garages to the rear.

Across the rest of the neighbourhood the houses retain the more innovative forms as designed by Redfern or Gordon. These take two main forms: the first are terraces of asymmetrical shallow-hipped houses, the front elevations of

which are steeply set-back to the left bay to allow for the incorporation of an entrance porch and garage as exemplified at The Wades and sections of Jule Road; the second terraced form is again of two-storey houses but with shallow mono-pitched roofs. The elevations of these are notable for the minimal glazing to the front, with a single window to the ground floor and a single horizontal slit window to the first floor. Facing into the interconnecting public footpaths or greens that provide access to the properties, these facades, indicating the location of kitchen and bathroom to the front of the house, preserve the privacy of the householder, the large windows lighting the living and bedrooms spaces facing on to the private rear garden. This arrangement of the fenestration, together with the use of contrasting brickwork and inset timber panelling, perhaps referred to the pattern used in the Span housing designed by Eric Lyons in the 1950s and 60s. In the southern section of Fairwater, these terraces are furnished with deep porches incorporating an outside store as exemplified at Hassocks Lea, which are absent on the other estates.

Figures 117 and 118: The innovative forms of CDC housing designed by Gordon Redfern at Jule Road and Hassocks Lea, Pace Road.

Fairhill, a discrete estate at the northern tip of the neighbourhood designed by the private practice of Alex Gordon and Partners, is differentiated by the laying out of terraces against the terrain, the sloping terraces forming a continuous mono-pitch roof from one end to the other. The building materials are uniform across the CDC- and privately-designed estates, with a greater use of exposed brickwork to the exteriors, complemented with the use of timber cladding. The latter material is particularly evident in the estates on the western side of Fairwater, where the austere elevations are lifted by the use of timber boarding across the facades, perhaps the best examples being either side of Neerings. With the exception of replacement of doors and windows with uPVC, the majority of houses retain an original external form.

Figure 119. Terraces at the Fairhill estate by Alex Gordon & Partners.

Figure 120: The flats incorporated into the Fairwater shopping centre.

The only medium-rise housing in the neighbourhood are the four-storey flats adjacent to the unit centre, where exposed, shutter-boarded concrete staircases add textural variety to the brickwork elevations. The steeply mono-pitched roofs of the houses are mirrored by pitched brick parapets carried high above the roof lines, a technique also used at the Fairwater centre to create an increased sense of height above the two storey units. This centre provides one of the few examples of non-domestic architecture in the neighbourhood, others including the contemporary Fairhill Methodist Church and Cwmbrân High School/Fairhill leisure centre. The intention to make the shopping unit a sheltered and protected area through its enclosed form appears in recent years to have made it an isolated space and one that has suffered, as with the other unit centres, commercially through competition with the town centre.

Figure 121: The Methodist Church at Fairhill.

A substantial section of Coed Waun-fyr survives as a mature woodland either side of the western end of Fairwater Way with open recreational fields on its southern edge. Extant parts of Maes-y-rhiw Woods form the northern boundary with Greenmeadow. Within the estates, open grassed courts, greens and walkways break up the dense terraces of houses which are provided with private, but relatively small rear gardens.

7.8 St Dials (including Old Cwm-brân)

7.8.1 Background

St Dials is a hilly 188 acres (76 hectares) in the centre of the Designated Area, immediately to the south-west of the Town Centre. Bounded to the north and north-east by Colomendy Road (now Greenforge Way) and to the south and west by the proposed Parkway (now Henllys Way to the south, Bleinheim Road to the west), it included most of the historic village of Cwm-brân. By the time of designation Cwm-brân comprised the historic streets of Commercial Street, Wesley Street, Oak Street and Abbey road to the west of the Eastern Valleys Line and canal. This had a relatively well-developed centre furnished with shops, St Dials Junior school, and the Abbey

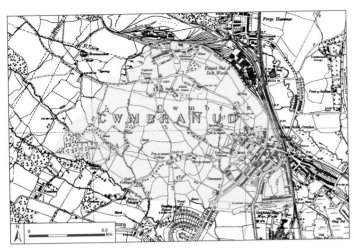
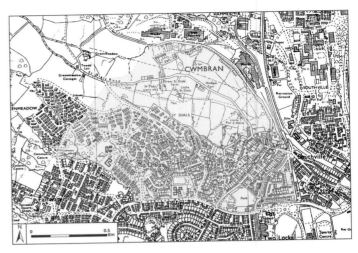

Figure 122: The area of St Dials depicted on the OS Mapping of 1948 and 1972.

Hotel public house.[316] St Gabriel's Anglican Church had been built in the early twentieth century to supplement the nineteenth-century nonconformist chapels, Elim Independent Chapel and the Wesleyan Methodist Chapel, and Our Lady of the Angels Catholic Church of 1883.

The remainder of the area was in agricultural use or wooded, seen as one of the least spoilt neighbourhoods, with a population of just 1,420 prior to the New Town development, targeted to rise to 4,300. The steepest sloping areas in the north and north-eastern part of the neighbourhood were due to be left undeveloped for topographical and climatic reasons.[317] This area included the site of St Dials 'chapel', a potential medieval chapel located on the pilgrimage route from Llantarnam Abbey to Pen-rhys demarcated by above

ground remains of a medieval barn and field system.[318] The development of the St Dials neighbourhood was part of the final major phase of development of the original designated area, along with Coedeva and Greenmeadow as the 'southwestern area'. Survey of these areas started in 1953, with public consultation on schools, council housing and planning proposals taking place in 1956.[319]

Henllys Way was designated as the main road to serve the south-western neighbourhoods with preparation starting in 1956 when the first housing scheme St Dials I was also approved.[320] Construction started on 34 houses during that year, though the overall scheme for the neighbourhood was not approved until 1959, by which time ground-work preparation was also underway for 280 dwellings in St Dials

Figure 123: The form of housing introduced by Chief Architect Gordon Redfern for St Dials Phase III, in distinct contrast to the traditional gabled-roofed forms used previously, undated.

II.[321] Delays on decisions and approval were at this point being complicated by ongoing discussions regarding the raising of the target population. J. C. P. West was replaced by Gordon Redfern as Chief Architect in 1962 and the style of dwellings in subsequent phases changed radically, with the use of new flat-roofed forms and a diversity of materials including timber and stone applied to the exterior of dwellings. In 1964 St Dials III, III(b) and III(c) of some 600 dwellings including 66 maisonettes and 'flatlets' in 11 four-storey blocks were approved and started, with III(a) and (b) completed by 1966. Phase III(c) was marked by the use of increased levels of prefabrication to save both time and money, though the annual reports were keen to point out that all dwellings complied with standards recommended in 'Homes for Today and Tomorrow'. [322]

The historic shopping core around Commercial Street was initially supplemented by a small sub-unit centre, at the junction of Henllys Way and Greenmeadow Way, comprising four shops, four houses and 10 garages. This was subsequently deemed insufficient for new residents and led to a second neighbourhood centre being developed. The unit centre at Blenheim Road, developed between 1963 and 1966, comprised six further shops and 12 garages.[323] This scheme was demolished in 2013, partly replaced with the smaller Blenheim Stores unit.

A new St Dials Infant school, now Ysgol Gymraeg, was built by the Monmouthshire Architects Department in 1960-61, on the southern boundary of the neighbourhood on Henllys way. Designed by Colin Jones, it followed the standard pattern of light brick, well-lit, airy buildings demarcated by a two-storey tower. To the front of the school 'Kate's Bears', commissioned by the Welsh Arts Council in 1973 and completed 1975, is by the artist Anthony Stevens who also taught at the Newport College of Art.[324]

Figure 124: The former St Dials Infant School, Henllys Way, with 'Kate's Bears' sculpture of 1975.

In 1974 St Dials was chosen as the site for the Wales and West of England Police Training Centre, CENTREX. This sizable complex was designed by James Russell and included a swimming pool, bar and assembly hall. Demolished in 2015, the site has been redeveloped for housing.

The Salvation Army had been using the Wesleyan Chapel on Wesley Street for worship since 1928. In 1968, wanting to improve its accommodation, it requested a new site from the CDC, in response to which it was allocated a plot for a new building on Victoria Street. Deciding instead to upgrade the building it already used, the congregation stayed on Wesley Street carrying out renovations. In 1994 they rebuilt on the same site, constructing the building that exists today.

The 2001 census recorded the population of St Dials as the neighbourhood was delineated at that point as 3,665.[325]

7.8.2 Character of area

St Dials neighbourhood has well-defined boundaries to the east, formed by the A4051, and with Coedeva to the south via Henllys Way. To the west and north-west the boundaries with Fairwater, a later neighbourhood partially formed from St Dials, and Greenmeadow are less well defined. The topography across the east-west orientated area rises from the lower-lying valley floor to the east, to the higher, hillier ground of the north-west.

The neighbourhood encompasses the greatest part of the nineteenth-century village of Cwm-brân. Comprising Commercial Street, Wesley Street, Oak Street, Star Street, Abbey Road and Bellvue Road, this historic core sits in the easternmost section of St Dials, bounded by the A4051. This

Figure 125 and 126: The historic centre of 'Old Cwmbrân' village – The Social Club and Halfway House.

area is distinguished by a diverse variety of building types and dates. Later nineteenth- and early twentieth-century terraced housing form long stretches of these main streets, the narrow frontages of which are set in unbroken rows with frontages directly onto the pavement. Of both stone and brick construction, the majority have later render and pebble dashing to the exterior and replacement uPVC glazing, but subtle variations in the use of dressings and moulded terracotta to indicate different phases and grades of construction are still visible. In contrast, the terrace on Clomendy Road, of stone and with enclosed garden frontages, includes grander villas with double-storey pedimented canted bays, which survive.

The historic commercial core is centred around the intersection of Commercial Street and Wesley Street. The pavement-frontage shops include some good surviving examples of simple, but higher-quality plate glass shopfronts from the late nineteenth century, all with residential accommodation above. Two public houses display contrasting architecture: the Mount Pleasant is built in the simple vernacular; while The Halfway House uses elements of the Italianate that came to define Victorian and Edwardian public houses. The most prominent buildings hin the area are religious, standing within open, defined grounds that enhance the visual impact provided by their distinctive architecture. Elim United Reformed Church, typical in its early nineteenth-century use of a Classical facade to announce its place as a nonconformist chapel, and with a particularly fine architrave to the central door, stands dominantly in the centre of the village. St Gabriel's, sitting on an elevated site, contrasts with its use of highly decorative Perpendicular architecture. This use of Gothic is replicated in the less conspicuously located Our Lady of Angels Catholic Church on Wesley Street.

There are substantial amounts of inter-war and New Town infilling in this historic centre. The brick-built, semi-detached houses of the inter-war period on Wesley Street and extending down Cocker Avenue sit sympathetically with the earlier terraces, as does the CDC estate of traditional housing at Bellevue Close.

West of this historic core, smaller pockets and individual properties of nineteenth- and earlier twentieth-century date are dominated by CDC New Town development. This is divided into distinct sections on the style and layout of the dwellings. To the centre of St Dials, in the areas of southern Greenmeadow Way and Shakespeare Road, the houses are predominantly those found in the earlier neighbourhoods of the 1950s and early 1960s, traditionally styled on inter-war local authority housing. Brick built and largely rendered and pebble-dashed, they sit in short terraces and semi-detached pairs, staggered where appropriate to the undulating topography. Uniform in design, there is little in the way of variety other than that provided by individual modernisation. Layout again comprises curving estate roads, branching into a series of culs-de-sac that break up the uniform lines of dwellings, becoming more regimented to the west as the

increasingly hilly topography dictated the lines of terraces that follow the contours. A small number of two-storey maisonettes are interspersed among the houses, with a continuous line of single-storey dwellings at Melbourne Court, forming sheltered housing with an accompanied warden's dwelling. A more notable infill development is that at Cwm-y-nant, where geometric forms, varying roof levels and first-floor interconnecting walkways are combined with the tile-hung elevations to form a successful complex of sheltered flats.

Figure 127: Sheltered housing scheme and warden's house at Melbourne Court, St Dials.

To the north-west, architectural change and the segregation of houses from the estate and access roads represent the advent of Gordon Redfern's tenure as Chief Architect. In the area encompassed by the northern curve of Bleinheim Road, Amroth Walk and Farlow Walk the housing consists of short terraces of austere, bold, flat-roofed houses. More angular than the traditional designs, each unit is delineated by extended end walls and wide pilasters of roughcast render, the front and rear facades displaying a diverse range of finishing. Timber panelling is predominant to these, with horizontal and vertical boarding used in a variety of natural or painted colours. Austerity is confirmed by the limited number of windows to the front elevations, small in size and grouped in small clusters. This both maximises the expanse of facade and the privacy of inhabitants, with the terraces more closely set than elsewhere and with access via public footpaths along the frontages. The main living areas are located to the rear of the houses where large windows overlook the private gardens. Rear extensions to some of the properties add to the angularity of the architecture, while interspersed within the estate are 14 blocks of flats, rising to three storeys and with high, steeply mono-pitched roof. Originally of dark-orange brickwork, with dark-stained vertical timber panels that contrasted with the housing, these have been externally clad in recent years with a white rendered finish. North of Blenheim Road and Greenmeadow Way, the narrow terraces set at sharp angles reflecting the terrain continue, but the design softens. A return to pitched roofs accompanies a greater use of mellow brickwork, combined with partial timber cladding, tile hanging or render. The segregated layout is retained, regular terraces set at right angles to through roads.

Figures 128 and 129: CDC terraced housing on Farlow Walk and Coleford Path, interspersed with higher-rising flats.

Bleinheim Road Stores, built c. 2010, has replaced the original unit centre, but the smaller sub-unit centre on Greenmeadow Way survives. Two units have been combined to create a larger, chain, convenience store, the other two remaining as a local independent and post-office. Adjacent to this, the Ysgol Gymraeg retains its original form, together with 'Kate's Bears', with little alteration.

The layout of the housing estates accommodated private gardens for all houses, with front gardens for many. Areas of open green space left as communal and recreational ground within the estates include retained historic woodland and CDC-planted trees, notably along the northern section of Blenheim Road and the Dowlais Brook. There are two principal areas of open space: Cwmbrân Park is a managed area of recreational ground including tarmacked courts, bowling green and children's playground. To the north of the neighbourhood is the substantial area of retained agricultural and woodland, preserved by the CDC as difficult to develop and important green space at the heart of the town. This has seen recent development in the western section for the Cwrt Celyn housing estate, which has included the site of Little St Dials.

7.9 Coedeva (including Two Locks)

7.9.1 Background

The Coedeva neighbourhood is located to the south-west of the New Town centre and was originally made up of 161 acres (65 hectares) bounded by the proposed Parkway (Henllys Way) and the canal to the north and east, by Two Locks Road to the south and by the 110 metre contour line to the west.[326] Throughout the nineteenth century this area had remained very sparsely populated, being largely agricultural, although the tramway between the Henllys Colliery and the Oakfield industries ran through the southern portion of the neighbourhood. The woodland bounding the area to the west, Coed Meyrick-Moel, again is recorded as abbey coppice woodland.[327] The small village of Oakfield sat on the eastern boundary with the Oakfield neighbourhood, and a small amount of nineteenth-century housing extended westwards from here along Two Locks Road.[328] The CUDC had started a small amount of post-war development along Cocker Road, most notably with the building of The Crescent and The Circle, and Ton Road but, along with Greenmeadow and St Dials, Coedeva was considered among the least spoilt part of the Designated Area.

The development of the South-Western Areas, comprising St Dials, Coedeva and Greenmeadow, was the final major phase in the development of the New Town as first envisaged and in total consisted of some 427 acres (173 hectares) to house 14,000 persons, with Coedeva to house 5,454 of these.[329] Survey of the area started in 1953, but site works for Coedeva I did not start until 1964, when design layouts for Coedeva II and III were also underway.[330] This was partly because of negotiations that were taking place in the late 1950s over the raising of the population of the designated area to 45,000 as, with the higher than expected density achieved in the earlier neighbourhoods, design of the neighbourhood and building could not begin until the question of a raised target population had been resolved.[331] Eventually, with no decision on the population increase, the CDC submitted a proposal to build 300 to 350 houses together with a new primary school and shops in the north-west portion of Coedeva that would take the town to the approved 35,000; this was designated as a new neighbourhood of Fairwater (see Section 6.7).

With the population target resolved in 1960, Coedeva I was approved to develop the south-eastern part of Coedeva, bounded to the west by Henllys Way, in 1963. Generally undulating open countryside, it contained New House Farm and its associated woodland, both of which it was decided to retain for open spaces and playing fields, the farmhouse to be used for community purposes.[332] The layout of the scheme for 234 dwellings under new Chief Architect Gordon Redfern commenced in 1965, and was particularly concerned with increasing car provision to 100 per cent. This first phase allowed for a mixture of garages and parking lots, though owing to the high costs of renting the garages, subsequent schemes were planned solely with parking lots. The layout

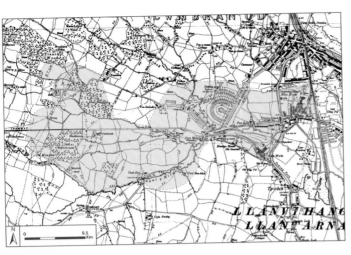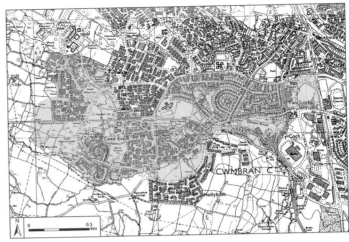

Figure 130: The Coedeva area depicted on the OS mapping of 1948 and 1984.

aimed for the complete segregation of pedestrians and cars as used at Fairwater, including the provision of some 14 underpasses costing £4,250 each.[333] The existing Henllys Lane and disused tramway were both preserved to form part of the extensive footpath system that would ensure the safety of people in moving round the neighbourhood. Coedeva I also included the building of a 'Children's Home' providing temporary accommodation for those in need; the home and school for girls was built by Monmouthshire County Council in 1976-77.[334] Coedeva II commenced in 1968 with 294 houses, some of which were designed for a moderately priced sales market, with the lowest tenders coming from industrial

method housebuilders.[335] Meanwhile, Coedeva III was redesignated as Fairwater.

The houses themselves were built in terraces that could follow the contours of the land, with a group of flats and maisonettes accentuated further by being located on the high ridgeline to the centre of the site. Gordon Redfern's more innovative use of architectural form and fabric came into play, with flat and shallow mono-pitched roofs and prefabricated panels in timber and other materials, together with innovative construction techniques adding to the aesthetic diversity and attractiveness. Particular attention was paid to the cost per unit, introducing a new two-bedroom, four-person dwelling,

Figure 131: The CDC housing scheme at Green Acre, Two Locks, undated.

while meeting the full Parker Morris standards (increasingly important in the other south-western areas) was sacrificed in favour of price to create 'utility' houses.[336] Despite this, the scheme went on to win awards for good house design.[337]

In addition to the CDC schemes, Coedeva was home to several private development schemes. Coedeva IV, Phases I to IV, originally a CDC scheme including better quality 'managerial housing', Coedeva V and Coedeva Mill were all developed privately between 1973 and 1983, including by Barratt.[338] Two acres of land at Coed Eva Mill was also provided for the development of 32 dwellings by a local housing society in 1972.[339]

With the unit centre at Blenheim Road, and the larger shopping centre planned for Fairwater, facilities at Coedeva were reduced from the unit centre originally planned at Ton Road/Coed Eva Mill Road. With the decision that the south-western areas would otherwise have one pantry shop for every 650 people, Coedeva I was provided with two pantry shops and a doctor's house, with further two serving Coedeva II and IV.[340] Community facilities were provided through the conversion of Coedeva Farm for a Scout headquarters in 1968-69, and the building of a community hall to be shared between the Coedeva and Hollybush neighbourhoods completed in 1973. The following year saw the opening of the neighbourhood pub, The Blinkin' Owl, and betting office.[341]

The building of a secondary school commenced in 1960 and was completed the following year, to a design by the Monmouthshire architect's department. While following many of the stylistic traits of Colin Jones's earlier schools, the complex made substantial use of dark timber panelling between the horizontal glazing lines of the classroom ranges, adding visual variation to the exposed brickwork used elsewhere. An additional range was constructed to provide facilities for adult education and community use, a strategy that had been successful at Croesyceiliog previously.[342] After the construction of Fairwater Comprehensive School in 1971, the CDC planned for this to be given for use by the Roman Catholic Church as a school, but instead the complex was reused as the Hollybush Primary School from 1972.[343] After the construction of the Nant Celyn School on the school grounds in 2010, the complex was demolished in 2012, the remainder of the site being used for housing. Coedeva Junior and Infant School was opened in 1967, designed not by the Monmouthshire architect's department, but by Stephen Thomas of Newport.[344] A two-storey, steel-framed complex, it differed from the earlier 'county style' set by Colin Jones. The school was heavily damaged by fire at the beginning of 2016, with one block subsequently demolished.

7.9.2 Character of Area

Coedeva is a large east-west orientated neighbourhood with poorly defined boundaries to the west and south, and with topography rising gently from east to west. The eastern

section of the neighbourhood now forms the smaller suburb known separately as Two Locks.

The main focus of pre-New Town development was the small, nineteenth-century village of Oakfield. Building occurred along the south side of Two Locks Road where a small number of individually built, two-storey properties survive, contrasting with the terraces of workers' housing seen in other historic cores. Most notable is Ebenezer Chapel, its imposing stone facade and internal gallery typical of mid-nineteenth-century chapel building. Outside of this core, scattered properties reflect the predominantly agricultural nature of the area, including the two pairs of red-brick houses on Ton Road, Carnsville and GlenView, both dating from 1902 and nearby Woodfield Cottage. A second, smaller focus for development was Coedeva Mill, the location of a corn-mill disused by the beginning of the twentieth century. The Mill Tavern has been recently demolished, but part of the Post-medieval mill complex survives as a dwelling, 'The Old Mill' to the rear of 'Ton Felin', a detached Edwardian house.

Figures 132 and 133: Inter-war and post-war local authority housing on The Crescent and Waun Road, built in advance of the Designation.

A substantial development of inter- and post-war local authority housing is located around The Crescent, The Circle, Cocker Avenue and Ton Road, situated towards the centre of the neighbourhood. The inter-war housing, which forms the largest part of this development, is formed of semi-detached pairs, brick built, hipped roofed and originally with render to the first floor of the front elevation. There are moulded concrete sills and lintels to the window and moulded concrete corbels support a flat canopy over the front door as exemplified at numbers 61, 63 and 65 The Crescent. The smaller amount of later, post-war, local authority housing is illustrated near the junction of Cocker Avenue and Henllys Way and along Waun Road, these white rendered properties marked out by their wider frontages, gabled roofs and open, concrete-slab porches.

The earliest CDC-built housing in the west of the neighbourhood, dating from the earlier 1960s, is concentrated around Coed Glas, Trem Trwybarlwm, Waun Road and Ton Road, and follows these traditional forms. On an area of flat ground, wide-fronted houses are set as semi-detached pairs or short terraces, laid out around informally arranged roads. Some have small single-storey stores adjacent to the front door with extended roofs forming a canopy to the entrance. These houses sit behind small enclosed front gardens, with larger gardens to the rear. Though there is some provision of garage blocks, the lack of parking has led to some front gardens being converted to driveways, while there has been universal modernisation of windows and doorways using uPVC. Open spaces that are left between the terraces and to corner plots are set with mature trees, with a larger area of open land to the centre of the area being separated into formal and informal recreational space.

In the south-west of the neighbourhood, across the area from Teynes to West Roedin, the houses reflect the intervention of Gordon Redfern in their design. More densely packed terraces are set in a complex pattern of right-angled courts and clusters that adapt to the hilly terrain, around a series of short access roads from which the majority of dwellings are accessed by foot. The houses take a very different form from the traditional dwellings in the eastern section of the neighbourhood, with steeply mono-pitched roofs and an austere, angular design that may be influenced by Eric Lyons 'Span' estates. This austerity is enhanced by the provision of only two small first-floor windows to the front elevations, supplemented by a small horizontal light adjacent to the front door lighting the hallway, with the main living space lit by large windows facing on to the private rear garden. There is a diversity of materials with brick-end elevations and pilasters separating timber-boarded facades, originally stained black but now of a variety of natural and painted colours. Timber boarding runs horizontally, vertically and diagonally across different properties providing some sense of variation. Further south, at Oxtens and Stiels, even this diversity of materials is removed, the elevations formed entirely of pale brickwork.

Figures 134 and 135: The mono-pitched roofs and austere façades of the CDC housing at Teynes and Stiels.

The majority of facades are unaltered apart from replacement uPVC glazing, with only small numbers of additional windows or porches added or the timber cladding replaced with render. Among these houses are a small number of three-storey blocks of flats. These are flat-roofed and combine vertical lines of rendered block walls with horizontal lines of timber panelling and continuous glazing. A more substantial complex of flats is located at Offway. A linear development, using the same combination of pale brick, render and timber panelling, Norwoods House avoids the same austere feeling as the remainder of the south-western estates, the facades displaying a variety of recessed bays, balconies and first- and second-floor projected windows and the flat rooflines punctuated with taller, mono-pitched, stair towers.

A small number of single-storey dwellings are scattered throughout Coedeva. Continuous lines of sheltered housing schemes are exemplified at Llwyn Celyn, Two Locks Road, with its sheltering canopy and inbuilt storage to the side of each front door and Nolton Place. A series of six bungalows on Coedeva Mill has been more heavily modified with the addition of dormer windows and external cladding to the majority.

A small, discrete development from the late 1960s or 1970s is found at Glan-y-nant/Garth Road. Semi-detached pairs of hipped-roof, brick-built houses are marked out by full height glazing to the front-facing living room and the use of tile hanging to the front elevations. Canopy porches to the front doors, supported by steel posts, have been largely replaced as

Figures 136 and 137: The CDC sheltered housing at Llwyn Celyn and Garth Road houses.

has the original glazing. Towards the east end of the development, larger gabled pairs generally retain their brightly stained timber panels, contrasting with pale brickwork and extensive glazing.

Recent housing developments include Gifford Close and Heol y Groes, both small, densely built estates of detached and semi-detached traditionally built houses.

There is little non-domestic development in the neighbourhood. There are no surviving historic commercial properties on Two Locks Road and with the proximity of the Fairwater Unit centre the pantry shops built by the CDC no longer operate. The Blinkin Owl public house on Oxtens is a simple design that owes more to the traditional domestic architecture of the CDC than the surrounding dwellings. Two Locks Nursery and Hollybush Primary School have both been demolished, the latter rebuilt as Nantcelyn School on a reduced site with land given over for the Heol y Groes estate. Coed Eva Primary (the former Junior and Infant School) has had one block removed after severe fire damage. The remaining two-storey range has had its external framing replaced with uPVC coverings that are considerably thicker and heavier looking than the original steel framing, but otherwise retains its original character.

In addition to the green spaces provided by the CDC in the estate layouts, larger areas of recreational and natural land

Figure 138: Coed Eva Primary School, Teynes.

were retained. Both the Nant y Milwr and Dowlais Brook Run through the neighbourhood, partly culverted but planted with mature trees along the natural stretches. Areas of previously agricultural ground were preserved for unstructured recreation within each estate, west of The Crescent, north of Offway and south of Coedeva School, allowing easy access to open ground for all residents. A children's playground is provided in the first, but no other structured recreational facilities exists. Woodland depicted on nineteenth-century mapping at New House (immediately south of the Hollybush Primary School complex) has been partially encroached upon to provide allotments.

7.10 Greenmeadow

7.10.1 Background

Greenmeadow was designated as a residential area in the 1951 Master Plan to cover an area of 177 acres (72 hectares) to the west of the Town Centre. A steeply sloping area, it contained the Dowlais Brook with Greenmeadow and Graig-Fawr Woods and was described in the Masterplan as 'attractive' and 'a delightful area with fine sites overlooking the town'. There was no existing residential development in the neighbourhood other than Greenmeadow Farm, which was scheduled for preservation. Consequently, the neighbourhood was designated as suitable for low density new housing with a proposed maximum population of 3,600.[345]

The development of the South-Western Areas, comprising Greenmeadow, St Dials and Coedeva, was the final major phase in the development of the New Town as first envisaged and in total consisted of some 427 acres (143 hectares) to house some 14,000 persons. Survey of the area started in 1953, but layout and site preparation work for Greenmeadow did not start until the early 1960s because of ongoing negotiations in the late 1950s over raising the target population.[346]

The designs for Greenmeadow I again followed Gordon Redfern's preferred pattern of completely segregating

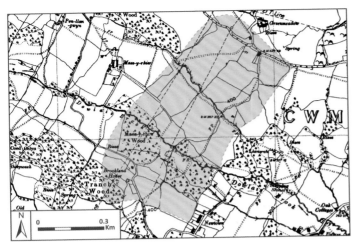
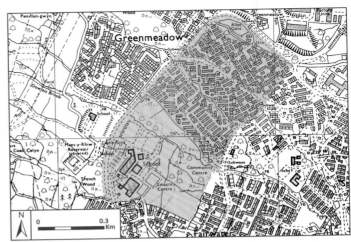

Figure 139: The area of Greenmeadow depicted on the OS mapping of 1948 and 1984–85.

vehicular and foot traffic with separate systems of roads and footpaths. Greenmeadow I included 366 dwellings, of which 10 maisonettes and 30 'flatlets' were provided in five-storey blocks, and one local shop. Phase 1A comprised 163 dwellings, 61 garages and 26 carports (the first time a carport design had been introduced) and cost £458,000. Phase 1B comprised 187 dwellings, 57 garages and 54 carports and cost £492,000. New housing was built by the contractor John Laing & Sons, with Phase IB housing originally intending to use the 'Easiform' system, but in the event this proved too expensive.[347] These schemes again differed from those in the older neighbourhoods by conforming to the Parker Morris standards laid out in 'Homes for Today and Tomorrow', while wide frontages and shallow plans dealt more efficiently with the steeper terrain. Many were designed with either the flat or shallow mono-pitched roofs used at Fairwater and Coedeva. In addition, Phase I introduced a larger five-bedroom, seven-person house for the first time, claimed to be the first of this type in Wales.[348] In 1968 there was a commendation for the house designs in this phase, although by 1982 the flat roofs were already causing problems with a programme of reroofing being required.[349] Phase 1B included the pantry shop with a residential maisonette, designed to meet the day-to-day shopping needs of the community in the south-west corner of the site, and 10 dwellings for older people in the final stage in the development of the area.[350] The main shopping needs of the neighbourhood were to be provided at the Fairwater unit centre.

Plans for Greenmeadow II and III were implemented in 1969 with the expansion of the population in Cwmbrân.[351] Greenmeadow III was the first to start being constructed in 1971, the 273 CDC dwellings supplemented by 24 pensioners' cottages, a warden's house and a hall built by the CUDC.[352] Greenmeadow II, a further 103 dwellings, commenced in 1972, with both phases being completed by 1974.[353] In the mid- to late-1980s private housing developments were taken over by both Westbury Homes and Barratt Developments.

By 1968 the 'Threepenny Bit' community centre had been constructed, an unusual hexagonal, brick-built structure.

Figure 140 and 141: Terraced CDC housing running across the steeply sloping terrain at Ravenscourt and sheltered housing scheme at Byways.

Managed by the neighbourhood association, it was reported as successful and well used day and night.[354] This was supplemented by a tenants' hall as part of the Greenmeadow III development in 1971-77, constructed adjacent to the care home development so as to enable use as a day-centre for residents of the bungalow complex.[355] In 1973-74 land was made available for a public house, which opened in 1976 as The Golden Harvest, while in the 1974-75 financial year work finished on the new Greenmeadow Primary School.[356]

One of the most prominent historic buildings in the neighbourhood was Greenmeadow Farm, at that point a Grade III Listed Building.[357] In 1979 it was proposed to repair and improve the complex to create a community facility, potentially as a riding and trekking centre. The centre was later developed as a community farm.

The 2011 census recorded a population of 5,229.[358]

7.10.2 Character of Area

Greenmeadow sits on the western slopes of the Lwyd Valley with views over Cwmbrân. The only pre-New Town building in the neighbourhood is Greenmeadow Farm, a Post-medieval complex of stone farmhouse and barns on the northern edge of the neighbourhood.

Bounded to the north-east and north-west by Greenmeadow Way and Ty Gwyn Way and to the south-east by Fairhill Way, the area is dominated by the dense housing development of the 1960s and 1970s. The layout of the neighbourhood is formed by a loose network of roads, with Ty Gwyn Road as the main through road connecting the boundary roads and the remainder acting as estate roads or culs-de-sac. With the segregation of the pedestrian and car at the heart of the design, the buildings sit at right angles to the roads forming blocks of short terraces that mainly alternate between a south-west to north-east or an east-west orientation as following the line of the contours. Between the terraces a denser network of footpaths run parallel to the properties.

Housing estates are made up of predominantly two-storey CDC-designed housing, with that to the centre and southern parts of the neighbourhood, such as Byways and the southern side of Ty Gwyn Road, characterised by grey, roughcast rendered exteriors set with contrasting smooth-rendered panels and flat roofs. North of Ty Gwyn Road, and in the western area of Barnets, the housing is built in a contrasting exposed brick with steeply mono-pitched roofs laid with pantiles. Across all estates, terraces are offset and staggered in places to break up the uniformity of the otherwise flat facades, which apart from the occasional later addition, are devoid of porches, garages or other features that would add depth. There are a small number of three-storey houses interspersed within the terraces, representing the larger model introduced. Front doors open directly onto the pathways, with only a nominal strip of forecourt garden either side of the step. Windows to the front elevations facing on to the pedestrian ways are therefore kept to a minimum and are

Figure 142: Greenmeadow neighbourhood from the air, 2006.

small, maintaining a level of privacy, while large windows overlook the rear gardens. The complex of pensioners' bungalows and warden's house sits at the eastern end of Ty Gwyn Road forming a small, contained estate, the terraces of which are interlinked with covered walkways and set among communal gardens. Separate from the estate housing, two private, architect-designed properties, which sit at the northern end of Bowleaze, date from the same period.

Figure 143: The Greenmeadow pantry store, Byways.

Figure 144: The 'Threepenny Bit', the Greenmeadow community centre, the most architecturally interesting of the New Town community halls.

The unit centre public house, the Golden Harvest, situated in the northern half of the neighbourhood has been converted into a Tesco Express in the period between 2008 and 2016, supplementing the original pantry shop on Byways, which remains as an independent grocery retailer. The Threepenny Bit remains, but has used by a local charity since 2012.

There has been little later development; Maybury House represents the most substantial recent building, being a five- to six-storey development of private flats adjacent to Fairhill Way. Despite problems with the flat roofs, the majority of the housing remains unaltered in form and appearance.

The dense setting of the terraces allows for the green network of footpaths and rear gardens, but open recreational space within the estates is confined to a few small areas of grassed land. A spine of mature woodland runs through the centre of the neighbourhood, with another line of woodland surviving along the former St Dials Road, while CDC planting along Ty Gwyn way provides a level of shielding for the neighbourhood from the busy ring road. The Ty Gwyn allotments provide another area of green space, which is well used by local residents.

7.11 Thornhill

7.11.1 Background

Thornhill was a later neighbourhood developed in Cwmbrân after the decision to raise the target population to 55,000 in 1961 and the subsequent expansion plan. It was constructed on the north-west edge of the town when the CDC decided to take advantage of the closure of Guest Keen Nettlefolds in 1971. It acquired the land, cleared it, and combined it with the site of the former Cwmbrân Colliery: land towards the Town Centre would be redeveloped as the Springvale Industrial Estate, while the higher, and more attractive land towards the north-west outskirts was designated for housing.[359] The whole neighbourhood was initially referred to as Springvale after a terrace of cottages associated with the former colliery, but was quickly renamed as Thornhill.

The overall structure of the Thornhill housing area of 712 dwellings was approved in November 1974, and detailed proposals for the first phase were submitted in February 1975.[360] The quality of the 'natural' landscape in this locality was recognised as important from the outset, with hedgerows being designated for preservation and reinforced with specialist planting, though existing housing at Springvale and Woodland Cottages were not so respected. The fact that this was an elevated, visible site also meant that the CDC required it to be an aesthetically pleasing environment both when viewed from within and when seen from a distance.[361]

Phase I at Thornhill consisted of the construction of the south-eastern part of the area, bordering Thornhill Road and Ty Gwyn Way to the east, Greenmeadow Wood to the south and Graig Fawr Wood to the north. This original neighbourhood of Thornhill consisted of 129 dwellings to house 550 people, the vast majority of being two-, three- and four-bedroom houses, with eight one-bed bungalows and ten

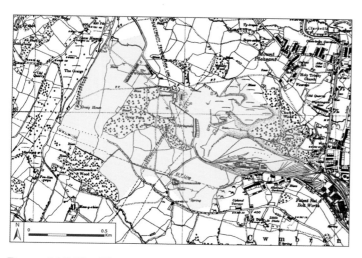
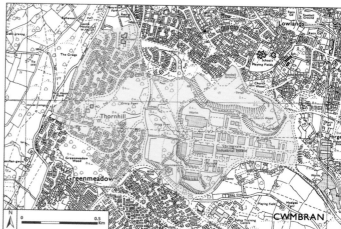

Figure 145: The Thornhill area depicted on the OS mapping of 1948 and 1985.

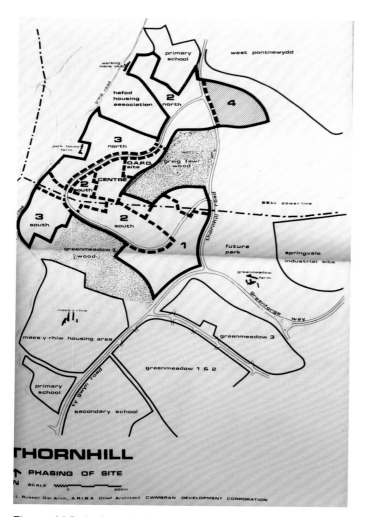

Figure 146: A phased plan of the Thornhill neighbourhood depicting development scheme Thornhill 1-4, 1975.

flats (one block of these being three storeys in height). Later, there was an increase in bungalow numbers as a direct response to Welsh Office Circular 42/75 'Housing: Needs and Action', which had identified an increasing need to provide smaller single-storey units.[362]

Thornhill I was designed on what was termed at the time the 'mixer court' principle of mixed pedestrian and car traffic within the housing courts where the speed of traffic was deemed safe, and segregated pedestrian routes on the main spine routes providing safe routes to shops, school and public transport. Parking was provided at a ratio of 11 spaces for every ten dwellings, entirely as open spaces on driveways or within the courts, with no provision made for garages. Designed by the then Chief Architect J. L. Russell, the houses returned to a more traditional form and materials than those designed under Redfern in the 1960s.

The recreational needs of younger children were to be met through the provision of what were termed 'tod-lots' and 'kick-about' areas, with the nearby 'important natural environments' of Graig Fawr and Greenmeadow Woods giving additional amenity and leisure space. In addition to the retention of existing woodland and trees, the elevated nature of Thornhill Road led to particular landscape treatment and substantial tree planting, and tree planting within the housing courts was considered essential to retain the wooded nature of the neighbourhood. This character was in part responsible for the return to 'mellow brick and tile simply detailed' that were able to 'blend quietly with the landscape'.[363]

The design for Thornhill Phase II was put forward in October 1975 by the J. L. Russell. The site of this scheme was the lower slopes of Mynydd Maen with particularly fine views of the ridge and upper slopes of this hill. The development of the local centre effectively divided this second phase of the neighbourhood into two parts, which subsequently became Phase II South and Phase II North. Phase II South was built first and followed the pattern of layout and dwellings type set in Phase I, being situated to the north-west of the first phase. Phase II South consisted of 129 dwellings across 10.5 acres (4.25 hectares) that extended up as far as the neighbourhood centre to the north and was contained to the south and west by Greenmeadow Wood and by land identified for the later Phase III.[364] By October 1977 both Thornhill Phase I and Phase II South were complete and Phase II North consisting of 136 dwellings and the unit centre of two shops was under construction. Both Phase II schemes were completed in 1980.[365]

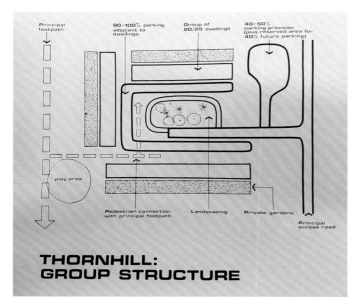

Figure 147: Example group structure plan from Thornhill 2 explaining the housing court layout, 1975.

Phase III of Thornhill was also divided into Phase III South and Phase III North, with 235 dwellings built across the two areas. The construction of Phase III South started at the end of 1977 on the western edge of the neighbourhood while Phase III North followed in October 1978. The Phase III North development had a roughly triangular shape bound by St Dials Lane and Hafren Road and sat on the lower slopes of Mynydd Maen. This meant it had fine views over Graig Fawr Wood and across to Wentwood and Usk, although it was recognised that the site was exposed to the north and east winds and generally steeply sloping. The site included the garden of Park House Farm, which it was decided should be preserved as open space and supplemented with further tree planting, including to provide screening to the outbuildings. Of the 140 dwellings in the Phase, 10 were flats and seven bungalows, the rest being two- to four-bedroom houses, none more than two-storey in height. The steepest parts of the site were dealt with by introducing a new, split-level design that placed the living room on the first floor to make the most of views and garden access.[366]

Thornhill IV, tucked into the north-east corner of the neighbourhood, was a relatively small scheme, the proposals for which were added in 1979. The six acres, previously known as 'Woodlands', were bounded by playing fields and woodland apart from its western edge where it adjoined Thornhill Phase II North. The site was bisected by the raised line of a nineteenth-century tramline, excluded from development owing to cost and therefore assigned as an adventure play area for older children. Development was also excluded from the southern section of the site where the

National Coal Board recorded a colliery adit less than 35.5 metres below ground level.

Of the 108 dwellings, 48 were to be flats in three-storey blocks and two bungalows for paraplegic people; the 58 houses were a mix of two- to four-bedroom houses, the four-bedroomed to be two-and-a-half storeys to add to the visual diversity. The mixer court principle was retained but reinterpreted to take account of the gradients to form meandering terraces following the contours, and served by informally planned culs-de-sac with shared vehicular/pedestrian access. As with the other Thornhill developments, no garages were provided with 100 per cent car parking available. [367]

A Hafod Housing Association scheme was also built in the neighbourhood between 1977 and 1979, consisting of 147 dwellings.[368]

The shopping needs for the Thornhill Phase I residents were initially provided through the building of a single shop unit as part of the original scheme.[369] The Thornhill Local Centre with its three shop units then opened in 1977 when the Thornhill Phase II South development was completed. The enlarged Centre Unit, located at the geographical heart of the neighbourhood, was built a little later mainly between 1977 and 1979, with 33 additional flats also included as part of the scheme and completed in 1981.[370] It was decided that those in the northern areas of the neighbourhood were also able to use the Maendy Square sub-unit centre.

In 1976 the new infant and junior school for the neighbourhood was started at The Woodlands designed by what was by now the Gwent Architects Department. The new school opened in the spring of 1977, from where at secondary school age children could proceed to Fairwater Comprehensive School.[371]

The Springvale Industrial Estate development commenced in 1975 with approval for 47 Advanced Factory Units (AFUs) varying in size from 1,250 square feet to 10,000 square feet (116 sq. m to 929 sq. m), built by the CDC in order to attract manufacturing to the town. These were built to a modular

Figure 148: Layout plan of the Springvale Industrial Estate, undated.

pattern to promote flexibility of use and allow them to be tailored to demand.[372] Thirty-four of these were completed the following year, together with a 170-space car park and design work for a custom Siebe Gorman factory.[373] The success of the AFUs was such that another 12 units were approved in 1979, with sites including larger factories such as that for Lucas Girling at over 10,000 square metres.[374] By early 1982 the CDC were looking to expand the industrial estate, with further AFUs of various sizes built up until the winding up of the CDC.

Enclosing three sides of the industrial estate and flowing into the Town Centre, the CDC allocated 100 acres (40 hectares) for the Springvale Leisure Park. This was to form an area for informal sports and hobbies for a wide range of the population, but was also initially intended to include facilities such as an artificial ski slope and toboggan run.[375] Space was also allocated for a helicopter landing pad.[376]

The whole Thornhill area was finally completed in 1983.[377]

7.11.2 Character of Area

Thornhill can be divided into two areas – the higher, sloping ground to the west, which is used for residential purposes, and the lower, flatter ground to the east which is the location for the Springvale Industrial Estate. Previous built elements of the landscape in the form of nineteenth-century workers' housing have been built over by the New Town development.

The southern residential areas of Thornhill, which were the first to be developed, have a varied, winding road pattern

Figures 149 & 150: The CDC Housing schemes at Sirhowy Court and Taff Court.

corresponding to the topography, with short staggered, stepped or winding terraces of houses following accordingly. These form a series of 'mixer courts' around which many of the houses are set giving a more inward feel to the estate. The majority of these have at least a small 'green' to the centre, as well as wide verges and occasional areas of open ground planted with mature trees and shrubs giving much needed open space to the densely set housing. This is also aided by the narrow nature of the estates, which are bounded by surviving areas of woodland which form a continuous skyline background to the views from all parts of the estates. The mainly two-storey housing displays a mix of hipped, shallow-pitched and mono-pitched roofs, combined with the use of brick header string courses to the walls and recessed porches. There is limited use of blocks of three-storey flats to the western area which, through their form and materials, blend into the estates rather than provide points of visual impact.

The fourth phase of Thornhill, Woodlands, again gives careful consideration to the contours of the sloping site, the design well integrated with the grain of the topography. The two-storey housing uses a similar combination of stepped and staggered layouts, with an integrated use of occasional mono-pitched roofs to punctuate the otherwise hipped rooflines. The use of a darker brickwork with lighter, contrasting mortar adds a level of texture, as does the occasional use of timber-boarded panels and, at Taff Court, the introduction of a modernised form of oriel window.

The unit centre, set into the slope of the hill, is unusually inconspicuous with the single-storey shop located below road level and the public house orientated away from the road. A modest surgery and pharmacy complete the grouping, the pharmacy being the most prominent building of the group. A community centre is separated from the unit centre, located rather remotely at the end of a cul-de-sac. At the northern end of the neighbourhood, Woodlands School occupies a large open site with excellent far-reaching views over the town and valley. The buildings fail to take advantage of this, being single-storey and forming an inward-looking courtyard plan.

The eastern section of the neighbourhood sits in contrast to these residential areas. A lower lying area of flat ground, this is dominated by the 100-acre Springvale Industrial Estate. The layout here is an ordered grid pattern ensuring easy and logical access to variously sized factories and workshop units. A substantial number of the advance factories developed by the CDC survive, noted by their dark green or silver corrugated steel cladding and mono-pitched or saw-toothed rooflines, with surprisingly small amounts of redevelopment and rebuilding indicating the strength of original design and build of these work spaces. Brickwork is used only for the smaller rows of small workshop units, which again appear to be well used.

Immediately south of the Springvale Estate is the Greenmeadow Farm, retaining its Post-medieval farmhouse

Figure 151: Advance factory units on the Springvale Industrial Park.

and barns though little in the way of earlier field boundaries. Surrounding the farm and industrial estate and occupying the land between these and the residential areas to the west, are substantial areas of mature woodland. These are partially formed from extant remains of Graig Fawr and Church Wood but a substantial programme of reclamation work on land of the former Cwmbrân Colliery and tree planting on behalf of the CDC on former industrial and agricultural ground has increased the woodland area. Substantial areas of open ground within and adjacent to the woodland area supplement this, though the only formal recreation facility is a recently constructed court for ball games off Sirhowy Court.

7.12 Hollybush

7.12.1 Background

The Hollybush neighbourhood was developed from the early 1970s, the first to be implemented after the decision to raise the target population to 55,000 and expand the Designated Area. At the extreme southern edge of the town, the scheme was on a prominent north-facing slope populated with 'fine trees and hedgerows' and 'extensive views of the town', the planting being retained as much as possible.[378] There was no pre-existing settlement of this area.

The first plans for Hollybush I were drawn up in 1970-71, and were defined by the fact that, although initially for rent, they were ultimately destined for sale.[379] The plans were reconsidered in 1972 after the CDC stated that people had been reluctant to buy dwellings in areas with the pedestrian/car segregation that had been a consistent feature since the days of Gordon Redfern; with the rapid rise in car ownership, residents now wanted to be able to bring and keep their car at their house.[380] In light of this the plans were altered and Hollybush I (Phase I) of 163 dwellings, including 20 pensioners' bungalows and a warden's house, commenced in 1974 with each house provided with space for two cars, including garaging. The houses continued to be clustered in groups of 15-25 around culs-de-sac and, as at Thornhill, the designs by Jim Russell, at this time Deputy Chief Architect, returned to a more traditional form of pale coloured brickwork, tile hanging or render, with hipped, tiled roofs. Hollybush I (Phase II) of 127 dwellings with neighbourhood shops followed later the same year with the same design.[381]

Hollybush II, consisting of 171 dwellings and a pantry shop, offered a slightly modified design. Also intended as properties for sale, the slope of the site forced a return to longer terraces along a central linear access road that could follow the lines of the contours. While those terraces adjacent to the road were still able to have on-site parking, those on the lower slopes had only pedestrian access.[382] Hollybush III proposals were approved in 1981 as part of the Henllys Expansion Area, with the designs carried out in light of the Welsh Office 'Housing Project Control System' that aimed to ensure that publicly funded housing was not of a standard higher than its market sale value or a rental value that would need to be subsidised. This marked government abandonment of the Parker Morris standards and other space and design guides recommended by the Department of the Environment. This meant that the floor space of the 79 dwellings in this scheme was reduced and statutory features including pram spaces, separate W.C.s and garden stores were eliminated from the designs. The layout returned to the 'mixer-court' of other recent developments, with shared pedestrian and vehicular access to

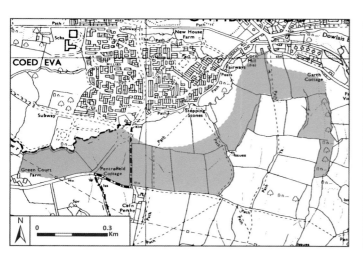
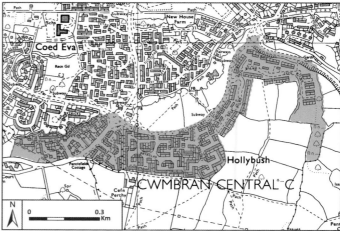

Figure 152: The Hollybush area depicted on the OS mapping of 1972 and 1984.

properties, though without the provision of garages.[383] This scheme was completed in 1983, by which time Hollybush I and II were the most sought-after estates in Cwmbrân.[384]

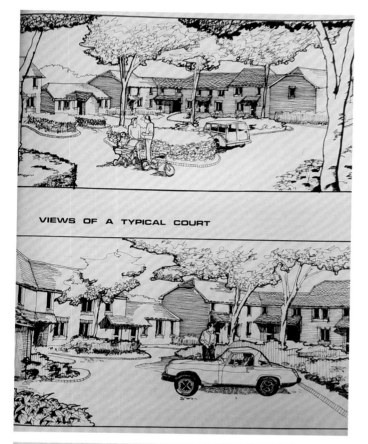

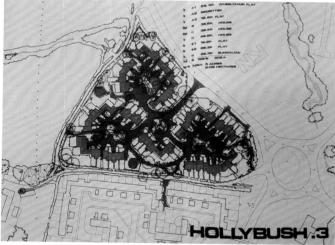

Figures 153 and 154: The estate court plan for Hollybush 3 and architect's sketches of a typical court, 1981.

The size of the neighbourhood did not warrant a sub-unit centre, and instead plans were made for a pantry shop with living accommodation above. This was constructed in 1976 to 1977. Some play spaces were allocated between the courts and terraces, but the main recreational area was the large playing fields provided between Hollybush I and II.

7.12.2 Character of Area

Hollybush is a narrow, extended neighbourhood located along the southern edge of the Designated Area built within a ten-year period. With gently sloping topography, the area can be visually split into its three components by the layout and design of the properties.

The higher, eastern ground occupied by Bryn Milwr and Cefn Milwr are characterised by longer, sinuous rows of semi-detached, two-storey houses that follow the contours supplemented by short, staggered terraces at right angles to these. The houses follow a traditional design, lifted by the markedly extended garages to the front elevation that break up the otherwise unornamented plain brickwork facades. Some visual variation is provided by the regular insertion of link-detached blocks of three-storey flats. Wide verges to the roads are planted with mature trees while substantial open areas between the roads provide space for garage blocks and parking courts, but also provide a 'village green' space. The spacing of the roads and their orientation ensures that the most is made of views across the valley.

Figure 155: Lower Cefn Milwr Road, Hollybush 1.

By contrast the central, flatter area of Trostrey and Brynglas is comprised of a denser network of terraces forming a series of inward-facing courtyards and culs-de-sac. Here, there is a greater diversity of hipped terraces, mono-pitched semi-detached houses and bungalows, the complex of sheltered housing at Trostrey with its inter-linked covered walkways particularly thoughtfully designed. The use of a variety of brick colours, timber boarding and contrasting tile hanging to the elevations provides a variety of textures in relation to each other and to the pan-tiled roofs of both houses and garages. Narrow pavements give way to small front courts and gardens, many concreted for further parking spaces. Further west, the layout becomes far less formal, with the sweeping curves of Perthy Close and Glan Rhyd lined with varied pairs, clusters and groupings of properties again with varying roof heights and frontages. The provision of larger forecourts, and the retention of a higher percentage of them as green garden space, together with a number of mature trees to the roadsides, provide a 'greener' feel to this part of the neighbourhood.

Figures 156 and 157: Sheltered housing scheme at Trostrey Close and the close layout at Glan Rhyd.

The only non-domestic building is the unit convenience store, an anonymous building which, from the road, is hard to differentiate from the surrounding domestic properties. The main facade faces into the estate, the elevation to the wider estate lacking the level of signage that is usual.

7.13 Maes-y-rhiw

7.13.1 History of Development

Maes-y-rhiw was a 15-acre estate built on the western extreme of the Designated Area immediately south of the Thornhill neighbourhood. Taking its name from Maes-y-rhiw Farm and Woods, the area was again a relatively steeply

sloping site on the bottom slopes of Mynydd Maen.[385] As an entirely agricultural area, the many mature trees on the site were retained as far as possible in order to contribute to the visual amenity of the development.

The initial development, approved in 1971, was for a private development of 120 houses, though a 98-house CDC housing scheme was added in 1974 designed by the private architectural practice of Diamond Redfern and Partners. Owing to the challenging topography, the layout reverted to flexible spinal access roads, off which culs-de-sac ran following the contours in an efficient manner. Traditionally constructed houses of concrete blockwork conformed to Parker Morris standards, with appropriate use of the split-level housing for the steepest areas.[386]

7.13.2 Character of Area

Maes-y-rhiw is a compact estate on the steep slopes of Mynydd Maen, divided between privately developed and CDC-built houses. The former, arranged in short, straight culs-de-sac forming the western section of Maes-y-rhiw off the longer estate roads of Wellington Drive, Leicester Drive and Norfolk Close, consist of sizable detached two-storey houses. Relatively uniform in design, they alternate between hipped and gabled forms using a combination of brick and render. A later development along Maes-y-Rhiw Court, dating to the early twenty-first century, consists of a mixture of two- and three-storey properties, which with their use of rooflines, extended bays, window and door dressings and fitting reference a 'Victorian villa' style.

To the west of this, along the more elevated Marlborough Road, is the denser-planned CDC development of detached, semi-detached and staggered terraced houses with steeply pitched roofs. Built to a set design and materials, this forms a very uniform estate with little in the way of later alterations beyond replacement windows and doorways and individual treatment to the gardens, the majority of which have been used at least partly for additional off-road parking. However, the use of mono-pitched porches and garages, and the

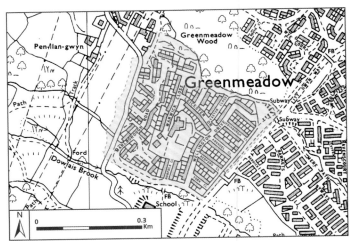

Figure 158: The Maes-y-rhiw area depicted on the OS mapping of 1948 and 1985.

Maes-y-Rhiw
Housing Development

Information Sheet No.HD3

Maes-y-Rhiw

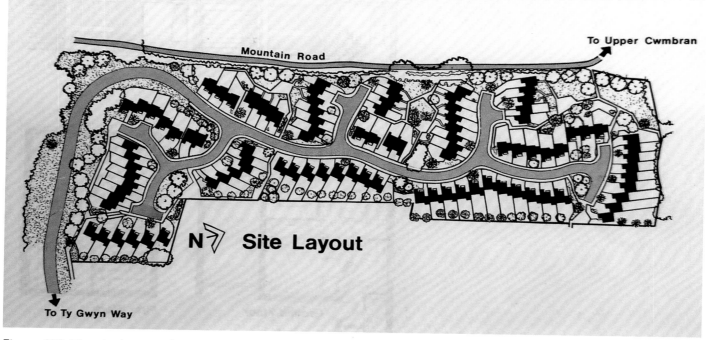

Figure 159: The site layout of the Maes-y-rhiw housing development, undated.

Figures 160 and 161: Diversity of higher quality detached one- and two-storey dwellings on Wellington Drive. These houses contrast with the denser CDC construction of Marlborough Road.

placement of houses both in terms of levels and along the longer roads, creates a variety of interesting visual lines that combine with fine views over the Lwyd valley.

There are no notable open spaces within the estate. An area of mature trees survives to the western boundary of the estate along Graig Road; many other small open areas and verges are now grassed. The recent Maes-y-Rhiw Court estate may have developed within an area of green space left at the heart of the area in the original planning with mature trees to its western boundary and south-east corner.

7.14 Henllys Expansion Area: Henllys and Tŷ Canol

7.14.1 History of Development

Negotiations between the Cwmbrân Development Corporation and the Welsh Office over the expansion of the Designated Area started in the early 1970s, the CDC arguing that the extra land was vital to reach the raised target population of 55,000.[387] Arguments against the expansion were fierce, particularly from the Heads of the Valleys Authorities Standing Conference (HOVASC), which was of the opinion that Cwmbrân had already adversely affected growth in the rest of Monmouthshire, particularly valley towns such as Tredegar. Others were concerned the expansion area encroached on the unofficial green belt that existed between Cwmbrân and Newport and failed to protect the natural

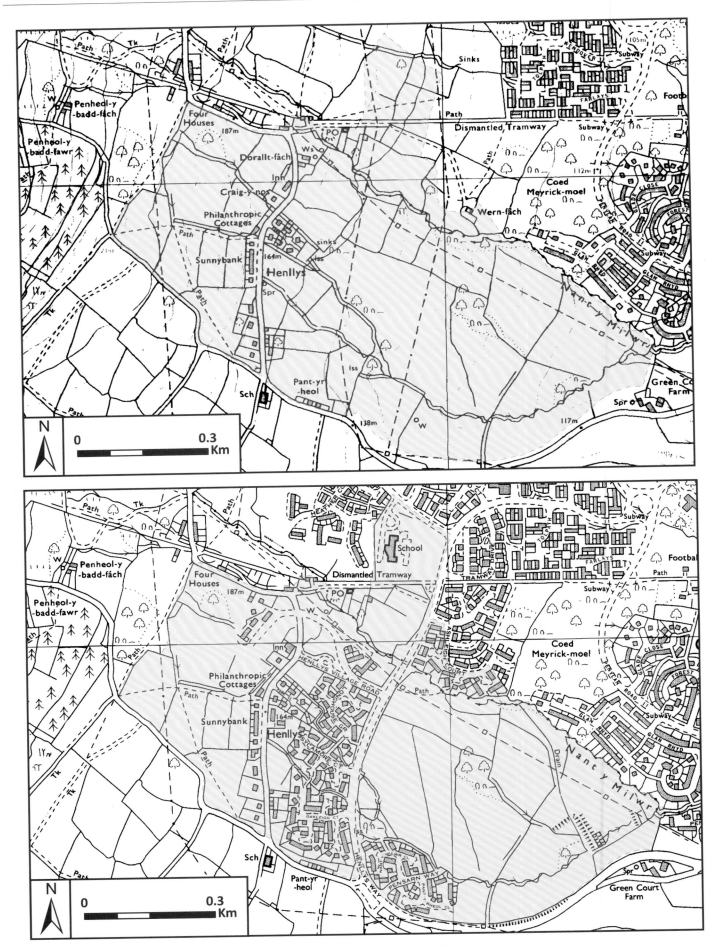

Figure 162: The Henllys area depicted on the OS mapping of 1948 and 1984.

environment around Henllys. At a public inquiry started in February 1976, CDC representation explained the need for extra land caused by the reduction in family sizes and the growth of second-generation 'Cwmbrâners'.

Alternative areas of expansion on the north side of Cwmbrân were assessed, but it was strongly felt that Henllys would preserve the shape and character of Cwmbrân, while having the least impact on the valley towns to the north. The inquiry supported the CDC's view that extra land was needed, while questioning HOVASC's view that if money was not spent at Cwmbrân it would be automatically allocated to improvement of the valley towns, and recommended the expansion be approved.[388] After awaiting a ministerial decision to accept this recommendation, the addition of 484 acres (196 hectares) to the south-west boundary of the Designated Area was finally approved in November 1977.[389]

The Expansion Area, which aimed to develop a further 1,800 dwelling to house c. 7,000 people, included additional land for existing neighbourhoods at Hollybush III, Fairwater IV and Coedeva V (included under neighbourhood sections). Henllys was a new neighbourhood on the south-west edge of Cwmbrân in the new Expansion Area, separated from the Coedeva neighbourhood by the Henllys Local Nature Reserve. Ty Canol was located immediately to the north of Henllys and provided a total of 191 dwellings.

Development at Ty Canol took place from 1983, including the first Shared Ownership Housing Scheme of 50 houses and six bungalows started October 1983 at Ty Canol 4A.[390] A second similar scheme was developed at Ty Canol 4B in 1985. A smaller number of individual plots for private development were allocated at schemes 4D and 3A.[391] Development continued through to 1987, when undeveloped plots were sold privately.

Little of Henllys was developed by the CDC outside of the new network of roads constructed in 1985-86. A Barratt development was completed by early 1985, but by early 1986 over 220 acres (89 hectares) of land was being sold to private developers for house building, with nearly 15 acres (six hectares) sold to Gwent County Council for the building of a County Church School and a County School.[392]

By the time of the winding up of the CDC in 1986, much of the land had not been developed and was offered on the open market to private developers.

7.14.2 Character of Area

Henllys and Ty Canol neighbourhoods consist almost exclusively of housing estates dating from the 1970s and 1980s. Pre-1970s buildings survive in the form of The Dorallt Inn and Cwrt Henllys Hotel, although the latter in a much-modified form. A handful of nineteenth-century stone cottages, such as New Row, and Cock-y-North Farm survive on the peripheries of the neighbourhoods representing the scattered, agricultural pre-New Town vernacular.

The topography of these areas is sloping. Ty Canol particularly is located on the steeply sloping hills of Mynydd Maen, and both have a meandering pattern of road layout that responds to the contours of this landscape, though little seems to have been done to maximise the views visible from this elevated location. The placement of housing is equally loose, varying between lines that follow the contours and those staggered against the slopes. All properties are set back from the road with the provision of front gardens, which have been modified in various ways to provide enclosed green space or parking courts, and medium-sized back gardens ensure open space between the lines of housing. The majority of properties are detached or semi-detached two-storey houses, a substantial amount being the former though often closely spaced together, with some use of short terraces of three houses in Ty Canol. Parking provision varies between garage parking for larger detached properties through to parking courts for semi-detached/terraced housing.

The housing is a mixture of CDC and privately developed, with little design difference between the two. The properties employ a variety of brick types and colours in conjunction with partial rendering and there is a wider variety in design, streetscapes mixing hipped and gabled roofs, catslide, gabled and open porches and casement and bay windows in an attempt to provide a level of individuality and visual interest. The privately developed estates are perhaps best indicated by an increasing use of 'historical' design elements including gabled windows, polychrome brickwork, terracotta tile hanging, 'stringcourses' and 'timber-framing'. Both areas contain a number of larger, individually designed properties, and a small number of bungalows. A small sheltered-housing scheme of terraced bungalows at Major Close has been supplemented by the Thistle Close Nursing and Residential Home, which replicates the general design of housing in the area.

Figure 164: The dwellings along Celandine Close, with their increasing use of historical references within the architecture.

Later development has included the building of the Henllys Village Hall in c. 2010 and a One Stop Store in c. 2012 providing amenities to areas otherwise largely dependent on other neighbourhoods or the Town Centre.

Within the estate some former field boundaries and copses are distinguished through surviving lines and groups of mature trees, but there is little in the way of designed landscapes or planting in shared open areas. Open recreational areas forming a central north-south strip through the heart of Henllys and open space at the heart of Ty Canol are formed from former agricultural land, that at Ty Canol formerly adjacent to the now demolished Ty Canol Farm that gave the neighbourhood its name.

Figure 165: The Henllys Nature Reserve.

The Henllys Nature Reserve forms the eastern boundary for Henllys, created from previous agricultural land and historic woodland. The Nant y Milwr runs along the north-east edge of the site. The north and north-eastern boundaries of Ty Canol are bounded by extant remains of Coed Celyn and Tranch Wood, one of the woodlands recorded to date back at least to the sixteenth century.

7.15 Ty Coch

7.15.1 Background

An important part of the expansion plans of the 1970s was the increased capacity for industry. With the closure of the Oakfield Steel Wireworks in 1966 and the acquisition of the land by the CDC, a mixed area of former industrial and agricultural land at the southern edge of the Designated Area was identified for industrial development. As well as the former wireworks site, this area included a major part of the existing village of Oakfield and the small settlement of Ty Coch. Focused around the main street of Llandowlais Place, Tranquil Place (originally Shop Row) and Hill Street by the time of designation, Oakfield was situated between the canal and the Great Western Railway Line, immediately south of the wireworks. Ty Coch was a linear development of houses adjacent to the canal, developed in the last quarter of the nineteenth century.[393]

The Ty Coch Industrial Estate was established by the CDC in the early 1970s with assessment given to its development in 1972.[394] This included the inclusion of a further 50 acres (20 hectares) of land outside the Designated Area in the expansion proposal put forward in 1972.[395] While this was initially approved in 1976, HOVASC, which had campaigned vigorously against this expansion on the grounds that any further industry should be located in the upper valleys, continued to protest against the decision. With reluctance on the part of the Welsh Secretary to accept the decision regarding Ty Coch sparking a further inquiry, this proposal was finally ruled against in 1978.[396]

One of the first developments was the construction of the 74,000 square feet (6,874 sq. m) Alfa Laval factory in 1973-75, designed by Keith Mainstone of the Percy Thomas Partnership.[397] In 1975 a major programme to clear the area and consolidate unstable industrial ground and tips commenced in advance of the construction of a number of warehouses and light industrial units and a distribution centre for Watney Mann, completed in 1978.[398] This was followed by the complex for Ferranti Computer Systems Limited (later GEC-Marconi) designed by J. L. Russell after his retirement as Chief Architect. Developed between 1980 and 1983 the complex included offices and lecture, computer and amenity facilities.[399]

In addition to industrial units, a fire station, an ambulance station for the Gwent Health Authority and Drill Hall for the Territorial Army were built, the last opened in November 1987 by Neil Kinnock, MP.

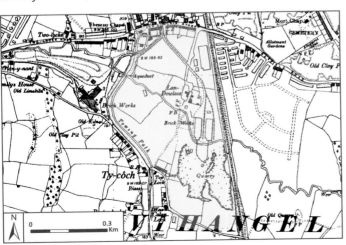
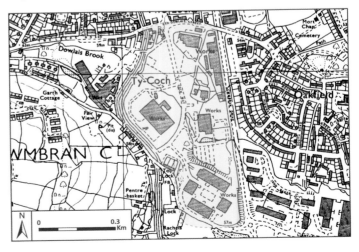

Figure 165: The Ty Coch area depicted on the OS mapping of 1954 and 1984.

7.15.2 Character of area

A north-south orientated area at the southern edge of Cwmbrân situated between the neighbourhoods of Oakfield and Coedeva, this flat-lying area is dominated by industrial development of the late twentieth century.

Nothing remains of the nineteenth-century Oakfield wire works, or the associated village of Oakfield, which has been cleared in its entirety. Historic dwellings are found along Ty Coch Lane in the southern part of the neighbourhood, comprised largely of late nineteenth-century workers' housing. These properties, situated in linear clusters along the canal, range from narrow-fronted stone-built terraces to more substantial detached stone cottages and brick villas exemplified by Oakland House, 1904. With long, narrow plots facing onto the canal, the majority of these still back on to agricultural land and sit within a semi-rural setting. A small estate, Cwrt Dowlas, built at the end of the twentieth century is formed of densely planned semi-detached brick houses set around two short culs-de-sac.

The dominant character of the area is industrial, however, forming the Ty Coch Industrial Estate. The Ferranti building, now Vantage Point House and offices of the South Wales Ambulance Service, has been retained in excellent original form externally. This red-brickwork complex has a range of three, equal height, storeys and equally spaced bays divided by alternating single and double pilasters, the repeating facades broken by projecting semi-hexagonal stair towers. The complex is set in expansive, well landscaped and planted grounds with the Dowlais Brook retained and incorporated to form attractive water features to the main entrance. On the opposite side of Ty Coch Road, the former Alfa-Laval building now houses Festive Productions. The largest unit on the estate, the original rectangular factory has been substantially expanded, but retains its original streamlined curtain-walled administration block to the front. Again, on a large plot, the factory is screened to all sides by mature trees with an open car park to the north.

Figure 166: Industrial units at the Hill Street Estate.

The remainder of the units are standard CDC-built, light-industrial units of corrugated metal upper structures on brickwork plinths, or later replacements in a similar style. Recent development has been concentrated in the northern section of the estate, with several new units constructed since 2000.

8 Statement of significance

8.1 Context

'*The building of a new town is not merely a great task of physical construction, it is also a great adventure in social construction, for the new towns must be lively communities with their own civic consciousness and civic pride*'[400]

The story of British New Towns originated in the industrialisation of late-eighteenth- and nineteenth-century Britain, resulting in urban inhabitants growing from 20% to 80% of the British population.[401] The ensuing living conditions for workers, overcrowded and with inadequate facilities, led to the growth of the Garden City movement at the end of the nineteenth and early twentieth century. Inspired by workers' settlements such as Saltaire, Bourneville and Port Sunlight, Ebenezer Howard's vision in *Tomorrow: A Peaceful Path to Real Reform* (1898) altered the way twentieth-century Britain thought about planning for urban growth and renewal. Howard imagined a network of settlements that provided for socially just and physically healthy societies through a combination of high-quality housing and jobs with open green spaces. Leading to the formation of the Garden Cities Association and the building of Letchworth Garden City (1903), in Wales these ideas were expressed most notably at Oakdale (1910-11), a planned village of 660 workers' houses, hospital, miners' institute and hotel by the Tredegar Iron and Coal Company, and Rhiwbina Garden Village (1912-23), a cooperative settlement of 189 houses on the northern outskirts of Cardiff designed by Parker and Unwin.[402]

The implanting of these ideals into UK national planning began through the 1918 campaign for 'Homes fit for Heroes', the 1918 Tudor Walters Report and 1919 Addison Act.[403] While many of the principles of Garden Cities were lost in the practical need to build substantial amounts of public housing at speed and low cost, large inter-war council estates built by

Figure 167: Y Groes, Rhiwbina Garden Village.

Figure 168: Gaer Estate, Newport c.1930.

local authorities such as Newport and Wrexham continued the more expansive, low-density development that remained in contrast to the dense industrial terraces of the nineteenth century. Newport Borough Council was one of the most enthusiastic builders of local authority housing in this period, including the initial phase of Y Gaer estate, 1933, later expanded as the Gaer-Stelvio estate in the immediate post-war period.[404]

The Building of Satellite Towns published 1925 by the self-named 'The New Townsmen' (a group of garden city proponents) introduced the idea of a ring of new towns around London for the first time. Likewise, the report of the Greater London Regional Planning Committee written in 1933 by Raymond Unwin, architect in the Garden City movement, prompted the formation of the Departmental Committee of Garden Cities and Satellite Towns. In 1938 the Barlow Commission was established to assess and report on the distribution of industrial population in the UK (reporting in 1940); in the same year the Green Belt Act was passed in recognition of the need to contain urban growth.[405] In the meantime, the efforts of both the GCA, renamed the Town and Country Planning Association in 1941, and the International Congresses of Modern Architecture (CIAM, from the French Congrès Internationaux d'Architecture Modern), maintained support for the Garden City principles of planning.[406]

The interest of the Modern Movement in Garden City planning brought a new emphasis on urbanised design, influenced by the views of those such as Le Corbusier who saw motorisation, and the associated urban expressways, ring roads and underpasses, as essential to new, technologically driven, societies. Early adopters of such an approach were largely American, including Robert Moses in his Depression-era transformation of New York and Frank Lloyd Wright's prototype design for Broadacre City, and were intertwined with the development of distinct zones separated and linked by these road networks.[407]

The substantial damage to towns and cities across the UK during the Second World War brought about opportunity to restructure urban areas and inner-city populations, and the idea of using Garden City principles of planning for this was immediate. *New Towns after the War*, originally published during the First World War, was republished by its author, socialist and Garden City supporter Frederic Osbourne, in 1942. In 1943-44 the County of London Plan/Greater London Plan were published by Patrick Abercrombie, the latter with its proposal of eight satellite towns allowing decentralisation for the worst inner-city slums.[408] In 1945 Lewis Silkin was appointed as Minister of Town and Country Planning and the New Towns Committee was created under John Reith. The resulting New Towns Act of 1946 enabled the designation of sites for new settlements by the state and the appointment of New Town Development Corporations, with full developer rights, to direct and accomplish the building of the towns.[409] This act has been described as the 'keystone in the

reconstruction of the so-called "New Jerusalem" promised by the Labour party' in its general election campaign of 1945.[410] The New Towns were part of Labour's welfare state, along with the NHS and state pensions that were intended to abolish poverty and exploitation.[411]

Despite the political divergence that had occurred between the proponents of Garden Cities and the Modern Movement, the planning for New Towns was ultimately a hybrid of both sets of planning ideals. The principles of Howard's 'Social City' were entrenched in the ethos of the first-generation New Town plans. The New Towns committee, which sat between 1945 and 1946, was a forum of politicians, planners, architects and social reformers, chaired by Reith. It discussed the founding principles of the towns and was heavily influenced by the likes of Osbourne, who was a key adviser.[412] The fourteen 'Mark I' New Towns aimed to be self-sustaining communities with good jobs, services and facilities, separated by open countryside but connected through good public transport. In contrast to these earlier settlements, which aimed to maintain a rural feel, they imbued CIAM's principles of urbanism.[413] The tone was set with the appointment of Frederick Gibberd, leading light in the Modern Architecture Group, as Chief Architect at Harlow, the first New Town to get underway. The contrast of planning based on the relationship between society and nature, and architectural design based on the relationship between society and technology, has been described as central to the unique character of British New Towns.[414]

The first to be designated was Stevenage, in November 1946, one of eight New Towns around London to relieve population pressure in the capital, along with Basildon, Bracknell, Crawley, Harlow, Hatfield, Hemel Hempstead and Welwyn Garden City. Similar pressures on Glasgow were alleviated through the designation of East Kilbride and Glenrothes. Cwmbrân, Peterlee, Newton Aycliffe and Corby were designated in response to industrial needs.[415]

A second generation of New Towns, including Runcorn, Skelmersdale, Telford (originally Dawley), Redditch and Washington, was initiated by the Conservative government's Town Development Act of 1952.[416] Running from 1959 and including the Expanded Town Programme, it answered the need for substantial quantities of housing to alleviate overcrowding in the northern conurbations of Liverpool and Birmingham, and addressed the post-war rise in the UK birth rate. More ambitious in scale were the third generation, created after the Labour government's New Town Act of 1965. These included both newly designated sites – the most well-known of which is Milton Keynes (1967) – and the expansion of existing towns such as Northampton, Peterborough and, in Wales, Newtown, Montgomeryshire. The latter was designated specifically to encourage economic growth in the region.[417]

The principles of planning developed rapidly in these second- and third-generation towns. The density of building was

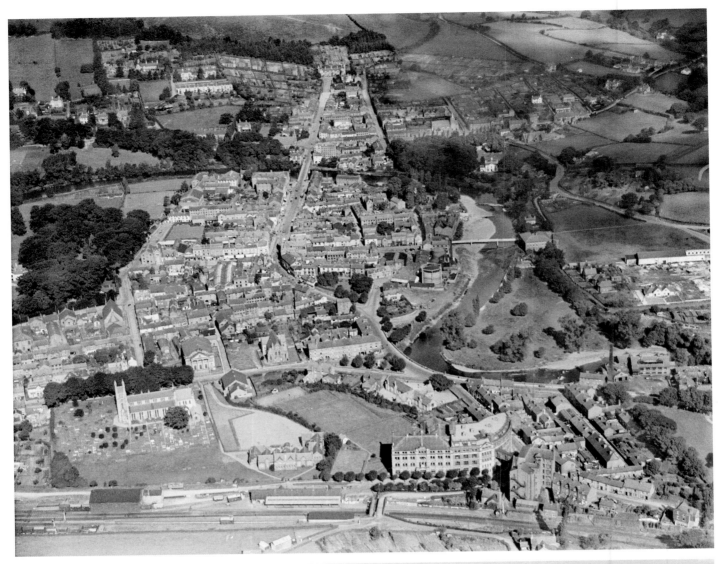

Figures 169 & 170: Newtown: the historic town from the air and New Town housing, 1970.

increased, zoning became less distinct and, fundamentally, the idea of the neighbourhood unit was dropped in favour of new sociological ideals of 'community without propinquity'.[418] This was partly in response to the rise of car ownership, with an acceptance that being able to drive increased mobility and that New Towns could be scaled up without losing a sense of community. Where Mark III New Towns were expansions of historic towns, their forms were determined to a greater extent than the newly designated settlements by existing architectural and planning narratives.

The only designated expanded town in Wales, Newtown, had its origins in a thirteenth-century planted settlement of Edward I, though the majority of the buildings date to the nineteenth century when the growth of the weaving industry quadrupled the population. Designation was intended to reverse the pattern of slow economic decline and depopulation of the area with a target population increase from 5,000 to 13,000. Political difficulties came into play, however, when it was suggested that, in order to meet this target, overspill population from the West Midlands be moved to the town – and the target and scale of development were subsequently reduced.[419]

Alongside this programme of decentralisation via New Town development, post-war planning in towns that had suffered from bomb damage during the war followed the same lines on a smaller scale. In these cities, including the south Wales examples of Newport, Cardiff and Swansea, the population was decentralised through the creation of a series of suburbs located around the edges of the city centres. Here planning was dominated by the similar themes of social changes, smaller households, changes in shopping customs, shorter hours of work and new communication systems.[420]

8.2 Essential Characteristics of Cwmbrân New Town

The New Town resident '*prefers segregation of home and work, has an innate love of nature, enjoys open air exercise – and, while demanding privacy for the individual family, likes some measure of community life***'**[421]

Many of the essential characteristics of Cwmbrân as a Mark I New Town can be classified as key components in common with other towns laid out under the 1946 Act. However, the differences of topography, industry, architectural treatment and the priorities and philosophies of the Cwmbrân Development Corporation as a whole, as well as the succession

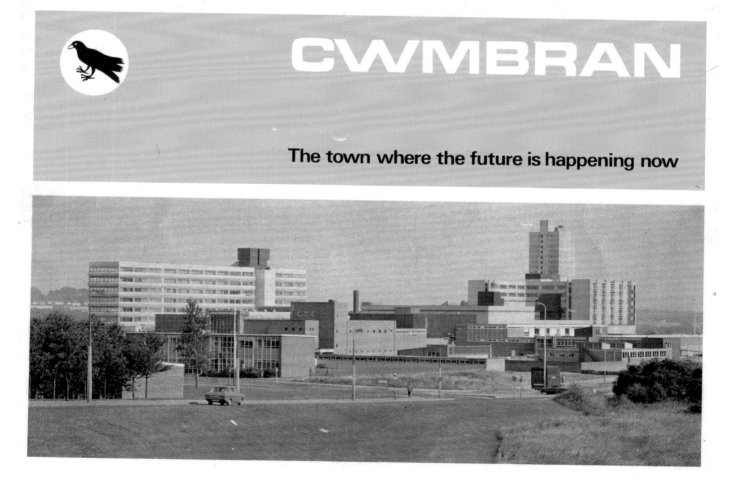

Figure 171: Cwmbrân: The town where the future is happening now...

of Chief Architects in particular, gave rise to Cwmbrân's individual character within the New Town grouping.

Fundamental to the design of Cwmbrân, as at other New Towns, was that its development was led by a development corporation as a publicly owned body, independent from government. The combination of its ability to create an uplift in land values by buying land at agricultural vales, allowing low-density development with a proliferation of open spaces, and establishing a long-term vision that focused on continuity of planning and design throughout and beyond its lifespan, can be seen as one of the most positive elements of the New Towns.[422]

Cwmbrân was planned with clear zoning of areas for residential, commercial and industrial use. This was partly determined by the challenging topography of the designated area, with industrial zones by necessity initially kept to the flatter areas of ground on the valley floor and centred around the substantial quantities of pre-existing industry, railways and regional road networks.

The bi-focal commercial and civic hub of the Town Centre was also informed by this topography, located on the flat valley floor, but still formed the central point around which the rest of the town was laid out. This centre was intended to be fully pedestrianised from its initial design by J. C. P. West in 1952 and was one of the earliest pedestrianised centres designed in

Figure 172: Cwmbrân Centre from the air, c.1980.

the UK alongside Coventry (from 1948) and Stevenage (opened in 1959).[423] The initial design for the latter, by Clifford Holliday, Gordon Stephenson and American 'consultant' Clarence S. Stein, was published in 1950 with Stephenson later explaining that there were 'no precedents to cite. The only examples to draw from would be Venice, the Kalverstraat in Amsterdam, Europe's first pedestrian shopping mall, Radburn and an exploratory suburban pedestrian shopping centre design executed by Clarence Stein and Matthew Nowicki'.[424] While the idea of small-scale market squares and shopping arcades had long been a feature of British towns, pedestrianisation as a recognised feature of urban planning was instigated by the rise of car ownership in the inter-war years when it was recognised that 'older shopping centres lost their interest as meeting places, and centres where once a happy atmosphere had prevailed now became death traps'.[425] Informed by developments in the US where car ownership had risen earlier, the idea of shopping precincts, separated from historic shopping areas and where segregation of pedestrians and traffic was key, was most notably advocated by Herbert Alker Tripp's idea of vertical layering in his 1942 *Town Planning and Road Traffic.*

Shoppers were protected from the surrounding ring road of traffic by the centre-facing shops, replicating on a smaller scale the network of small shopping streets and parades that would have developed over a long period of time in historic town centres. The outer face presents high walls to the surrounding traffic, a design that was subsequently criticised, along with the relentlessly flat nature of the rooflines, but which clearly define the centre.[426] Within the centre, the two focal points are formed are the Civic Square (the potential of which was not fulfilled) and Gwent Square, and connected by a central shopping spine. The location of the Town Centre is clearly signalled by the high-rise residential 'The Tower', which provides the modern equivalent of a church spire forming a landmark in the townscape.

Many of the retail centres in New Towns have been described as suffering from poor 'modern' design, which has driven shoppers to more traditional city centres. Milton Keynes has been described as standing 'in stark contrast … to the lacklustre economic performance and town centres of much smaller new towns such as Peterlee in the north-east of England, or the new towns in Wales'.[427] Cwmbrân, however, from its early conception as a supplement to the existing centres of Pontypool and Newport, has become the largest and most successful shopping centre in southeast Wales.[428] Part of this success was the forward thinking of the CDC in providing 3,000 free car parking spaces adjacent to the pedestrianised shopping area, a situation that was not always mirrored elsewhere. At Welwyn, for example, which had grown into a regional shopping centre by the 1960s, it was estimated that car parking provision would need to be increased by up to three times in the following 20 years to deal with the lack of parking.[429] The scale of its provision has become one of Cwmbrân's most publicly recognisable features, even passing

into popular culture.[430] However, the positivity of such accessibility for high levels of car use is now being called into question by the need to promote more sustainable modes of transport.

Despite later proposals to 'enhance' the centre, much of the scheme retains its original form. However, some landmark developments, such as the first Sainsbury's in Wales and the health centre, have been demolished and plans are currently in place for substantial redevelopment of Gwent Square including external remodelling of House of Fraser (David Evans) and the infilling of the Water Gardens. In comparison with the larger 'London ring' New Towns, only Stevenage, Harlow and Basildon offered the scope for wholly new Town Centres. Part of Harlow's town centre was demolished in 2018, rebuilding and alterations have taken place at Basildon and Crawley, while the planned centre at Basildon of 1963 has been largely replaced since 2013.[431]

The commercial and industrial core is surrounded by an array of residential neighbourhood units, fundamental to the planning ethos of the New Towns Committee and designed to be largely self-sustaining in day-to-day life. The concept of such a 'unit' where key amenities such as schools and shops were located within walking distance of a defined 'community', which would be both practical and encourage a sense of space, had been developed by American planner Clarence Perry and was most successfully deployed at Radburn, New Jersey.[432] Each neighbourhood had a central shopping unit, some of the largest supplemented by a sub-unit centre or pantry shops to ensure availability within easy walking distance of all homes. At Cwmbrân the architecture of these public buildings of the 1950s within the residential areas – mainly single-storey and simple structures – reflects West's desire not to create overbearing elements. With the increasing dominance of the town centre shops, only those at Llanyravon and Fairwater remain in their original form, but they demonstrate the potential to reinvigorate a more sustainable transport model of local shopping.

Fundamental to the creation of a recognisable identity around which a new community could form, a series of buildings was provided in all but the smallest neighbourhoods. A network of community halls was provided, in some cases in conjunction with a new public house as at Fairwater. Although architecturally unambitious – the most innovative design found at the octagonal 'Threepenny Bit' at Greenmeadow – these centres continue to thrive, offering facilities, gathering places and communal activities. Perhaps the greatest elements of design are to be seen in the new places of worship where the Methodist church deliberately set out to create buildings that would be distinctly recognisable and identifiable within the landscape.

Research indicates that New Towns generated strong communities, possibly stronger than those in established towns, evidenced by the higher levels of interaction with community activities from residents' association to clubs. This has been attributed partly to early residents being overwhelmingly white, working class and either young married couples or those with young families, the similarity making familiarity easier to generate.[433] The lack of existing family or social connections made people more open to joining new activities and forming new networks, and sociological research in the 1950s indicated that the majority of families participated in circles of mobility, sociability and leisure outside of their neighbourhood unit.[434] 'Transferable Lessons from New Towns', a Department of Communities and Local Government report of 2006, revealed that New Towns continue to have more community organisations than areas of older cities with comparable socio-economic characteristics.[435]

Also central to each neighbourhood community was the network of infant and junior schools, with secondary schools and places of worship towards the boundaries to allow joint use between adjacent neighbourhood units. Designed by Monmouthshire County Council architects' department, a strong unity of design was developed across those built in the 1950s and early 1960s. Unfortunately, some architecturally notable examples have already been demolished, including the first secondary school opened at Llantarnam, the Croesyceiliog Campus and Hollybush School, all in the County Style developed by Colin Jones.

Particularly successful was the dual use of school facilities for adult education classes and as community leisure facilities. In 1964 the Ministry of Housing and Local Government and the Department of Education and Science issued a circular to New Towns stating that in planning new facilities, the requirements of the communities should be taken into consideration and that dual use of amenities such as school playing fields and tracks should be encouraged to meet local needs. Subsequent plans at Telford and Skelmersdale, to create social and recreational buildings around schools for the community and to provide a greater range of activities for adults, were lauded.[436] At Cwmbrân, such provision was made early on, with adult education wings at Croesyceiliog and West Pontnewydd Primary built from 1959, although it was noted that by the mid-1960s such activity was declining in popularity.

The New Towns Committee was adamant that to 'secure a true social balance, dwellings of all class must be built in due proportions' and the Development Corporation 'should see that larger as well as smaller houses are built and houses for sale as well as letting', and that different income groups and classes should not be segregated into different areas of the town.[437] Owing to the nature of its designation, Cwmbrân was to some extent exempt from this ideal, with an acceptance that the existence of existing industry and associated commuter workforce would result in a population of working-class families employed by the manufacturing or service industries, with a small percentage of people working in management roles. This was reflected in the construction of a high proportion of houses for rent, with owner-occupation

limited to what were deemed the most attractive areas of the town. CDC housing was initially unambitious in design, dominated by two-storey houses set in semi-detached pairs or short terraces, with private gardens, and fronting an informal network of estate roads. Following a pattern set by local authority housing in the inter-war period, itself developed from the Garden Village layouts, the first innovations were in the use of materials and construction techniques, as exemplified by the 'demonstration houses' at Pontnewydd. Innovation in planning was initiated with the development of the neighbourhoods immediately north and south of the centre, which exhibited markedly more 'urban' characteristics, the denser housing including a higher percentage of three- and four-storey blocks of flats, while variety in design was prompted by the development of 'higher-quality' housing at Croesyceiliog and Llanyravon.

With the appointment of Gordon Redfern overseeing the development of the neighbourhoods to the south and west from the mid-1960s, the use of form and material became more experimental, though the number of mediumr-rise properties remained low because of a lack of demand for flats from either renters or buyers. Aesthetic variety was provided instead through using a range of external materials, roof forms and window arrangements and varying both the layout of pairs, short terraces or courts and the distance and angle of layout to the road. Adaptation to topography through design became more important as building moved to areas on the sloping valley sides. The rapid increase in car ownership had a discernible effect on the planning of estates both with increased provision of private parking adjacent to houses, and the introduction of Radburn-style systems for separating vehicular and foot traffic.[438]

The neighbourhoods were both connected and separated by a road network consisting of inner and outer ring roads, providing circulation around the town, in conjunction with a series of radial roads providing access between the Town Centre and the neighbourhoods. This internal network was tied into regional roads linking to out-of-town traffic. The separation of vehicular and pedestrian traffic, derived from the Radburn system, was fundamental to transport planning in four ways:

- vehicles, cyclists and pedestrians on the main radial and ring roads were segregated;

- no heavy traffic routes passed through the shopping or civic centres, or the residential neighbourhoods;

- adequate road widths were provided to ensure safe setting down and picking up of passengers where needed, such as at shopping centres/units; and

- the number of at-grade pedestrian crossings were limited through the use of overpasses and underpasses.[439]

Much of the circulation planning was predicated on the idea of foot traffic, particularly in determining the layout of the neighbourhood units and the placing of shops, schools and places of worship – an idea that quickly became outdated with the increase in car ownership. As the layout planning adapted to this, the Radburn principles of separation became more evident and sophisticated with the development of a strong network of discrete foot and cycle paths within and between neighbourhoods, and to the Town Centre. Despite criticism from later planners contemptuously describing that 'drive into any example of the garden city idea and you will lose your sense of direction in the wide streets that lead nowhere. Wide tarmac rivers wave off in every direction, any of them may be the way out', this facilitated both a safe system for foot travel and allowed for the quickest movement of traffic around the town.[440]

Criticism was forthcoming earlier, in 1953, for what was described as 'prairie planning', 'a feeling of hopelessness in the face of an eternity of wideness, punctuated at intervals by seas of concrete'.[441] The creation and retention of green spaces between and within the different elements of the town were seen as fundamental for recreational and environmental purposes, with on average 20% of the designated area left as open space.[442] They provided a continuous connection between areas with differnt characters and built elements, creating harmony within the town and between the urban nature of the new town and its rural setting. The preservation and conservation of important elements of the existing landscape, from individual trees to swathes of woodland, was supplemented by a substantial scheme of landscaping and planting by CDC, partly as an aesthetic compensation for the man-made nature of the urban scheme that they were imposing and partly as a deliberate environmental policy. This scheme of planting included 37,388 trees and 683,768 shrubs.[433]

The provision of recreational and sporting facilities, including playgrounds, represents the rounded idea of improved living offered by the New Town. When interviewed for the book 'Concretopia', Jim Griffiths, a retired planner living in Cwmbrân, lauded the 'space to breathe' and the 'green spaces buzzing with activity', which were in contrast to the previous experiences of so many escaping inner city living.[444] During the course of its existence, the CDC designated 43.6 hectares of public playing fields and 43.5 hectares of public parks and recreational areas, alongside a further 14.1 hectares of private playing fields.

The creation of such a large proportion of green space, generous gardens, playgrounds, public parks, sporting grounds and open areas, was one of the greatest achievements of the New Towns. Such consideration to the green infrastructure, for both aesthetic and environmental reasons, can be seen as prescient in the light of current environmental and planning policy, in particular the Welsh Government's Well-being of Future Generations (Wales) Act 2015, which puts emphasis on the creation of accessible and high-quality green spaces that create well-being, and the protection, promotion, conservation and enhancement of natural assets.[445]

8.3 Significant Assets and Recommendation for Further Study

'self-contained and balanced communities for work and living'

Figure 173: A CDC matchbox advertising Cwmbrân as the 'Garden City of Wales'.

Unfortunately, apart from the archive research, this study has taken place largely between March 2020 and December 2020. With travel and fieldwork severely limited by the COVID-19 pandemic, field visits and the study of individual assets have not been possible in the way anticipated, or likely to be possible for the foreseeable future. Likewise, it has not been possible to visit and assess building interiors. Based on the research carried out for this report, a number of notable assets that would benefit from further study can be highlighted. It is recommended that further research, recording and interpretation of individual sites in the town is carried out.

8.3.1 Town Centre Sites

One of the most notable features of the Town Centre of Cwmbrân is its pedestrianisation. No documentation has been found regarding West's inspiration for his design at Cwmbrân, but in date and design it is comparable with Town Centre developments at Coventry and Stevenage – both of which are recognised as pioneering and innovative developments – and with the Upper Precinct, Coventry, listed at Grade II as the earliest planned pedestrianised development in England.[446] Outside of the UK, Europe's first purpose-built pedestrianised street, the Lijnbaan, Rotterdam, built from 1952 to designs by Johannes van den Broek and Jacob Bakema, is also designated a national heritage site. This, together with the 'pedestrian type centre' at Vällingby, Stockholm, and plans by Frederick Gibberd for a pedestrianised shopping centre at the Lansbury Estate for the Festival of Britain, are cited as important contemporary influences for the Stevenage design. It would difficult to think that West, as a fellow Corporation Development Chief Architect, would not have been aware of these when producing what the Ministry of Housing, Communities and Local Government described as 'one of, if not the most interesting, New Town Centre schemes we have had'.[447]

While more recent commercial development around the Town Centre has been in the form of generic stores, particularly in the area of General Rees Square, the unity of design inherent in the original scheme, including the concrete planters and benches, has been retained and focus has remained on the tightly defined site at the centre of Cwmbrân. This has avoided the dispersal of 'out-of-town' shopping centres common in other towns and cities. Within Wales it is unique as a wholly planned and built pedestrianised Town Centre, and of outstanding importance within the context of post-war urban redevelopment of the historic city centres of Cardiff, Newport and Swansea. More detailed comparative work, both within Wales and to other UK New Towns, is suggested to properly highlight the significance of this development.

Monmouth House is an interesting example of a Town Centre building with mixed commercial and residential development. At the time of its opening in 1967, the Kibby's supermarket was the largest in Wales. The building is particularly notable for the large William Mitchell sculpture to the external lift shaft; this is one of only two large-scale sculptures by the artist in Wales and the only one to remain in-situ (the other removed and its whereabouts currently unknown). As of 2016, Historic England had listed six of his works in recognition of his eminence in the pantheon of post-war artists working in the public realm and a major assessment of Mitchell's work is currently in progress by Dr Dawn Pereira. Alongside this major sculpture, the William Mitchell reliefs to the retaining walls of the A4051, though simpler in form, should also be noted.

Gwent House is a strong design by Sheppard, Robson & Partners, a practice whose reputation was built on an expertise in concrete-shell public buildings. A number of their schemes outside Wales are also listed, and Gwent House may be considered at threat in terms of the potential decline in demand for Town Centre office sites. The 1972 building was carefully designed as a multi-functional building to bring both leisure and office facilities into a centre otherwise dominated by retail, diversifying the usage of the Town Centre. It is also notable for the inclusion of the Gwent murals by Henry Collins and Joyce Pallot. While Collins and Pallot created works UK wide, another example registered in Wales cannot be found at the time of writing. The set of three concrete murals are representative of the approach they took in extensively researching an area's history prior to design, including references to important figures and events in the final works. In conjunction with Gwent House was the development of the

Figures 174 and 175: Gwent House.

library, a two-storey structure that sits in contrast with the monumentality of Gwent House. The exterior has remained unaltered, including the brushed steel signage.

The David Evans store (currently House of Fraser) of 1964 is an excellent example of a post-war department store in original external condition. Unlike many high-street stores of this date, which adopted the trend for exposed curtain-walling and large plate glass windows, the store is strongly distinguished by its cladding of closely set vertical timbers to the upper floors. They sit in visual contrast to the horizontal concrete and glass lines that dominate the shopping area. With a planning application in process for major external alterations, the exterior character of the building is likely to be changed radically, which is regrettable. The building also risks being affected by the large-scale closure of high-street chains, with concerns about the changing nature of high street retail deeper than ever after COVID-19 lockdown.

The Moonraker Pub (currently the John Fielding) of 1964, is the only public house in the Town Centre. It unusually sits on the northern edge of the area, with the main social hub originally to be provided by the complex of bars and restaurants in Gwent House. Run by Watney Mann, as their first public house in Wales, both the interior and exterior have been heavily altered.

The Water Gardens at the south end of the shopping precinct are a striking example of post-war Town Centre planning. The carefully thought-out scheme combining texture, colour and sound by Gordon Redfern, brings imuch-needed green planting to the town and is an important representation of the interlinking of countryside and town, the rural and modernist ideals that underpin the ideology of the New Town movement. It can also be seen as unique in post-war urban centre planning in Wales. At the time of writing (March 2021), the Town Centre Water Gardens are under assessment for listing by Cadw as a central piece of civic centre planning in Wales's only fully planned New Town.

A major feature of the Town Centre was the provision of car parking. The two most distinctive elements of this are the Glyndwr Road car park and Llewelyn car park. The former is of eight storeys, constructed of pre-cast concrete cladding units. Carefully designed to deal with the sloping site, the design has been compromised by the removal of the vertical struts that enclosed each of the parking decks. The latter sits below the south-western corner of the shopping centre and is distinguished by the sweeping spiral of the external access ramp on Tudor Road. The shuttered concrete patterning of this contrasts with the bush hammered decoration to the protruding stair towers to the corners of the site.

To the south of this, the area designated as the 'Civic Square' was not developed as intended, reducing the impact of the pairing of magistrate's court and police station. The Congress Theatre, a striking design of 1972 developed as a major architectural addition to Gwent Square, has previously been heavily altered. The Tower, a significant structure in the

planning of point-block development in Wales and designed as the most visible landmark in the town, has had its impact compromised by unsympathetic over-cladding. Further assessment of the potential survival of original elevations below the over-cladding would be recommended for both buildings.

8.3.2 Neighbourhood Sites

The neighbourhood units that make up the majority of the town vary in terms of their completeness. Llanyravon and Fairwater unit centres are the two best surviving examples of local centres and illustrate contrasting principles of design from two very different Chief Architects. Fairwater, in its architectural response to the climate and topography, the needs of shoppers and use of innovative forms and materials, is particularly significant. Its form as an enclosed space, with car parking provided to the south and excluded by the high walls of the rear elevations to the shop units, pedestrianised walkways protected by exaggerated canopies to the shop fronts and a central playground is a mirroring, and further development, of the pedestrianised ideals of the Town Centre shopping area. Llanyravon is more modest in scale and form, but has been commercially the most successful of the unit centres and is still well used and maintained. Both centres would benefit from a reassessment in light of a renewed emphasis on the provision of local facilities and decentralisation from Town Centres and a reduction in car use.

St David's Catholic Church has been included in the recent pan-Wales Taking Stock programme to assess parish churches in the three Welsh dioceses. Opened in 1961, and immediately pre-Vatican II, the design is noted in the assessment as influenced by Basil Spence's Coventry Cathedral, in particular with its saw-toothed fenestration to the nave and staggered windows to the sanctuary. The conclusion classifies the church as of regional interest and meriting designation as a Historic Asset of Special Local Interest.[448] The Methodist chapels of Llanyravon and Fairhill, and Church of Latter-Day Saints (LDS) all fit into a programme of post-war chapel building that includes city centre redevelopment and suburban expansion, which is only now being studied methodically in Wales. The earliest LDS church still in use in Wales is that at Merthyr Tydfil of 1963, dating to the re-introduction of the LDS denomination into Wales in this period, so the example at Croesyceiliog is of interest within this context. Both the LDS church and two Methodist chapels would merit more detailed study.

Post-war schools are also currently undergoing a period of assessment as many are due to be replaced under the Welsh Government's 21st Century Schools and Colleges Programme. Cwmbrân was remarkable for its coherent scheme of buildings across primary and secondary schools. In light of the loss of three of the early secondary educational complexes by Colin Jones and his team at the Monmouthshire County Council architect's department in recent years, it would be prudent to make further assessment of surviving primary schools in the same idiom: West Pontnewydd, Croesyceiliog, Llanyravon and Ysgol Gymraeg. Another important feature is the use of curtain-walling, for which the breakthrough came with the building of Lever House, New York, in 1952 and which aided in its popularity from 1955-57 by development of aluminium and glass walling techniques by firms such as Pilkington's. Curtain-walling was illustrated in early use at schools at Oakfield (demolished) and Maendy in 1961 with that at Coedeva being later in date. The two latter examples are also recommended for further assessment.

Housing makes up the largest percentage of building carried out as part of the New Town development with over 10,000 dwellings built by the CDC. A small number of these were individually designed and built, the most significant grouping being the properties along Crown Road and Bryn Rhedyn. It is not within the scope to carry out individual research and assessment on these houses and more work on this development is recommended. There is exciting diversity and typology of housing style and form, as well of innovative construction techniques, over the 35-year history of housing schemes by the CDC, which merits a more detailed study in its own right. The Crescent and Ty Newydd schemes are good examples of post-war housing development as enacted by the local authority and the CDC respectively, while closer study of the surviving elements of the innovative demonstration houses at Pontnewydd is advised. The most significant demonstration of innovation in architectural form is displayed in the neighbourhoods of Fairwater, Greenmeadow and Coedeva under Gordon Redfern and Alex Gordon. Few twentieth-century workers housing or public 'estate' housing schemes in Wales are listed. Those houses forming the original core at Rhiwbina Garden Village are listed Grade II, but no examples of publicly built housing are designated from the post-war period. While later alterations to the housing in Cwmbrân are so widespread, it would be difficult to find individual properties in original condition to meet listing criteria, although assessment of the schemes as conservation areas or for local listing would be appropriate. From the last phase of development by the CDC, the building of Taliesin by MacCormac Jamieson Prichard (MJP) stands out as a thoughtfully designed and executed co-living scheme, and as an early example of such work by the practice.

Many of the most significant civic buildings outside of the Town Centre have already been demolished, most regrettably the County Hall, but also the Police Training Centre and Police Headquarters.

Currently only one asset relating to New Town development between 1951 and 1988 is on Cadw's Register of Listed buildings; this is Cadw record No. 87770, the Court Road Industrial Estate sign. Designated in 2019, the sign is listed as:

Included for its special architectural interest as a highly distinctive sign, a classic example of post war design that exemplifies the spirit of the age of the Cwmbrân new town

development. The establishment of Cwmbrân as the only major new town in Wales was a significant event in the post war period and was a major landmark in planning and development in Wales. This sign is of special historic interest as a rare surviving example of street furniture from the development of the new town, a type of sign used elsewhere in the industrial estates in the town and intended to promote the key role of industrial estates in that development.

Figure 176: Court Road Industrial Estate sign.

Industrial development by the CDC is distinguished by the quantity and success of their advance factory building programme, including the 10 factories by Powell & Alport on the Avondale Estate of 1963-64 (unfortunately demolished) and the group of saw-tooth-roofed buildings developed in a 'CDC style' on the Springfield Industrial Estate. Individual schemes for further assessment should include the Girling Engineering School by Cifford Tee & Gale of 1958-59 (their offices for Saunders Valve company, c.1961 now demolished) and the Alfa-Laval factory (Festive Productions) and GEC-Marconi (South Wales Ambulance Service offices) at Tŷ Coch.

Most notable is the group of well-designed high-tech units at the Llantarnam Industrial park, dating from the earlier 1980s. This includes Raglan House, the earliest high-tech unit, Brecon House and Tŷ Gwent.

8.4 Conclusion

'the great social adventure which they will embody, the fulfilment of their architectural possibilities, and the development of their industries should arouse a world-wide interest'[449]

The New Towns movement was a monumentally ambitious programme to transform the lives of people across Britain, resulting in 32 new or expanded communities housing 28 million people.[450] By 1969 the success of New Towns was being lauded, with a number of surveys conducted showing

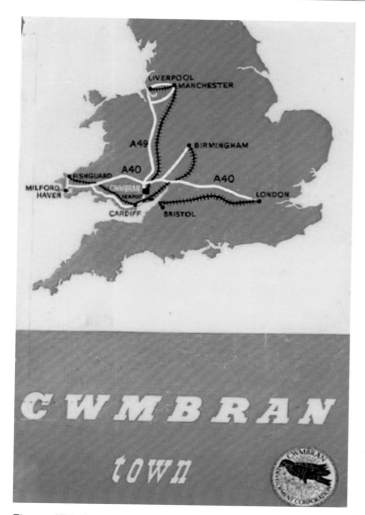

Figure 177: Cwmbrân New Town Handbook from 1962.

80% of New Town residents were pleased at having moved there.[451]

Cwmbrân's importance lies primarily in its designation as the only Mark I New Town in Wales. This first wave of New Towns was the first such organised network in the world and went on to influence and inform town planning globally. The Town Centre is of a date and design that is comparable to Coventry and Stevenage, both of which have received much greater attention as being in the vanguard of pedestrianisation and post-war planning, as well as levels of protection, though both are currently facing similar issues of redevelopment and alteration. It is the only settlement in Wales with a coherent plan of Town Centre, neighbourhoods and industrial zones, planned and built within a defined time period and with a consistent philosophy provided by the Development Corporation overview. Within this philosophy, it also illustrates the fast-paced development in innovative construction techniques, building form and urban planning that took place in the post-war period and was introduced through the series of chief architects attracted to working within the CDC.

While there has been post-CDC development that has moved away from these principles, such developments are relatively small and in areas to the outskirts or in small pockets of infilling, with much of the original character of the built landscape retained. More worrying is the impact of infill developments on the character of the open spaces and green areas. These were of equal importance in the original master plan in creating a town that provided balance between work and leisure by providing spaces for play, recreation and relaxation as well as the environmental and aesthetic benefits that the CDC's substantial planting schemes brought. A number of the other Mark I New Towns have recognised the importance of their mid-century built heritage and have introduced a range of responses: Stevenage Borough Council have stated that its regeneration scheme will build on 'treasuring and protecting the historic landmarks and countryside that make Stevenage unique… inspiration for many of the new buildings and developments draws from Stevenage's rich culture and heritage'. At Harlow a heritage assessment written to inform the Town Centre Area Action Plan noted the negative impact of the loss of New Town assets. And Hemel Hempstead can be looked towards for its exemplary restoration scheme of the New Town water gardens as part of the Town Centre regeneration.[452]

There has been substantial denunciation and mocking of the towns as a failed experiment from later planners. In addition to the claims of prairie planning, issues are recognised around the inability to create socially, racially and economically balanced communities and to attract a wider diversity of job opportunities, and failures with some of the most innovative housing materials and design.

However, the commitment to innovative and efficient housing, generous green spaces, community development, arts provision for all, civic provision and employment opportunities, can be strongly charted across the history of the CDC through the built environment of Cwmbrân today. With the increasing pressures of industrial and commercial development, the provision of higher quantities of inexpensively produced housing, rising land prices and reduced provision for car use, together with increasing focus on environmental sustainability of urban settlements, it is important to both protect the fundamental characteristics of this unique settlement in Wales and take these forward in planning new inclusive and sustainable communities for the future.[453]

Figure 178: The Cwmbrân Development Corporation logo as adapted for use on local road signs.

Acknowledgements

The report was produced with the co-operation and help of Torfaen County Borough Council and particular thanks go to Adrian Wilcock, Robert Murray and Rebecca McAndrew within Torfaen CBC.

We should like to acknowledge the considerable help of archive staff at both the Gwent Record Office, in particular Kai Michael (Senior Archivist), and the National Library of Wales. Many thanks also to Deborah-Anne Wildgust and Jonathan Smith of Torfaen Museum Trust for their generosity and help with images, to the South Wales Argus for allowing the use of photographs from their archives and to Architectural History Practise.

Many thanks to Jonathan Vining of WYG for contributing his advice and considerable expertise on twentieth century architecture and planning to this report, to Dr Dawn Pireira for sharing her knowledge of William Mitchell. Colleagues at the Royal Commission are thanked for their contributions to the production of the report, in particular Jon Dollery for the production of the maps, Penny Icke for help with copyright, Reina van der Wiel for copyediting the text, Meg Ryder for archiving photographs, and David Billingsley for aiding with background research.

We would also like to thank all the staff of the Cwmbrân Development Corporation who created such detailed records of their work and who had the foresight to deposit their records with the Gwent Record Office.

Note on the spelling of Cwmbrân: Cwmbrân is spelt in the form recommended by the Welsh Language Commissioner's *List of Standardised Welsh Place-names* except where the historical context demands a variant spelling. Thus: 'Cwmbrân New Town', 'Cwmbran Development Corporation', and 'Cwm Bran' (the historic O.S. form).

List of Images

Except where otherwise indicated, the images are Crown copyright and are reproduced with the permission of the Royal Commission on the Ancient and Historical Monuments of Wales (RCAHMW), under delegated authority from The Keeper of Public Records.

Cover Image: Gwent Archives: D2603/C/3477: Cwmbran Development Corporation: Photograph Album, Pontnewydd West

Figure 1: © Crown Copyright: RCAHMW – AP_2006_13153 (NPRN 408671)

Figure 2: © Crown Copyright: RCAHMW, 2021. This map is based upon Ordnance Survey material with the permission of Ordnance Survey on behalf of the Controller of Her Majesty's Stationery Office © Crown copyright. Unauthorised reproduction infringes Crown copyright and may lead to prosecution or civil proceedings. Licence number: 100022206

Figure 3: © Crown Copyright: RCAHMW – DS2021_034_005 (NPRN 307297)

Figure 4: National Library of Wales, Public Domain, via Wikimedia Commons

Figure 5: © Crown Copyright: RCAHMW, 2021. This map is based upon Ordnance Survey material with the permission of Ordnance Survey on behalf of the Controller of Her Majesty's Stationery Office © Crown copyright. Unauthorised reproduction infringes Crown copyright and may lead to prosecution or civil proceedings. Licence number: 100022206

Figure 6: © Crown Copyright: RCAHMW: Aerofilms Collection – WPW032472 (NPRN 415260)

Figure 7: Torfaen Museum Trust Collection

Figure 8: © Crown Copyright: RCAHMW, 2021. This map is based upon Ordnance Survey material with the permission of Ordnance Survey on behalf of the Controller of Her Majesty's Stationery Office © Crown copyright. Unauthorised reproduction infringes Crown copyright and may lead to prosecution or civil proceedings. Licence number: 100022206

Figure 9: Cwmbran New Town: A Master Plan, T.H. Huxley Turner 1951

Figure 10: Gwent Record Office C/MISCR/184: Monmouthshire CC, Reports: Cwmbran New Town: A Master Plan, T.H. Huxley Turner 1951

Figure 11: Cwmbran New Town: A Master Plan, T.H. Huxley Turner 1951

Figure 12: Torfaen Museum Trust Collection

Figure 13: Torfaen Museum Trust Collection

Figure 14: © Crown Copyright: RCAHMW – DS2021_017_001 (NPRN 45102)

Figure 15: © Crown Copyright: RCAHMW – DS2021_015_004 (NPRN 45076)

Figure 16: © Crown Copyright: RCAHMW – DS2021_025_002 (NPRN 422742)

Figure 17: © Crown Copyright: RCAHMW – DS2021_021_003 (NPRN 701510)

Figure 18: Photograph courtesy of South Wales Argus

Figure 19: © Crown Copyright: RCAHMW – DS2021_024_002 (NPRN 701511)

Figure 20: © Crown Copyright: RCAHMW – DS2021_027_003 & DS2021_027_004 (NPRN 415259)

Figure 21: © Crown Copyright: RCAHMW – DS2021_043_002 (NPRN 701527)

Figure 22: © Crown Copyright: Homes England available under the Open Government Licence; Gwent Record Office: D2603/C/3479: Cwmbran Development Corporation: Photograph Album, Fairwater, 1966-1967

Figure 23: Torfaen Museum Trust Collection

Figure 24: © Crown Copyright: RCAHMW – DS2021_035_001 (NPRN 701508)

Figure 25: © Crown Copyright: RCAHMW – DS2021_020_001 (NPRN 701515)

Figure 26: Copyright The Francis Frith Copyright Collection, C547021

Figure 27: © Crown Copyright: RCAHMW – DS2021_041_001 (NPRN 701528)

Figure 28: © *Crown Copyright: Homes England* available under the Open Government Licence; Gwent Record Office: D2603/C/3472: Cwmbran Development Corporation: Photograph Album, Oakfield, Undated

Figure 29: © *Crown Copyright: RCAHMW* – DS2021_057_001 (NPRN 701529)

Figure 30: © *Crown Copyright: RCAHMW* – DS2021_006_002 (NPRN 701524)

Figure 31: © *Crown Copyright: RCAHMW* – DS2021_027_009 (NPRN 415259)

Figure 32: © *Crown Copyright: RCAHMW* – DS2021_023_019 (NPRN 422686)

Figure 33: © *Crown Copyright: RCAHMW* – DS2021_039_001 (NPRN 701530)

Figure 34: © *Crown Copyright: Homes England* available under the Open Government Licence: Gwent Record Office: D2603/C/3472: Cwmbran Development Corporation: Photograph Album, Oakfield, Undated

Figure 35: © *Crown Copyright: RCAHMW* – DS2021_022_002 (NPRN 701513)

Figure 36: © *Crown Copyright: Homes England* available under the Open Government Licence, Gwent Record Office: D2603/C/3474: Cwmbran Development Corporation: Photograph Album, Greenmeadow, Undated

Figure 37: Copyright The Francis Frith Copyright Collection, C547084

Figure 38: © *Crown Copyright: RCAHMW* – DS2021_013_002 (NPRN 701509)

Figure 39: © *Crown Copyright: RCAHMW* – AP_2006_1349 (NPRN 408671)

Figure 40: © *Crown Copyright: RCAHMW* – DS2012_034_001 (NPRN 408671)

Figure 41: Copyright Jonathan Vining 2021

Figure 42: © *Crown Copyright: RCAHMW* – DS2021_030_002 (NPRN 701512)

Figure 43: © *Crown Copyright: RCAHMW* – DS2021_011_002, NPRN 701507

Figure 44: © *Crown Copyright: RCAHMW* – DS2021_001_005 (NPRN 701506)

Figure 45: © *Crown Copyright: RCAHMW* – DS2021_044_001 (NPRN 701531)

Figure 46: © *Crown Copyright: RCAHMW* – DS2021_040_001 (NPRN 422592)

Figure 47: Copyright The Francis Frith Copyright Collection, C547051

Figure 48: © *Crown Copyright: RCAHMW* – DS2021_033_003 (NPRN 13151)

Figure 49: © *Crown Copyright: RCAHMW* – DS2021_028_006 (NPRN 10724)

Figure 50: © *The Methodist Church* Gwent Archives, Gwent Archives: D2603/C/1455: Cwmbran Development Corporation: Correspondence File, Croesyceiliog South, Site for Methodist Church

Figure 51: © *Crown Copyright: RCAHMW* – DS2021_018_003 (NPRN 10719)

Figure 52: © *Crown Copyright: RCAHMW* – DS2021_002_002 (NPRN 307518)

Figure 53: © Architectural History Practise

Figure 54: © *Crown Copyright: RCAHMW* – AP_2006_1346 (NPRN 408671)

Figure 55: Courtesy of the South Wales Argus

Figure 56: ©Llyfrgell Genedlaethol Cymru – The National Library of Wales

Figure 57: © *Crown Copyright: RCAHMW* – DI_2021_054_009 (NPRN 701542)

Figure 58: Torfaen Museum Trust Collection

Figure 59: © *Crown Copyright: RCAHMW* – IMG_2900 (NPRN 422665)

Figure 60: © *Crown Copyright: RCAHMW* – IMG_2953; IMG_2953; IMG_2591 (NPRN 422665)

Figure 61: © *Crown Copyright: Homes England* available under the Open Government Licence

Figure 62: Torfaen Museum Trust Collection

Figure 63: © Crown Copyright: Homes England available under the Open Government Licence; Gwent Archives: D2603/C/3586: Cwmbran Development Corporation: Booklets: Cwmbran Garden City of Wales, CDC Information Sheets, Undated

Figure 64: © *Crown Copyright: Homes England* available under the Open Government Licence; Gwent Archives: D2603/C/1746: Cwmbran Development Corporation: Correspondence File: Town Centre: Civic Square inc Water Gardens S42(1), 28 July 1967

Figure 65: © *Crown Copyright: RCAHMW* – DI_2021_052_005 (NPRN 599)

Figure 66: © *Crown Copyright: RCAHMW* – DI_2021_042_001 (NPRN 422731)

Figure 67 © *Crown Copyright: RCAHMW* – IMG_2939 (NPRN 422740)

Figure 68: © *Crown Copyright: RCAHMW* – DI2011_0587 (NPRN 599)

Figure 69: Torfaen Museum Trust Collection

Figure 70: © *Crown Copyright: RCAHMW* – DI_2021_056_001 (NPRN 701526)

Figure 71: © *Crown Copyright: RCAHMW* – DI_2021_056_002 (NPRN 701526)

Figure 72: © *Crown Copyright: RCAHMW, 2021*. This map is based upon Ordnance Survey material with the permission of Ordnance Survey on behalf of the Controller of Her Majesty's Stationery Office © Crown copyright. Unauthorised reproduction infringes Crown copyright and may lead to prosecution or civil proceedings. Licence number: 100022206

Figure 73: Gwent Archives: D2603/C/3477: Cwmbran Development Corporation: Photograph Album, Pontnewydd West, Undated (photograph 1954)

Figure 74: Gwent Archives: D2603/C/3477: Cwmbran Development Corporation: Photograph Album, Pontnewydd West, Undated (photograph February 1953)

Figure 75: Gwent Archives: D2603/C/3477: Cwmbran Development Corporation: Photograph Album, Pontnewydd West, Undated (photograph September 1955)

Figure 76: © *Crown Copyright: RCAHMW* – DI_2021_051_008 (NPRN 415259)

Figure 77: © *Crown Copyright: RCAHMW* – DI_2021_053_002 (NPRN 701530)

Figure 78: © *Crown Copyright: RCAHMW* – DI_2021_026_001 (NPRN 415259)

Figure 79: © *Crown Copyright: RCAHMW, 2021*. This map is based upon Ordnance Survey material with the permission of Ordnance Survey on behalf of the Controller of Her Majesty's Stationery Office © Crown copyright. Unauthorised reproduction infringes Crown copyright and may lead to prosecution or civil proceedings. Licence number: 100022206

Figure 80: © *Crown Copyright: RCAHMW* – DI_2021_020_004 (NPRN 701515)

Figure 81: Copyright The Francis Frith Collection, C547048

Figure 82: © *Crown Copyright: RCAHMW* – AP_2018_2880 (NPRN 408671)

Figure 83: © *Crown Copyright: RCAHMW* – DI_2021_022_004 (NPRN 701513)

Figure 84: © *Crown Copyright: RCAHMW* – DI_2021_029_001 (NPRN 701514)

Figure 85: © *Crown Copyright: RCAHMW, 2021.* This map is based upon Ordnance Survey material with the permission of Ordnance Survey on behalf of the Controller of Her Majesty's Stationery Office © Crown copyright. Unauthorised reproduction infringes Crown copyright and may lead to prosecution or civil proceedings. Licence number: 100022206

Figure 86: © *Crown Copyright: Homes England* available under the Open Government Licence; Gwent Archives: D2603/C/3471: Cwmbran Development Corporation: Photograph Album, Croesyceiliog, Undated

Figure 87: © *Crown Copyright: Homes England* available under the Open Government Licence; Gwent Archives: D2603/C/3471: Cwmbran Development Corporation: Photograph Album, Croesyceiliog, Undated

Figure 88: © *Crown Copyright: Homes England* available under the Open Government Licence; Gwent Archives: D2603/C/3471: Cwmbran Development Corporation: Photograph Album, Croesyceiliog, Undated

Figure 89: © *Crown Copyright: RCAHMW – DI_2021_007_022* (NPRN 422687)

Figure 90: © *Crown Copyright: RCAHMW – DI_2021_007_018* (NPRN 422687)

Figure 91: © *Crown Copyright: RCAHMW – DI_2021_007_006* (NPRN 422687)

Figure 92: © *Crown Copyright: RCAHMW – DI_2021_007_009* (NPRN 422687)

Figure 93: © *Crown Copyright: RCAHMW – DI_2021_007_015* (NPRN 422687)

Figure 94: © *Crown Copyright: RCAHMW – DI_2021_007_003* (NPRN 422687)

Figure 95: © *Crown Copyright: RCAHMW – DI_2021_008_001* (NPRN 701516)

Figure 96: © *Crown Copyright: RCAHMW – DI_2021_004_004* (NPRN 701542)

Figure 97: © *Crown Copyright: RCAHMW, 2021.* This map is based upon Ordnance Survey material with the permission of Ordnance Survey on behalf of the Controller of Her Majesty's Stationery Office © Crown copyright. Unauthorised reproduction infringes Crown copyright and may lead to prosecution or civil proceedings. Licence number: 100022206

Figure 98: © *Crown Copyright: Homes England* available under the Open Government Licence; Gwent Archives: D2603/C/3476: Cwmbran Development Corporation: Photograph Album, Llanyravon, Undated

Figure 99: © *Crown Copyright: Homes England* available under the Open Government Licence; Gwent Archives: D2603/C/3476: Cwmbran Development Corporation: Photograph Album, Llanyravon, Undated

Figure 100: © *Crown Copyright: RCAHMW – DI_2021_019_013* (NPRN 701517)

Figure 101: © *Crown Copyright: RCAHMW – DI_2021_019_010* (NPRN 701517)

Figure 102: © *Crown Copyright: RCAHMW – DI_2021_019_026* (NPRN 701517)

Figure 103: © *Crown Copyright: RCAHMW – DI_2021_019_004* (NPRN 701517)

Figure 104: © *Crown Copyright: RCAHMW – DI_2021_019_007* (NPRN 701517)

Figure 105: © *Crown Copyright: RCAHMW, 2021.* This map is based upon Ordnance Survey material with the permission of Ordnance Survey on behalf of the Controller of Her Majesty's Stationery Office © Crown copyright. Unauthorised reproduction infringes Crown copyright and may lead to prosecution or civil proceedings. Licence number: 100022206

Figure 106: © *Crown Copyright: Homes England* available under the Open Government Licence; Gwent Archives: D2603/C/3472: Cwmbran Development Corporation: Photograph Album, Oakfield, Undated

Figure 107: Gwent Archives: D2603/C/3472: Cwmbran Development Corporation: Photograph Album, Oakfield, Undated

Figure 108: © *Crown Copyright: RCAHMW – DI_2021_023_015* (NPRN 422686)

Figure 109: © *Crown Copyright: RCAHMW – DI_2021_016_001* (NPRN 422686)

Figure 110: © *Crown Copyright: RCAHMW – DI_2021_023_005* (NPRN 422686)

Figure 111: © *Crown Copyright: RCAHMW – DI_2021_023_011* (NPRN 422686)

Figure 112: © *Crown Copyright: RCAHMW – DI_2021_023_013* (NPRN 422686)

Figure 113: © *Crown Copyright: RCAHMW – DI_2021_038_003* (NPRN 701506)

Figure 114: © *Crown Copyright: RCAHMW, 2021.* This map is based upon Ordnance Survey material with the permission of Ordnance Survey on behalf of the Controller of Her Majesty's Stationery Office © Crown copyright. Unauthorised reproduction infringes Crown copyright and may lead to prosecution or civil proceedings. Licence number: 100022206

Figure 115: © *Crown Copyright: Homes England* available under the Open Government Licence; Gwent Archives: D2603/C/3591: Cwmbran Development Corporation: Booklets etc, Fairwater 4 CDC, 9 July 1982

Figure 116: Gwent Archives: D2603/C/150: Cwmbran Development Corporation: Correspondence File, Fairwater Shopping Centre, 14.2.1964-13.10.1967

Figure 117: © *Crown Copyright: RCAHMW – DI_2021_010_012* (NPRN 701502)

Figure 118: © *Crown Copyright: RCAHMW – DI_2021_010_002* (NPRN 701502)

Figure 119: © *Crown Copyright: RCAHMW – DI_2021_010_018* (NPRN 701502)

Figure 120: © *Crown Copyright: RCAHMW – 636738* (NPRN 422746)

Figure 121: © *Crown Copyright: RCAHMW – DI_2021_009_001* (NPRN 10719)

Figure 122: © *Crown Copyright: RCAHMW, 2021.* This map is based upon Ordnance Survey material with the permission of Ordnance Survey on behalf of the Controller of Her Majesty's Stationery Office © Crown copyright. Unauthorised reproduction infringes Crown copyright and may lead to prosecution or civil proceedings. Licence number: 100022206

Figure 123: © *Crown Copyright: Homes England* available under the Open Government Licence; Gwent Archives: D2603/C/3473: Cwmbran Development Corporation: Photograph Album, St Dials 3c, Undated

Figure 124: © *Crown Copyright: RCAHMW – DI_2021_031_001* (NPRN 701521)

Figure 125: © *Crown Copyright: RCAHMW – DI_2021_050_005* (NPRN 422689)

Figure 126: © *Crown Copyright: RCAHMW – DI_2021_050_007* (NPRN 422689)

Figure 127: © *Crown Copyright: RCAHMW – DI_2021_032_011* (NPRN 422689)

Figure 128: © *Crown Copyright: RCAHMW – DI_2021_032_006* (NPRN 422689)

Figure 129: © *Crown Copyright: RCAHMW – DI_2021_032_002* (NPRN 422689)

Figure 130: *Crown Copyright: RCAHMW, 2021.* This map is based upon Ordnance Survey material with the permission of Ordnance Survey on behalf of the Controller of Her Majesty's Stationery Office © Crown copyright. Unauthorised reproduction infringes Crown copyright and may lead to prosecution or civil proceedings. Licence number: 100022206

Figure 131: © *Crown Copyright: Homes England* available under the Open Government Licence; Gwent Archives: D2603/C/3473: D2603/C/3472: Cwmbran Development Corporation: Photograph Album, Oakfield, Undated

Figure 132: © *Crown Copyright: RCAHMW* – DI_2021_005_037 (NPRN 422685)

Figure 133: © *Crown Copyright: RCAHMW* – DI_2021_005_049 (NPRN 422685)

Figure 134: © *Crown Copyright: RCAHMW* – DI_2021_005_019 (NPRN 422658)

Figure 135: © *Crown Copyright: RCAHMW* – DI_2021_005_006 (NPRN 422658)

Figure 136: © *Crown Copyright: RCAHMW* – DI_2021_005_026 (NPRN 422658)

Figure 137: © *Crown Copyright: RCAHMW* – DI_2021_005_032 (NPRN 422658)

Figure 138: © *Crown Copyright: RCAHMW* – DI_2021_003_001 (NPRN 701521)

Figure 139: © *Crown Copyright: RCAHMW, 2021*. This map is based upon Ordnance Survey material with the permission of Ordnance Survey on behalf of the Controller of Her Majesty's Stationery Office © Crown copyright. Unauthorised reproduction infringes Crown copyright and may lead to prosecution or civil proceedings. Licence number: 100022206

Figure 140: © *Crown Copyright: Homes England* available under the Open Government Licence; Gwent Archives: D2603/C/3473: D2603/C/3474: Cwmbran Development Corporation: Photograph Album, Greenmeadow, Undated

Figure 141: © *Crown Copyright: Homes England* available under the Open Government Licence; Gwent Archives: D2603/C/3473: D2603/C/3474: Cwmbran Development Corporation: Photograph Album, Greenmeadow, Undated

Figure 142: © *Crown Copyright: RCAHMW* – AP_2006_1356 (NPRN 408671)

Figure 143: © *Crown Copyright: RCAHMW* – DI_2021_012_002 (NPRN 422682)

Figure 144: © *Crown Copyright: RCAHMW* – DI_2021_037_002 (NPRN 701501)

Figure 145: © *Crown Copyright: RCAHMW, 2021*. This map is based upon Ordnance Survey material with the permission of Ordnance Survey on behalf of the Controller of Her Majesty's Stationery Office © Crown copyright. Unauthorised reproduction infringes Crown copyright and may lead to prosecution or civil proceedings. Licence number: 100022206

Figure 146: © *Crown Copyright: Homes England* available under the Open Government Licence; Gwent Archives: D2603/C/3590: Cwmbran Development Corporation: Booklet: Thornhill Housing Phase II, South CDC, 10 Oct 1975

Figure 147: © *Crown Copyright: Homes England* available under the Open Government Licence; Gwent Archives: D2603/C/3590: Cwmbran Development Corporation: Booklet: Thornhill Housing Phase II, South CDC, 10 Oct 1975

Figure 148: © *Crown Copyright: Homes England* available under the Open Government Licence; Gwent Archives: D2603/C/3586: Cwmbran Development Corporation: Booklets: Cwmbran Garden City of Wales, CDC Information Sheets, Undated

Figure 149: © *Crown Copyright: RCAHMW* – DI_2021_036_001 (NPRN 701523)

Figure 150: © *Crown Copyright: RCAHMW* – DI_2021_036_003 (NPRN 701523)

Figure 151: © *Crown Copyright: RCAHMW* – DI_2021_030_013 (NPRN 701512)

Figure 152: © *Crown Copyright: RCAHMW, 2021*. This map is based upon Ordnance Survey material with the permission of Ordnance Survey on behalf of the Controller of Her Majesty's Stationery Office © Crown copyright. Unauthorised reproduction infringes Crown copyright and may lead to prosecution or civil proceedings. Licence number: 100022206

Figure 153: © *Crown Copyright: Homes England* available under the Open Government Licence; Gwent Archives: D2603/C/3587: Cwmbran Development Corporation: Booklet: Hollybush 3 CDC, 12 June 1981

Figure 154: © *Crown Copyright: Homes England* available under the Open Government Licence; Gwent Archives: D2603/C/3587: Cwmbran Development Corporation: Booklet: Hollybush 3 CDC, 12 June 1981

Figure 155: © *Crown Copyright: RCAHMW* – DI_2021_048_002 (NPRN 701509)

Figure 156: © *Crown Copyright: RCAHMW* – DI_2021_048_028 (NPRN 701509)

Figure 157: © *Crown Copyright: RCAHMW* – DI_2021_048_012 (NPRN 701509)

Figure 158: © *Crown Copyright: RCAHMW, 2021*. This map is based upon Ordnance Survey material with the permission of Ordnance Survey on behalf of the Controller of Her Majesty's Stationery Office © Crown copyright. Unauthorised reproduction infringes Crown copyright and may lead to prosecution or civil proceedings. Licence number: 100022206

Figure 159: © *Crown Copyright: Homes England* available under the Open Government Licence; Gwent Archives: D2603/C/3586: Cwmbran Development Corporation: Booklets: Cwmbran Garden City of Wales, CDC Information Sheets, Undated

Figure 160: © *Crown Copyright: RCAHMW* – DI_2021_049_018 (NPRN 701539)

Figure 161: © *Crown Copyright: RCAHMW* – DI_2021_049_007 (NPRN 701536)

Figure 162: *Crown Copyright: RCAHMW, 2021*. This map is based upon Ordnance Survey material with the permission of Ordnance Survey on behalf of the Controller of Her Majesty's Stationery Office © Crown copyright. Unauthorised reproduction infringes Crown copyright and may lead to prosecution or civil proceedings. Licence number: 100022206

Figure 163: © *Crown Copyright: RCAHMW* – DI_2021_046_014 (NPRN 701537)

Figure 164: © *Crown Copyright: RCAHMW* – DI_2021_045_010 (NPRN 701538)

Figure 165: © *Crown Copyright: RCAHMW, 2021*. This map is based upon Ordnance Survey material with the permission of Ordnance Survey on behalf of the Controller of Her Majesty's Stationery Office © Crown copyright. Unauthorised reproduction infringes Crown copyright and may lead to prosecution or civil proceedings. Licence number: 100022206

Figure 166: © *Crown Copyright: RCAHMW* – DI_2021_047_006 (NPRN 701540)

Figure 167: © *Crown Copyright: RCAHMW* – DS 2008_187_004 (NPRN 403393)

Figure 168: © *Crown Copyright: RCAHMW*: Aerofilms Collection – WPW041238 (NPRN 410436)

Figure 169: © *Crown Copyright: RCAHMW*: Aerofilms Collection – WPW040047 (NPRN 33188)

Figure 170: © *Crown Copyright: RCAHMW* – DI2009_1160 (NPRN 33188)

Figure 171: Torfaen Museum Trust

Figure 172: Torfaen Museum Trust

Figure 173: Author's personal collection

Figure 174: © *Crown Copyright: RCAHMW* – 636789 (NPRN 422665)

Figure 175: © *Crown Copyright: RCAHMW* – 636785 (NPRN 422665)

Figure 176: © *Crown Copyright: RCAHMW* – 636771 (NPRN 422744)

Figure 177: Torfaen County Borough Council

Figure 178: Torfaen Museum Trust

Back cover: © *Crown Copyright: RCAHMW* – DS2021_058_001 (NPRN 422740 and 422730).

Appendix I: Listed Buildings within the Designated Area

NGR	COMMUNITY	RECORD NUMBER	NAME	GRADE
ST3036396844	Croesyceiliog	3125	Pontrhydyrun Baptist Church	II
https://cadwpublic-api.azurewebsites.net/reports/listedbuilding/FullReport?lang=&id=3125				
ST3037696836	Croesyceiliog	81750	War Memorial in front of Pontrhydyrun Baptist Church	II
https://cadwpublic-api.azurewebsites.net/reports/listedbuilding/FullReport?lang=&id=81750				
ST3036996862	Croesyceiliog	81749	Enclosure railings, walls, gatepiers and memorials at the Conway Burial Yard	II
https://cadwpublic-api.azurewebsites.net/reports/listedbuilding/FullReport?lang=&id=81749				
ST3003597212	Croesyceiliog	3147	Pontrhydyrun House	II
https://cadwpublic-api.azurewebsites.net/reports/listedbuilding/FullReport?lang=&id=3147				
ST3055195823	Croesyceiliog	87806	2 Jim Crow Square	II
https://cadwpublic-api.azurewebsites.net/reports/listedbuilding/FullReport?lang=&id=87806				
ST2855494039	Cwmbrân Central	26986	Glan-y-nant Farm	II
https://cadwpublic-api.azurewebsites.net/reports/listedbuilding/FullReport?lang=&id=26986				
ST2916494856	Cwmbrân Central	20740	Elim United Reformed Church and attached Schoolroom	II
https://cadwpublic-api.azurewebsites.net/reports/listedbuilding/FullReport?lang=&id=20740				
ST2872193956	Cwmbrân Central	82034	Limekiln on S side of Garth Road	II
https://cadwpublic-api.azurewebsites.net/reports/listedbuilding/FullReport?lang=&id=82034				
ST2904894008	Cwmbrân Central	81859	Aqueduct over Dowlais Brook on Monmouthshire and Brecon Canal (partly in Cwmbrân Central community)	II
https://cadwpublic-api.azurewebsites.net/reports/listedbuilding/FullReport?lang=&id=81859				
ST2664694936	Fairwater	27060	Barn at Tŷ'r Ywen Farm	II
https://cadwpublic-api.azurewebsites.net/reports/listedbuilding/FullReport?lang=&id=27060				
ST2663494914	Fairwater	27059	Tŷ'r Ywen Farmhouse	II
https://cadwpublic-api.azurewebsites.net/reports/listedbuilding/FullReport?lang=&id=27059				
ST2976694533	Llantarnam	87770	Court Road Industrial Estate Sign	II
https://cadwpublic-api.azurewebsites.net/reports/listedbuilding/FullReport?lang=&id=87770				
ST3069793155	Llantarnam	3121	Church of St Michael and All Angels	II*
https://cadwpublic-api.azurewebsites.net/reports/listedbuilding/FullReport?lang=&id=3121				
ST3069493140	Llantarnam	3122	Churchyard cross at the Church of Saint Michael and All Angels	
https://cadwpublic-api.azurewebsites.net/reports/listedbuilding/FullReport?lang=&id=3122				
ST3066693174	Llantarnam	81870	Memorial to T. Leadbetter in churchyard of Church of St Michael and All Angels	II
https://cadwpublic-api.azurewebsites.net/reports/listedbuilding/FullReport?lang=&id=81870				
ST3066693174	Llantarnam	3137	Tŷ-coch Farmhouse	II
https://cadwpublic-api.azurewebsites.net/reports/listedbuilding/FullReport?lang=&id=3137				
ST3069793155	Llantarnam	26082	Brook House and railings	II
https://cadwpublic-api.azurewebsites.net/reports/listedbuilding/FullReport?lang=&id=26082				
ST3069493140	Llantarnam	3123	The Greenhouse Public House	II
https://cadwpublic-api.azurewebsites.net/reports/listedbuilding/FullReport?lang=&id=3123				
ST3029194734	Llanyrafon	27026	Llanyrafon Mill	II
https://cadwpublic-api.azurewebsites.net/reports/listedbuilding/FullReport?lang=&id=27026				
ST3032894587	Llanyrafon	3140	Llanyrafon	II*
https://cadwpublic-api.azurewebsites.net/reports/listedbuilding/FullReport?lang=&id=3140				
ST2872796269	Pontnewydd	23533	Church of the Holy Trinity	II
https://cadwpublic-api.azurewebsites.net/reports/listedbuilding/FullReport?lang=&id=23533				
ST2878796658	Pontnewydd	80862	Culvert taking Blaen Bran under Monmouthshire and Brecon Canal	II
https://cadwpublic-api.azurewebsites.net/reports/listedbuilding/FullReport?lang=&id=80862				

Listed Buildings outside the Designated Area but closely related to the town

NGR	COMMUNITY	RECORD NUMBER	NAME	GRADE
ST3133692952	Llantarnam	81871	Porth Mawr gateway, lodge, walls and railings at Llantarnam Abbey	II
https://cadwpublic-api.azurewebsites.net/reports/listedbuilding/FullReport?lang=&id=81871				
ST3123792982	Llantarnam	81860	Bridge on drive at Llantarnam Abbey	II
https://cadwpublic-api.azurewebsites.net/reports/listedbuilding/FullReport?lang=&id=81860				
ST3074493236	Llantarnam	85246	Llantarnam Abbey	II*
https://cadwpublic-api.azurewebsites.net/reports/listedbuilding/FullReport?lang=&id=85246				
ST2974393270	Llantarnam	81868	Garden walls and gates at Llantarnam Abbey	II
https://cadwpublic-api.azurewebsites.net/reports/listedbuilding/FullReport?lang=&id=81868				
ST3064693137	Llantarnam	81867	Forecourt walls and gates at Llantarnam Abbey	II
https://cadwpublic-api.azurewebsites.net/reports/listedbuilding/FullReport?lang=&id=81867				
ST3115192913	Llantarnam	81874	Two statues in garden to E of Llantarnam Abbey	II
https://cadwpublic-api.azurewebsites.net/reports/listedbuilding/FullReport?lang=&id=81874				
ST3111992927	Llantarnam	81872	The Cottage and attached walls of walled garden at Llantarnam Abbey	II
https://cadwpublic-api.azurewebsites.net/reports/listedbuilding/FullReport?lang=&id=81872				
ST3111792896	Llantarnam	81873	The Monks Cell at Llantarnam Abbey	II
https://cadwpublic-api.azurewebsites.net/reports/listedbuilding/FullReport?lang=&id=81873				
ST3120693015	Llantarnam	3128	Ruins of barn at Llantarnam Abbey	II
https://cadwpublic-api.azurewebsites.net/reports/listedbuilding/FullReport?lang=&id=3128				
ST2944592318	Llantarnam	81862	Canal bridge at Rachels Lock on Monmouthshire and Brecon Canal	II
https://cadwpublic-api.azurewebsites.net/reports/listedbuilding/FullReport?lang=&id=81862				
ST2952691864	Llantarnam	81863	Canal bridge at Shop Lock on Monmouthshire and Brecon Canal	II
https://cadwpublic-api.azurewebsites.net/reports/listedbuilding/FullReport?lang=&id=81863				
ST2935592574	Llantarnam	81864	Canal bridge at Top Lock on Monmouthshire and Brecon Canal	II
https://cadwpublic-api.azurewebsites.net/reports/listedbuilding/FullReport?lang=&id=81864				
ST3042192755	Llantarnam	81865	Canal bridge at Tredegar Lock on Monmouthshire and Brecon Canal	II
https://cadwpublic-api.azurewebsites.net/reports/listedbuilding/FullReport?lang=&id=81865				

Appendix II: Llantarnam Grange: Gazetteer of monastic landscape features from Proctor, 2019
https://ore.exeter.ac.uk/repository/handle/10871/37371

Monastic holding or landscape feature name (with variant spellings/ first dates for these)	Monastic holding or landscape feature type	Grange or manor containing the feature	Location	Notes	Sources
Cefn-mynach Grange (Apud veterem Abbathiam, 1291; Kevan y mynach, 1542; Kevenvynocke, 1553; Kevenminnick, 1582; Cefn-y-fynach; Cefn-vynoche; Kilsant; Cilsant, 1801; Pentry, 1704; Pentrea bach, 1634; Pentra-bach, 1779; Pentre-bach)	Grange	Cefn-mynach	Pentre-bach Farm, Llantarnam, Torfaen (ST285921)	Valley grange in Magna Porta manor. Possibly the original site of the abbey. Situated at the foot of a long, broad ridge to the north which probably gave the grange its name; alternatively, named for the sharper Castell-y-bwch ridge immediately to the west and overlooking it. Extensive building by Morgan family became settlement of Pentre-bach with extant Grade II Tudor farmhouse and 17th century hall, later converted into a large barn. Substantial earthworks in field below/west of house (Round field), could be fishpond or remains of a moated site (ie perhaps separate/ pre-dating house?); strong potential for further survey/ investigation as not recorded. Large semi-oval enclosure to west of farmstead, with two more to the north. Field names of interest: Cae Crwn (round field), Caeven y Perthy/ Coed y Perthy (the boundary or limit hedge or bush field/ the hedge wood), Gwain Vellin Vach (little mill meadow), Perthlan Vawr (great church hedge), Perthlan y Pisstell (spout or drainage ditch of the church hedge), the langott (church wood).	Taxatio Ecclesiastica, 1291; William Morgan Will, 1542
Coed-cefin-y-perthi (Coed Mawr, 1846)	Wood	Cefn-mynach	Pentre-bach Farm, Llantarnam, Torfaen (ST282929)	Extensive area of coppice woodland surrounding large oval enclosure north of the grange farm divided into allotments, with Coed-yr-Helygos (willow wood) and Pentre-bach Wood (now smaller, Limekiln Wood), only partially remaining; included a section known as The Langott (possibly 'church wood') in 1779.	Llantarnam Estate Map, 1779; Llanfihangel Llantarnam Tithe Map, 1846
Groes-mawr (Transemawre, 1536; Trawsechawre, 1539; Transmaur, 1582; Troes Mawr, 1779; Traws Mawr, 1886)	Farmstead	Cefn-mynach	Traws Mawr, Llantarnam, Torfaen (ST293917	Recorded as a 'tenement', 'one messuage with the appurtenances' of the abbey, within Magna Porta manor (1536). Perhaps an out-farm of Cefn-mynach grange. Possible location, modern farm yard and wooded enclosure on edge of Cae Troes Mawr (great cross field, 1779) near to post-modern Traws Mawr House. Alternatively, possibly associated with Tranch Wood?	Ministers Accounts, 1536/7; William Morgan Inquisition post mortem, 1582; Llantarnam Estate Map, 1779; OS 1st Edition Map, 1887
Coed-cefn-coch (Coedkevancoch, 1634)	Wood	Dorallt		Abbey coppice woodland.	Magna Porta Manor Survey, 1634
Dorallt Grange (Torald, 1291; Doralt, 1841; Dorallt-fawr, 1842)	Grange	Dorallt	Site of Dorallt-fach farm, Cwmbrân Central or Henllys. Torfaen (ST266940)	Hillside grange in Magna Porta manor. Grange name is likely a reference to a promontory jutting out from slopes of Mynydd Henllys above the farmstead, or perhaps the prominent Castell-y-bwch ridge overlooked to the south-east. Actual site of grange farm and boundary of lands not known, possibly site of Dorallt-fawr farm. Several cwrt field-names may indicate a more significant medieval grange steading. Lower lands now housing within Cwmbrân. Field names of interest: Cae Cwrt Bach (little court field), Coed y Cwrt (wood of the court), Cae Coed y Cwrt (wood of the court field), Cae Groes (cross field), Warren. Two Pandy (a fulling mill associated with wool production) place names near Dorallt are perhaps indicators in medieval sheep-rearing on the grange.	Taxatio Ecclesiastica, 1291; Henllys Tithe Map, 1844; OS 1st Edition Map, 1887

Gelli-las Grange (Gelli Las, 1536; The Grange, 1554; Kellilace, 16th century; Gelly Lase, 1634; Gelli-laes, 1846; Llantarnam Grange)	Grange	Gelli-las	Llantarnam Grange Arts Centre (site of Llantarnam Grange farm), Cwmbrân, Torfaen (ST297953)	Valley grange in Magna Porta manor. Grange farm now location of Llantarnam Grange Arts Centre, lands now Llantarnam Grange Industrial Estate in Cwmbrân. Approach road from abbey called Grange Road. The 1846 tithe map includes ninety-six acres (thirty-nine ha.) of 'Part of Gelly-las', it is unclear from the apportionment where the rest of the grange's lands were located. Field-names of note: Cae'r Coed Ycha and Issa ('upper and lower wood field'), Gwern y Gwair ('alder trees or swampy meadow of the hay'), Gwern y Ceffyloy ('alder trees or swampy meadow of the horses'), Gwern y Gwartheg ('alder trees or swampy meadow of the cattle').	Ministers Accounts, 1536/7; Plan of Gelli-las, 1751; Llanfihangel Llantarnam Tithe Map, 1846
Hollow Lane	Track	Llanderfel	Fairwater, Torfaen (ST273962)	Part of pilgrim way from Llanderfel to Penrhys, via chapels at St. Dials and Llanderfel	
Llanderfel Chapel (Llanderfol, 1412; St. Dervalli, 1535; St. Darvally, 1536; Llantherval, 1577; Llanderfil, 1886)	Chapel	Llanderfel	Llanderfel Farm, Fairwater, Torfaen (ST264953)	Scheduled pilgrimage cell, tavern and enclosure, with possible late 11th or early 12th century origin. Postulated as chapel for nearby grange or perhaps the site of the grange farm itself. Possible site of early medieval church, perhaps also supported by local place-name evidence including nearby farmstead, Pen-llan-gwyn ('headland of the white church'), maybe a reference to the whitewashed walls of the chapel, and the wooded hillside of Coed Gwern-esgob ('wood on the bishop's moor').	Valor Ecclesiasticus, 1535; Ministers Accounts, 1536/7; Saxton Map of Monmouthshire, 1577; Llanfihangel Llantarnam Tithe Map, 1846; OS 1st Edition Map, 1887
Llanderfel Grange (Coitca mynachlog; Landerval, 1634; Llanderfil, 1886; Llanderfel House; Llanderfel Farm)	Grange	Llanderfel	Llanderfel Farm, Fairwater, Torfaen (ST266954)	Upland grange of Magna Porta manor occupying assarted hillside shelf below Mynydd Maen around Grade II listed late 16th/ early 17th century longhouse of Llanderfel Farm (150 acres of tithe free land, plus surrounding land from Craig-y-Llwarch, Ty'r-ywen and Upper House post-medieval farmsteads). Not listed in Taxatio Ecclesiastica, 1291 or Valor Ecclesiasticus, 1535. Grange centre either at Llanderfel or Craig-y-Llwarch farm or enclosure and ruin previiusly identified as Llanderfel chapel; or possibly on site of Henllys Colliery, Henllys, Torfaen (ST258943). St. Darvel's was possibly the grange chapel. The post-medieval farmstead of Penllangwyn ('end of white church') perhaps suggests the limit of the lands of the white chapel grange. Pits above the chapel site are possible site of open-cast coal mining; immediately north of the probable grange boundary, at Gelli-gravog, many other small abandoned workings have been observed.	Ministers Accounts, 1536/7; Llanfihangel Llantarnam Tithe Map, 1846; OS 1st Edition Map, 1887; Bradney, 1993
Afon Llwyd (Torfaen; Yr avon awr; Afon; Saturn; River Avon, 1634)	River	Magna Porta		Known as Torfaen ('breaker of stones'), Yr avon awr ('the rough river'), Afon or Saturn before late seventeenth century industrialisation led to Lwyd ('grey'), named for the discolouration of the water downstream from Pontypool ironworks.	
Clwyd-y-brawd (Clawdd y Brawdd, 1634)	Boundary marker	Magna Porta	Cwm Bran, Fairwater, Torfaen (ST267965)	Part of the northern manor boundary – dyke, hedge or fence.	Magna Porta Manor Survey, 1634
Coed-cored	Wood	Magna Porta	Pontnewydd, Cwmbrân, Torfaen (ST298965)	Abbey coppice woodland. Now built over by Cwmbrân urban development.	Llanfihangel Llantarnam Tithe Map, 1846; OS 1st Edition Map, 1887

Coed-waun-fyr	Wood	Magna Porta	Fairwater, Cwmbrân, Torfaen (ST275944)	Abbey coppice woodland, still partially extant within Cwmbrân urban development.	Llanfihangel Llantarnam Tithe Map, 1846; OS 1st Edition Map, 1887
Colomendy (Clo-mendy, 1886)	Dovecote	Magna Porta	Cwmbrân, Torfaen (ST292949)	Possible site of monastic dovecote.	Llanfihangel Llantarnam Tithe Map, 1846; OS 1st Edition Map, 1887
Craig-fawr	Wood	Magna Porta	Thornhill, Cwmbrân, Torfaen (ST278959)	Abbey coppice woodland, still extant within Cwmbrân urban development.	Llanfihangel Llantarnam Tithe Map, 1846; OS 1st Edition Map, 1887
Cwm-bran Brook	Stream	Magna Porta	Cwmbrân, Torfaen (ST280969)	Stream that marks the northern boundary of Magna Porta manor. Also name of a stream along western edge of Gelli-las grange, now largely subsumed within Cwmbrân urban development).	Magna Porta Manor Survey, 1634
Dowlais Brook (Dowlas, 1634; Dowlas Brooke, Dowlace, 1787)/ fishponds	Stream/ fishponds	Magna Porta	Llantarnam Abbey, Llantarnam, Torfaen (ST315926)	Forms southern boundary of abbey site (and probably of the precinct). Two fishpond indicated along course of stream on tithe map with a number of weirs upstream.	Magna Porta Manor Survey, 1634
Graig Road	Track	Magna Porta	Fairwater, Torfaen (ST271952)	Road up to Mynydd Maen from abbey.	
Graig Wood	Wood	Magna Porta	Graig Wood, Caerleon, Newport (ST316925)	Remnant of park woodland.	OS 1st Edition Map, 1887
Greenmeadow	Farmstead	Magna Porta	Greenmeadow, Thornhill, Cwmbrân, Torfaen (ST279956)	Possible medieval farmstead on edge of abbey lands. Now a community farm within Cwmbrân town.	OS 1st Edition Map, 1887
Llantarnam Abbey (Emsanternon; Nant-teyrnon; Dewma, Deuma, 14th century; Caerleon upon Usk; Caerleon; Vallium, 1244; Lanterna, 1273; Kerlyon, 1291; Karliun; Karlyn; Karlioun, 1317; Lanternan, 1396; Karlion alias Lanternam, 1398; Karelyon, alias Lanternam, 1465; Lant'na, 1535; Lantarnum House, 1704; Llantorfaen, Lantarnam; Llantarnam House)	Abbey	Magna Porta	Llantarnam Abbey, Llantarnam, Torfaen (ST312929)	Site of medieval abbey, replaced by 16th century gentry house then Grade II* listed 19th century mansion, which may contain some fabric of the earlier buildings. Used as a convent since the 1950s. Precinct area laid out as post-medieval park then 19th century park and formal gardens, with listed features. Precinct boundary/ wall not identified, possible linear feature in parkland to south/ east of abbey identified on LiDAR which could be the line of the boundary or an old water ditch. Field names of interest in the probable precinct area: Abbey Orchard, Cae Lletty (possibly visitor accommodation), The Llangott (possibly church wood), The Warren. New housing estate built on the Abbey Fields, part of the outer court.	Cistercian General Chapter, 1273; Taxatio Ecclesiastica, 1291; Valor Ecclesiasticus, 1535; Ministers Accounts, 1536/7
Llantarnam Abbey 'tithe' barn	Barn	Magna Porta	Llantarnam Abbey, Llantarnam, Torfaen (ST312930)	Scheduled and Grade II listed home manor 'tithe' barn, date unknown, possibly medieval, 16th century or later. Foundations found near the barn may point to a larger agricultural infrastructure around the abbey.	Llantarnam Estate Map, 1779

Llantarnam mill (Abbey mill, 1885; Abbey Farm)	Mill	Magna Porta	Llantarnam, Torfaen (ST309932)	Post-medieval corn mill, fulling mill (Tuck mill) and farmstead, probably on site of monastic mill; demolished and site now cut by Trunk Road. Served by mill races (from Afon Lwyd, Cwm Bran Brook and Dowlais Brook), some sections still operating as watercources, with system of sluices, and a mill pond. Known as Abbey Farm by the late nineteenth century. 'Pandy' field-names adjacent to the mill site support a joint corn and fulling mill operation. A dam structure on a small stream leading from Pen-y-Parc to Pill-Mawr has been interpreted as related to another possible long-abandoned medieval mill.	Ministers Accounts, 1536/7; Llanfihangel Llantarnam Tithe Map, 1846; OS 1st Edition Map, 1887
Llantarnam Park/ Ton-y-groes (Ton y Grose, 1634; old Park, 1634)	Park	Magna Porta	Pen-y-park farm, Llantarnam, Torfaen (ST312927)	Ton-y-groes is perhaps the pre-existing name for the area in which the abbey was established, then used as name of park. Area of post-medieval parkland, encompassing the abbey precinct, now mostly new woodland/ housing/ bypass/ cultivated fields, with some remaining parkland trees; monastic park probably covered undulating land to south of abbey around Pen-y-park and Wilderness (Reference to Old Park in 1634 and fields known as Old Park on tithe map). 1787 reference to 'residue of the Park known as Rayle Ffawothoog' (beech road, from heol). 'Fish Pool' reference, 1634; field-names recording a fishpond or series of ponds ('pisscodlyn') cascading down to The Wilderness, 1779. Area around Park Farm part of the larger (and possibly later) lordship park of Caerleon abbutting the abbey park and possibly encroaching on abbey land. Some sources have implied that the area around Park Farm and Park Wood up to Lodge Wood, within the bounds of Caerleon's King's Park, was part of the abbey's estate, but there is no evidence to support this.	Saxton Map of Monmouthshire, 1577; Magna Porta Manor Survey, 1634; Llantarnam Estate Map, 1779; Llanfihangel Llantarnam Tithe Map, 1846
Maes-mawr	Wood	Magna Porta	Oakfield, Cwmbrân, Torfaen (ST302937)	Wood formally within Scybor Cwrt grange, now built over by Cwmbrân urban development. Name perhaps indicates that this was previously a common or open field.	Llanfihangel Llantarnam Tithe Map, 1846; OS 1st Edition Map, 1887
Maes-y-rhiw Wood	Wood	Magna Porta	Fairwater, Cwmbrân, Torfaen (ST276948)	Abbey coppice woodland, still largely extant within new town context.	Llanfihangel Llantarnam Tithe Map, 1846; OS 1st Edition Map, 1887
Meyrick-moel (Merick-Mole, 1634; Tir Myrick Mile, 1804; Meyrick Mole, 1846)	Farmstead	Magna Porta	Coed Eva, Cwmbrân, Torfaen (ST276936)	Possible medieval farmstead.	Magna Porta manor survey, 1634
Meyrick-moel Wood (Coed Eva, 1886)	Wood	Magna Porta	Coed Eva, Cwmbrân, Torfaen (ST274939)	Abbey coppice woodland.	Llanfihangel Llantarnam Tithe Map, 1846; OS 1st Edition Map, 1887
Nant-brane (Nant y Ffrwd, 1751; Cwm Bran Brook, 1886)	Stream	Magna Porta	Forge Hammer, Cwmbrân, Torfaen (ST285958)	Forms part of boundary of Magna Porta manor and Gelli-las grange.	Magna Porta manor survey, 1634; Gelli-las Estate Map, 1751; OS 1st Edition Map, 1887
Nant-y-milwr (Nant Milur)	Stream	Magna Porta	Coed Eva, Cwmbrân, Torfaen (ST273928)	Forms part of boundary of manor/ parish.	Magna Porta manor survey, 1634

St. Dial's Chapel (Llantylull, c877?; St Darvally, 1535; St Tylull)	Chapel and possible grange	Magna Porta	St. Dial's, Cwmbrân Central, Torfaen (ST285953)	Little documented chapel on pilgrimage route from abbey to Penrhys (on old lane called St. Dial's Road). Perhaps on the site of an early medieval church mentioned in the Llandaff Charter. Perhaps an unidentified grange, or sub-unit of one of the surrounding granges (tithes for some of the Saint Dials farmstead were paid to the owner of Llanderfel may indicate a sub-unit of that grange), occupying the centre ground of Magna Porta manor. Medieval barn remains and field systems with boundary banks still extant within Cwmbrân urban development.	Valor Ecclesiasticus, 1535; Ministers Accounts, 1536/7
St. Dial's Lane	Track	Magna Porta	St. Dial's, Cwmbrân Central, Torfaen (ST285953)	Part of pilgrim way from Llanderfel to Penrhys, via chapels at St. Dials and Llanderfel.	
St. Michael's Church, Llantarnam (Capella St. Michis juxta monastiu, 1535; Llanfihangel Llantarnam)	Church	Magna Porta	St. Michael's Church, Llantarnam, Torfaen (ST307931)	Grade II* listed church, mostly 15th century with some possible 12th/ 13th century fabric. Functioned as a chapel for the tenants of Magna Porta manor during the monastic period, though possibly the foci of a pre-Norman parish named Deuma with unknown boundaries.	Valor Ecclesiasticus, 1535
Tranch Wood	Wood	Magna Porta	Tranch Wood, Fairwater, Cwmbrân, Torfaen (ST271947)	Abbey coppice woodland, still largely extant within new town context.	Ministers Accounts, 1536/7; Llanvihangel Llantarnam Tithe Map, 1846
Le Therweis (Cae Thurwen, 1779; Court Wood, 1904)	Wood	Scybor Cwrt	Oakfield, Cwmbrân, Torfaen (c ST302935)	Thirty acre wood. Perhaps around Cae Thurwen at northern end of grange lands (1779) or Court Wood.	Llantarnam Estate Map, 1779
Scybor Cwrt Grange (Cwt Grange, 1291; Scybor, Skyborcourt, 1535; Skibery Court, 1704; Scyborau, 1707; Skybbercourt; Ysgubor Court; Scybor Court; Skibor y Court, 1783; The Court Farm, 1779; Skibbor-y-court, 1803; Cwrt Mawr, 1846; Skibbery Court, 1853; Llantarnam Court)	Grange	Scybor Cwrt		Valley 'home' grange in Magna Porta manor. Field names of interest: Cae Groos (cross field), Cae Gross Mawr (great cross field), Cae Gross Vach (Little cross field), Cae Llan y Door Usha and Isha (upper and lower field of the church water), Cae Porth (gate field), Cae Skibbor (barn field), Gwain Vawr (great meadowland), Maes Mawr (great meadow).	Taxatio Ecclesiastica, 1291; Valor Ecclesiasticus, 1535

Appendix III: List of NPRNs for historic assets in Cwmbrân

408671: Cwmbrân Town
307898: Llantarnam Abbey (Cistercian)
45089: Llantarnam Abbey (House)
85124: Brecknock and Abergavenny Canal
85125: Monmouthshire Canal
415260: Patent Nut & Bolt Works: Guest Keen & Nettlefold Cwmbran Works

The Town Centre

599: Cwmbrân Town Centre
422592: Congress Theatre, Gwent Square
422665: Gwent House
422730: The Civic Square
422731: Gwent Square
422732: Central Bus Station
422735: Bandstand, Gwent Square
422739: The Tower Block
422740: Monmouth House
422742: The Central Police Station, Tudor Road
422743: The Moonraker (John Fielding) Pub, Caradoc Road
422749: Family Group, Llantarnam Arts Centre
701510: Magistrates' Court, Tudor Road
701525: David Evans Department Store (House of Fraser), Gwent Square
701526: The Water Gardens, Monmouth Square
701531: The Scene Cinema, Monmouth Square
701532: Glyndwr House
701545: Taliesin Housing Scheme

Pontnewydd

415259: Pontnewydd Neighbourhood
10729: Richmond Road Baptist Chapel
13159: Hope Wesleyan Methodist Chapel
13160: St David's Roman Catholic Church, Pontnewydd
13161: Ebenezer Congregational Hall
415418: Avondale Tinplate Works
415481: Ty Newydd Tinplate Works
701503: Mount Pleasant Primary School (Pontnewydd Primary)
701530: Tŷ Newydd
701544: Maendy Unit Centre, West Pontnewydd
701547: West Pontnewydd Community Association Hall

Northville

701513: Northville Neighbourhood
422747: Pontnewydd Walk, Northville
701515: Maendy County Primary School

Southville

701514: Southville neighbourhood

Croesyceiliog

422687: Croesyceiliog Neighbourhood
10724: Pontrhydyrun Baptist Chapel
307518: The Church of Jesus Christ of Latter Day Saints
415846: County Hall, Croesyceiliog
422688: Croesyceiliog Secondary School, Woodland Road
701505: Croesyceiliog Infants School, the Highway
701516: Edlogan Square Unit Centre
701524: Croesyceiliog Health Centre
701542: Croesyceiliog Infants and Junior School, Croesyceiliog
701548: Jim Crow's Cottage

Llanyravon

701517: Llanyravon Neighbourhood
40069: Llanyrafon Mill
45076: Llanfrechfa Grange
45102: Llanyrafon Manor
307520: Llanyrafon Wesleyan Methodist Chapel
701508: The Crow's Nest Public House
701511: The County Police Headquarters
701527: Llanyravon Unit Centre
701541: Crow Valley Recreational Park

Oakfield

422686: Oakfield Neighbourhood
307297: The Church of St Michael and All Angels
20984: Tŷ Coch
36997: The Greenhouse Public House
307489: Gospel Hall
308308: Weston's Biscuit Factory (Burton's Biscuits)
422041: Cwmbrân Stadium
422744: Court Road Industrial Estate Sign
701503: Oakfield Primary School
701504: Llantarnam Secondary School
701518: Llantarnam Gardens
701506: Brecon House
701519: Tŷ Gwent
701546: Llantarnam Industrial Park
701549: Oakfield Unit Centre

Fairwater

701520: Fairwater Neighbourhood
10719: Fairhill Methodist Chapel
422745: Fairwater Unit Centre
422746: 20 Fairwater Square
701528: Fairwater Comprehensive School

St Dials

422689: St Dials Neighbourhood
10711: Elim Independent Chapel
13149: Our Lady of the Angels Roman Catholic Church
13151: St Gabriel's Church
307501: Cwmbrân Salvation Army
701502: Police Training Centre
701521: St Dials Infant School (Ysgol Gymraeg)

Coedeva

422685: Coedeva Neighbourhood
36921: Glan-y-nant
13147: Penywaun Independent Chapel
13150: Ebenezer Baptist chapel
413682: Coedeva Corn Mill
701522: Coed Eva Infant and Junior School, Teynes
701550: The Crescent and The Circle

Greenmeadow

422682: Greenmeadow Neighbourhood
422683: Greenmeadow and St Dials Community Hall, Pandy
422684: Greenmeadow Primary School
701501: The Threepenny Bit Community Hall

Thornhill

701523: Thornhill Neighbourhood
701512: Springvale Industrial Park
701529: Woodlands Road Primary School
701551: Thornhill Unit Centre

Hollybush

701509: Hollybush Neighbourhood

Maes-y-rhiw

701536: Maes-y-rhiw Neighbourhood

Henllys and Tŷ Canol

701537: Henllys Neighbourhood
701543: Tŷ Canol Neighbourhood
701538: Henllys Nature Reserve

Tŷ Coch

701539: Tŷ Coch Neighbourhood
701507: Ferranti Computers (GE Marconi)
701552: Alfa Laval Factory

Bibliography

Published Sources:

Alexander, Anthony, *Britain's New Towns* (Abingdon: Routledge, 2009

Boughton, John, *Municipal Dreams: The Rise and Fall of Council Housing* (London: Verso Press, 2018)

Bradley, Martha Sonntag, 'The Cloning of Mormon Architecture', *The Dialogue Journal*, 14: 1 (Spring 1981)

Bromwich, Rachel (ed.), *Trioedd Ynys Prydein*, 3rd ed (Cardiff: University of Wales Press, 2006)

Bullock, Nicholas, *Building the Post-War World: Modern architecture and reconstruction in Britain* (Abingdon: Routledge, 2002)

Central Office of Information, *The New Towns of Britain*: Reference Pamphlet 44 (London: HMSO, 1969)

Clapson, Mark 'The English New Towns since 1946: what are the Lessons of their History for their Future?' in *Société française d'histoire urbaine*, Volume 50, Issue 3 (2017)

Cwmbran Development Corporation, *Cwmbran: Its Concept and Development* (Cwmbrân: Cwmbran Development Corporation, 1974)

Cwmbran Development Corporation, *Cwmbrân – Garden City of Wales* (Cwmbrân: Cwmbran Development Corporation, 1978)

Cwmbran Development Corporation, *Cwmbran: Garden City of Wales* Information Sheet no. HD3 'Maes-y-Rhiw' (1975)

Cwmbran Development Corporation, *Cwmbran: Garden City of Wales* Information Sheet no. HD4 (1975)

Cwmbran Development Corporation, *Cwmbran: Garden City of Wales* Information Sheet no. HD6, 'Thornhill 1' (1975)

Cwmbran Development Corporation, *Cwmbran: Garden City of Wales* Information Sheet no. HD7 (1975)

Cwmbran Development Corporation, *Cwmbran Garden City of Wales* Information Sheet no. ID1 'Springvale' (1975)

Cwmbran Development Corporation, *Cwmbran Garden City of Wales* Information Sheet no. OS1 'Springvale' (1975)

Cwmbrân Development Corporation, *Cwmbran: Garden City of Wales* Information Sheet no. R1 'Hollybush 1' (1975)

Cwmbran Development Corporation, *Cwmbran: Garden City of Wales* Information Sheet no. R2 'Hollybush 2' (1975)

Davies, Sioned, *The Mabinogion* (Oxford: Oxford University Press, 2007)

Grindrod, John, *Concretopia: A journey around the rebuilding of postwar Britain* (Brecon: Old Street Publishing, 2013)

Hadfield, C, *The Canals of South Wales and the Borders* (Cardiff: University of Wales Press, 1960)

'Industrial offices, Cwmbran, South Wales' in *The Architectural Review*, 132, Number 786 (12th August 1962)

Jones, Peter W. & Hitchman, Isabel, *Dictionary of Artists In Wales* (Llandysul: Gomer Press, 2015)

Lock, Katy & Ellis, Hugh, *New Towns: the Rise, Fall and Rebirth* (London: RIBA Publishing, 2020)

Mason, E., 'Henry Collins and Joyce Pallot', *C20 Magazine*, (Winter, 2012)

Ministry of Health & Ministry of Works, *Housing Manual 1944* (London: HMSO, DATE)

Minoprio & Spencely and P. W. Macfarlane, *Cwmbran New Town: A Plan Prepared for the Cwmbran Development Corporation* (London: np, 1951)

Nairn, Ian 'Centre – and off-centre', *The Observer*, (October 8th, 1967).

Newman, John, *The Buildings of Wales: Gwent/Monmouthshire* (London: Penguin Books, 2000)

Port, M, *Six Hundred New Churches: The Church Building Commission 1818-1856*, 2nd ed (Reading: Spire Books Ltd, 2006).

Priestley, Joseph, *Historical Account of the Navigable Rivers, Canals, and Railways of Great Britain* (Cambridge: Cambridge University Press, 2015)

Michael Quick, *Railway Passenger Stations in Great Britain: A Chronology*, 4th edn (Oxford: Railway and Canal Historical Society, 2009).

Reports of the Aycliffe, Basildon, Bracknell, Corby, Cwmbran, Harlow, Hemel Hempstead, Peterlee, Stevenage, Welwyn Garden City & Hatfield Development Corporations for the period ending 31 March 1950 (London: HMSO)

Reports of the Aycliffe, Basildon, Bracknell, Corby, Cwmbran, Harlow, Hemel Hempstead, Peterlee, Stevenage, Welwyn Garden City & Hatfield Development Corporations for the period ending 31 March 1951 (London: HMSO)

Reports of the Aycliffe, Basildon, Bracknell, Corby, Cwmbran, Harlow, Hemel Hempstead, Peterlee, Stevenage, Welwyn Garden City & Hatfield Development Corporations for the period ending 31 March 1952 (London: HMSO)

Reports of the Aycliffe, Basildon, Bracknell, Corby, Cwmbran, Harlow, Hemel Hempstead, Peterlee, Stevenage, Welwyn Garden City & Hatfield Development Corporations for the period ending 31 March 1953 (London: HMSO)

Reports of the Aycliffe, Basildon, Bracknell, Corby, Cwmbran, Harlow, Hemel Hempstead, Peterlee, Stevenage, Welwyn Garden City & Hatfield Development Corporations for the period ending 31 March 1954 (London: HMSO)

Reports of the Aycliffe, Basildon, Bracknell, Corby, Cwmbran, Harlow, Hemel Hempstead, Peterlee, Stevenage, Welwyn Garden City & Hatfield Development Corporations for the period ending 31 March 1955 (London: HMSO)

Reports of the Aycliffe, Basildon, Bracknell, Corby, Cwmbran, Harlow, Hemel Hempstead, Peterlee, Stevenage, Welwyn Garden City & Hatfield Development Corporations for the period ending 31 March 1956 (London: HMSO)

Reports of the Aycliffe, Basildon, Bracknell, Corby, Cwmbran, Harlow, Hemel Hempstead, Peterlee, Stevenage, Welwyn Garden City & Hatfield Development Corporations for the period ending 31 March 1957 (London: HMSO)

Reports of the Aycliffe, Basildon, Bracknell, Corby, Cwmbran, Harlow, Hemel Hempstead, Peterlee, Stevenage, Welwyn Garden City & Hatfield Development Corporations for the period ending 31 March 1959 (London: HMSO)

Reports of the Aycliffe, Basildon, Bracknell, Corby, Cwmbran, Harlow, Hemel Hempstead, Peterlee, Stevenage, Welwyn Garden City & Hatfield Development Corporations for the period ending 31 March 1960 (London: HMSO)

Reports of the Aycliffe, Basildon, Bracknell, Corby, Cwmbran, Harlow, Hemel Hempstead, Peterlee, Stevenage, Welwyn Garden City & Hatfield Development Corporations for the period ending 31 March 1961 (London: HMSO)

Reports of the Aycliffe, Basildon, Bracknell, Corby, Cwmbran, Harlow, Hemel Hempstead, Peterlee, Stevenage, Welwyn Garden City & Hatfield Development Corporations for the period ending 31 March 1964 (London: HMSO)

Reports of the Aycliffe, Basildon, Bracknell, Corby, Cwmbran, Harlow, Hemel Hempstead, Peterlee, Stevenage, Welwyn Garden City & Hatfield Development Corporations for the period ending 31 March 1965 (London: HMSO)

Reports of the Aycliffe, Basildon, Bracknell, Corby, Cwmbran, Harlow, Hemel Hempstead, Peterlee, Stevenage, Welwyn Garden City & Hatfield Development Corporations for the period ending 31 March 1966 (London: HMSO)

Reports of the Aycliffe, Basildon, Bracknell, Corby, Cwmbran, Harlow, Hemel Hempstead, Peterlee, Stevenage, Welwyn Garden City & Hatfield Development Corporations for the period ending 31 March 1968 (London: HMSO)

Reports of the Aycliffe, Basildon, Bracknell, Corby, Cwmbran, Harlow, Hemel Hempstead, Peterlee, Stevenage, Welwyn Garden City & Hatfield Development Corporations for the period ending 31 March 1969 (London: HMSO)

Reports of the Aycliffe, Basildon, Bracknell, Corby, Cwmbran, Harlow, Hemel Hempstead, Peterlee, Stevenage, Welwyn Garden City & Hatfield Development Corporations for the period ending 31 March 1970 (London: HMSO)

Reports of the Aycliffe, Basildon, Bracknell, Corby, Cwmbran, Harlow, Hemel Hempstead, Peterlee, Stevenage, Welwyn Garden City & Hatfield Development Corporations for the period ending 31 March 1971 (London: HMSO)

Reports of the Aycliffe, Basildon, Bracknell, Corby, Cwmbran, Harlow, Hemel Hempstead, Peterlee, Stevenage, Welwyn Garden City & Hatfield Development Corporations for the period ending 31 March 1972 (London: HMSO)

Reports of the Aycliffe, Basildon, Bracknell, Corby, Cwmbran, Harlow, Hemel Hempstead, Peterlee, Stevenage, Welwyn Garden City & Hatfield Development Corporations for the period ending 31 March 1973 (London: HMSO)

Reports of the Aycliffe, Basildon, Bracknell, Corby, Cwmbran, Harlow, Hemel Hempstead, Peterlee, Stevenage, Welwyn Garden City & Hatfield Development Corporations for the period ending 31 March 1974 (London: HMSO)

Reports of the Aycliffe, Basildon, Bracknell, Corby, Cwmbran, Harlow, Hemel Hempstead, Peterlee, Stevenage, Welwyn Garden City & Hatfield Development Corporations for the period ending 31 March 1975 (London: HMSO)

Reports of the Aycliffe, Basildon, Bracknell, Corby, Cwmbran, Harlow, Hemel Hempstead, Peterlee, Stevenage, Welwyn Garden City & Hatfield Development Corporations for the period ending 31 March 1976 (London: HMSO)

Reports of the Aycliffe, Basildon, Bracknell, Corby, Cwmbran, Harlow, Hemel Hempstead, Peterlee, Stevenage, Welwyn Garden City & Hatfield Development Corporations for the period ending 31 March 1977 (London: HMSO)

Report of the Cwmbran Development Corporation for the period ending 31 March 1979 (London: HMSO)

Report of the Cwmbran Development Corporation for the period ending 31 March 1980 (London: HMSO)

Report of the Cwmbràn Development Corporation for the period ending 31 March 1982 (London: HMSO)

Report of the Cwmbran Development Corporation for the period ending 31 March 1983 (London: HMSO)

Report of the Cwmbran Development Corporation for the period ending 31 March 1984 (London: HMSO)

Report of the Cwmbran Development Corporation for the period ending 31 March 1985 (London: HMSO)

Report of the Cwmbran Development Corporation for the period ending 31 March 1986 (London: HMSO)

Report of the Cwmbran Development Corporation for the period ending 31 March 1987 (London: HMSO)

Report of the Cwmbran Development Corporation for the period ending 31 March 1988 (London: HMSO)

'RIBA Awards 1986' in *RIBA Journal*, Volume 93, Number 8, (August 1986)

Riden, Phillip, *Rebuilding a Valley* (Cwmbrân: Cwmbran Development Corporation, 1988)

Saumarez Smith, Otto, *Boom Cities* (Oxford: Oxford University Press, 2019)

Toulmin Smith, L, (ed.). *The Itinerary in Wales of John Leland... 1536–1539* (London: G. Bell and Sons, 1906)

'Training Schools' in *The Architects' Journal*, Volume 135, Number 20 (16th May 1962)

'Unit Factories' *The Architects' Journal*, Volume 143, Number 9 (2nd March 1966)

Welsh Office Circular 42/75, 'Housing: Needs and Actions', 1975

Wyn Owen, Hywel, & Morgan, Richard, *Dictionary of the place-names of Wales* (Llandysul: Gwasg Gomer, 2008)

Unpublished Sources:

Apportionment of the rent-charge in lieu of tithes in the parish of Llanvrechva in the County of Monmouth, 1842

Architectural History Practice, 'Our Lady of the Angels: Statement of Significance' (2019)

Architectural History Practice, 'St David, Cwmbrân: Statement of Significance' (2019)

Cwmbrân Development Corporation, Board Report 1954-55

Cwmbrân Development Corporation, Board Minutes 8 March 1951

Gwent Record Office, D 2603 A 000135: 'Lands/Plots/Houses Quarterly Housing Returns 1979-1983'

Gwent Record Office, D 2603 000137: 'Housing Services for the Elderly'

Gwent Record Office, D 2603 000159: 'Housing Crown Rd. Area'

Gwent Record Office, D 2603 000183: 'Monmouth House Official Opening'

Gwent Record Office, D 2603 A 000140: 'Open House Town Centre'

Gwent Record Office, D 2603 000141: 'Housing-Demonstration Types'

Gwent Record Office, D 2306 000149: 'Fairwater III'

Gwent Record Office, D 2306 000150: 'Fairwater Shopping Centre'

Gwent Record Office, D 2603 A 000153: 'Housing Greenmeadow I'

Gwent Record Office, D 2603 000155: 'Greenmeadow I, including Report on the Condition of Rented Housing'

Gwent Record Office, D 2603 000167: 'Housing Town Centre South now called Southville'

Gwent Record Office, D 2603 000459: 'Report by Chief Architect on Preliminary Layout and House Types for Crown Road Area, Llanfrechfa'

Gwent Record Office, D 2603 000459: 'Photo Album Fairwater Centre'

Gwent Record Office, D 2603 001586: 'Tudor House – Civic Block'

Gwent Record Office, D 2603 001746: 'Town Centre – Civic Square (including Water Gardens)'

Gwent Record Office, D 2603 001414: 'Churches 1963 + Church Sites Committee'

Gwent Record Office, D 2603 001415: 'Churches: Cwmbran Assemblies of God'

Gwent Record Office, D 2603 A 001416: 'County Hall Site'

Gwent Record Office, D 2603 001451: 'Housing: Croesyceiliog Areas'

Gwent Record Office, D 2603 001455: 'Croesyceiliog South (Llanyravon) Site for Methodist church'

Gwent Record Office, D 2603 001448: 'Tŷ Newydd Housing'

Gwent Record Office, D 2603 001451: 'Croesyceiliog Areas General'

Gwent Record Office, D 2603 001555: 'Town Centre – Civic Square (Including Water Gardens)'

Gwent Record Office, D 2603 000166: 'Housing-Town Centre'

Gwent Record Office, D 2603 001666: 'Fairhill Methodist church'

Gwent Record Office, D2603 000168: 'Submission Housing North of Town Centre'

Gwent Record Office, D 2603 000214: 'Town Centre Decorative Features'

Gwent Record Office, D 2603 002620: 'Fairwater Shopping Centre'

Gwent Record Office, D 2603 003325: 'Town Centre, Central Building, Gwent Square'

Gwent Record Office, D 2603 003329: 'Town Centre'

Gwent Record Office, D 2603 003471: 'Croesyceiliog Photograph Album'

Gwent Record Office, D 2603 003472: 'Oakfield Photograph Album'

Gwent Record Office, D 2603 003473: 'St Dials Photograph Album'

Gwent Record Office, D 2603 003474: 'Greenmeadow Photograph Album'

Gwent Record Office, D 2603 003477: 'Pontnewydd West Photograph Album'

Gwent Record Office, D 2603 003478: 'Fairwater Photograph Album'

Gwent Record Office, D 2603 003587: 'Hollybush 3'

Gwent Record Office, D 2603 003588: 'Thornhill IV'

Gwent Record Office, D 2603 003589: 'Thornhill Housing Phase Three north'

Gwent Record Office, D 2603 003590: 'Thornhill Housing Phase II South'

Gwent Record Office, D 2603 003591: 'Fairwater 4'

Gwent Record Office, D 2603 003592: 'The Development and General Improvement of Pontnewydd Old Village'

Gwent Record Office, D 2603 003596: 'Cwmbran Centre Offices'

Gwent Record Office, D 2603 003596: 'Cwmbran Hotel and Shopping'

Gwent Record Office, D 2603 003597: 'South Western Areas Development'

Gwent Record Office, D 2603 003599: 'South Western Areas Fairwater III A&B'

Lambeth Palace Library, Incorporated Church Building Society Files, Ref. No. 5193

Lambeth Palace Library, Incorporated Church Building Society Files, Ref. No. 10498

London, The National Archives, SC 6/HENVIII/2497: 'Monmouth: Monastic Possessions of the Dissolved Abbey of Llantarnam'

Quarterly Meetings of the Cwmbran Urban District Council and the Cwmbran Development Corporation, 25 January 1957

Proctor, Edward, 'The Topographical Legacy of the Medieval Monastery: Evolving Perceptions and Realities of Monastic Estate Landscapes in the Southern Welsh Marches' (unpublished PhD thesis, University of Exeter, 2019)

Vining, Jonathan, 'Modernism in Wales' (Unpublished MSc Thesis, University of Bath, 2014)

Websites:

Aneurin Bevan University Health Board: http://www.wales.nhs.uk/sitesplus/866/page/61210

Bam: <https://www.bam.com/en>

British Geological Survey: <https://mapapps.bgs.ac.uk/geologyofbritain/home.html>

The Church of Jesus Christ of Latter-Day Saints: <https://aec.churchofjesuschrist.org/aec/home/>.

Cinema Treasures: <http://cinematreasures.org/>.

Cof Cymru: <https://cadw.gov.wales/advice-support/cof-cymru>

Coflein: <https://coflein.gov.uk/en>

Coleg Gwent: <https://www.coleggwent.ac.uk/campuses/torfaen-learning-zone>.

Dialogue Journal: <https://www.dialoguejournal.com/>

National Archives: <https://www.nationalarchives.gov.uk/>

Office for National Statistics, 2011 Census: <https://www.ons.gov.uk/census/2011census>

Polly Hope: <http://www.pollyhope.com/about.html>.

South Wales Argus: <https://www.southwalesargus.co.uk/news/8375908.torfaens-newest-school-opens-doors/>

St Mary's Church History <http://www.webster.uk.net/In-the-Community/St-Marys-Church/History.aspx>

VADS Online Database: <https://vads.ac.uk/>

Welsh chapels: <http://www.welshchapels.org/>

Maps:

Ordnance Survey, Monmouthshire Sheet XXIII Six-inch to the mile mapping, 1881

Ordnance Survey, Monmouthshire Sheet XXVIII Six-inch to the mile mapping, 1881

Ordnance Survey, Monmouthshire Sheet XXIII.SE Six-inch to the mile mapping, 1899

Ordnance Survey, Monmouthshire Sheet XXVIII.NE Six-inch to the mile mapping, 1889

Ordnance Survey, Monmouthshire Sheet XXIII.SW Six-inch to the mile mapping, 1899.

Ordnance Survey, Monmouthshire Sheet XXIII.11 25-inch to the mile mapping, Revised edition 1917

Ordnance Survey, Monmouthshire Sheet XXIII.SE Six-inch to the mile OS mapping, Revised edition 1917

Ordnance Survey, Monmouthshire Sheet XXVIII.NE OS Six-inch to the mile mapping, Revised edition 1938

Ordnance Survey, ST29NE: A Series: 1:10,000 Surveyed / Revised 1880 to 1964. published: 1965

Ordnance Survey, ST29NE: A Series: 1:10,000 Surveyed / Revised 1961 to 1971. published: 1972

Ordnance Survey, ST29NE: B Series: 1:10,000 Surveyed / Revised 1961 to 1983. published: 1985

Ordnance Survey, ST39NW: A Series: 1:10,000 Surveyed / Revised: Pre-1930 to 1964: published: 1964

Ordnance Survey, ST39NW: A Series: 1:10,000 Surveyed / Revised: 1962 to 1971: published: 1971

Ordnance Survey, ST39NW: A1 Series: 1:10,000 Surveyed / Revised: 1962 to 1994: published: 1995

Ordnance Survey, ST29SE: A Series: 1:10,000 Surveyed / Revised: 1876 to 1963: published: 1964

Ordnance Survey, ST29SE: A Series: 1:10,000 Surveyed / Revised: 1954 to 1972: published: 1972

Ordnance Survey, ST29SE: B Series: 1:10,000 Surveyed / Revised: 1961 to 1984: published: 1984

Ordnance Survey, ST39SW: A Series: 1:10,000 Surveyed / Revised: 1930 to 1964: published: 1964

Ordnance Survey, ST39SW: A Series: 1:10,000 Surveyed / Revised: 1959 to 1972: published: 1972

Ordnance Survey, ST39SW: B Series: 1:10,000 Surveyed / Revised: 1959 to 1981: published: 1983

Endnotes

1   Newtown, Montgomeryshire, was designated as an 'Expansion Town' in December 1967 as part of the 'third-generation' of UK New Town planning.

2   Cwmbran Development Corporation, *Cwmbran – Garden City of Wales* (Cwmbrân: Cwmbrân Development Corporation, 1978), p.4; Sioned Davies, *The Mabinogion* (Oxford: Oxford University Press, 2007), p. 22; and Rachel Bromwich (ed.), *Trioedd Ynys Prydein*, 3nd edn (Cardiff: University of Wales Press, 2006), pp.290-92.

3   Hywel Wyn Owen & Richard Morgan, *Dictionary of the Place-names of Wales* (Llandysul: Gwasg Gomer, 2008) p.109.

4   Newtown, Montgomeryshire, was designated as an expansion town in 1967. Here plans involved the development of housing estates and industry around a substantial existing town core.

5   Royal Commission on the Ancient and Historical Monuments of Wales, *National Monuments Record of Wales* (*NMRW*), NPRN 93391: Gaerllwyd Burial Chamber <https://coflein.gov.uk/en/site/93391/details/gaerllwyd-burial-chamber>.

6   *NMRW*, NPRN 409091: Bwllfa Cottages Henge <https://coflein.gov.uk/en/site/409091/details/bwllfa-cottages-henge>.

7   *NMRW*, NPRN 420979: Ysgryd Fach Defended Enclosure <https://coflein.gov.uk/en/site/420979/details/ysgyryd-fach-little-skirrid-defended-enclosure>.

8   *NMRW*, NPRN 414953: Malthouse Road Defended Enclosure <https://coflein.gov.uk/en/site/414953/details/malthouse-road-defended-enclosure-west>.

9   *NMRW*, NPRN 93753: Caerwent Roman City <https://coflein.gov.uk/en/site/93753/details/caerwent-roman-city-venta-silurum>.

10 *NMRW*, NPRN 306925: Abergavenny Roman Settlement <https://coflein.gov.uk/en/site/306295/details/abergavenny-roman-settlement-gobannium>.

11 *NMRW*, NPRN 95647: Caerleon Roman Fortress <https://coflein.gov.uk/en/site/95647/details/caerleon-isca-legionary-fortress>.

12 *NMRW*, NPRN 93470: Usk Roman Site <https://coflein.gov.uk/en/site/93470/details/usk-roman-site-burrium>.

13 *NMRW*, NPRN 307891: Coed-y-Caerau Enclosures <https://coflein.gov.uk/en/site/307891/details/coed-y-caerau-enclosures-pen-toppen-ash-roman-fort>.

14 *NMRW*, NPRN 301351: Pen-y-Coedcae Roman Camp <https://coflein.gov.uk/en/site/301351/details/pen-y-coedcae-roman-camp>.

15 Cadw, *Register of Listed Buildings in Wales*, Ref. No. 85246: Llantarnam Abbey <https://cadwpublic-api.azurewebsites.net/reports/listedbuilding/FullReport?lang=&id=85246>.

16 *NMRW*, NPRN 43276: Llantarnam Tithe Barn <https://coflein.gov.uk/en/site/43276/details/tithe-barn-llantarnam-abbey>. *Register*, Ref. No. 3128: Ruins of barn at Llantarnam Abbey <https://cadwpublic-api.azurewebsites.net/reports/listedbuilding/FullReport?lang=&id=3128>.

17 Edward Proctor, 'The Topographical Legacy of the Medieval Monastery: Evolving Perceptions and Realities of Monastic Estate Landscapes in the Southern Welsh Marches' (unpublished PhD thesis, University of Exeter, 2019), Appendix 4 (Llantarnam – Gazetteer of monastic landscape features).

18 *Register of Listed Buildings*, Ref. No. 3121: Church of St Michael and All Angels <https://cadwpublic-api.azurewebsites.net/reports/listedbuilding/FullReport?lang=&id=3121>. Proctor, Appendix 4.

19 *Register of Listed Buildings*, Ref. No. 85246: Llantarnam Abbey <https://cadwpublic-api.azurewebsites.net/reports/listedbuilding/FullReport?lang=&id=85246>.

20 Cadw, *Register of Landscapes Parks and Gardens of Special Historic Interest in Wales*; PGW(Gt) 25.

21 *Register of Listed Buildings*, Ref. No. 85246 Llantarnam Abbey <https://cadwpublic-api.azurewebsites.net/reports/listedbuilding/FullReport?lang=&id=85246>.

22 Minoprio & Spencely and P. W. Macfarlane, *Cwmbran New Town: A Plan Prepared for the Cwmbran Development Corporation* (London: NP, 1951), p.16.

23 Joseph Priestley, *Historical Account of the Navigable Rivers, Canals, and Railways of Great Britain* (Cambridge: Cambridge University Press, 2015), pp.453-55.

24 Hadfield C: *The Canals of South Wales and the Borders* (Cardiff: University of Wales Press, 1960) pp.131 & 139.

25 *Cwmbran New Town, CDC, The Official Handbook* (Ed J Burrow & Co ltd, Publishers, Cheltenham and London) pp.18-20.

26 Monmouthshire six-inch OS mapping 1872-1949.

27 Cwmbran Development Corporation, *Cwmbran – Garden City of Wales* (Cwmbrân: Cwmbrân Development Corporation, 1978), p.2.

28 Cwmbran Development Corporation, *Cwmbran – Garden City of Wales* (Cwmbrân: Cwmbrân Development Corporation, 1978), p.4.

29 British Geological Survey website <https://mapapps.bgs.ac.uk/geologyofbritain/home.html>.

30 For background, see Nicholas Bullock, *Building the Post War World: Modern Architecture and Reconstruction in Britain* (London: Routledge, 2002), Alexander Arnold, *Britain's New Towns: Garden Cities to Sustainable Communities* (London: Routledge, 2009) and Katy Lock & Hugh Ellis, *New Towns: Rise and Fall* (London: RIBA Publishing, 2020). Further discussion in Section 7: Statement of Significance.

31 Phillip Riden, *Rebuilding a Valley* (Cwmbrân: Cwmbran Development Corporation, 1988), pp.21-22.

32 Minoprio & Spencely and P. W. Macfarlane, p.5.

33 *Reports of the Aycliffe, Basildon, Bracknell, Corby, Cwmbran, Harlow, Hemel Hempstead, Peterlee, Stevenage, Welwyn Garden City & Hatfield Development Corporations for the period ending 31 March 1951* (London: HMSO) pp.151.

34 Minoprio & Spencely and Macfarlane, p.5.

35 *Reports of the ... Development Corporations for the period ending 31 March 1950*, pp.152-53.

36 Sir Anthony Minoprio (1900–1988), architect and planner at the Liverpool School of Architecture under Professor Charles Reilly. In the late 1930s, in partnership with Hugh Spencely, Minoprio designed Fairacres, a large-scale residential development at Roehampton. Now listed, it was distinctive for its modernist form and the prominence given to landscaping, alongside respect for traditional materials and methods of construction. Minoprio prepared plans for post-war development of Chelmsford and Worcester 1944-46 and developed the Master Plan for Crawley in 1947. A key feature of each was the prominence given to public open space and parkland. In the 1950s and 60s Minoprio produced designs for New Towns in the middle-east (Baghdad and Kuwait City) and in the Indian sub-continent (Dhaka and Chittagong).

37 *Reports of the ... Development Corporations for the period ending 31 March 1952*, pp.207-08.

38 J C P West had previously been a student of Louis de Soissons at Welwyn Garden City; Gordon Redfern had previously worked at Architects Co-operative Partnership, moving from his post at Cwmbrân to work as part of the Northampton Development Corporation; James Russell, born in Pontnewydd, came to the Cwmbrân Development Corporation from the Newport Borough Architects Department in 1960, becoming Chief Architect of the Mid-Wales Development Corporation as part of the shared service scheme before taking on the role at Cwmbrân.

39 Minoprio & Spencely and Macfarlane, pp.9-15.

40 Minoprio & Spencely and Macfarlane, pp.16-18.

41 Based on research by the Social Survey Division of the Central Office of Information, 1948.

42 Minoprio & Spencely and Macfarlane, pp.19-29.

43 Minoprio & Spencely and Macfarlane, pp.30-31.

44 Minoprio & Spencely and Macfarlane, p.32.

45 Minoprio & Spencely and Macfarlane, p.33.

46 Minoprio & Spencely and Macfarlane, p.5.

47 Minoprio & Spencely and Macfarlane, pp.35-38.

48 *Reports of the ... Development Corporations for the period ending 31 March 1953*, p.199.

49 *Reports of the ... Development Corporations for the period ending 31 March 1969*, p.141.

50 *Report of the Cwmbran Development Corporation 31 March 1979* (London: HMSO) p.3.

51 'Torfaen Learning Zone', Coleg Gwent website <https://www.coleggwent.ac.uk/campuses/torfaen-learning-zone>.

52 'The Grange University Hospital (SCCC)', Aneurin Bevan University Health Board website <http://www.wales.nhs.uk/sitesplus/866/page/61210>.

53 Gwent Record Office, DRO 2603 A 000140: Open House Town Centre.

54 Minoprio & Spencely and Macfarlane, p.39.

55 John Newman, *The Buildings of Wales: Gwent/Monmouthshire* (London: Penguin Books, 2000) pp.195-96.

56 Newman, p.203.

57 Gwent Record Office, D 2603 001416: County Hall Site.

58 Gwent Record Office, D 2603 001416: County Hall Site.

59 Scottish architectural partnership of Robert Marshall and Stirrat Johnson-Marshall, originated 1956, became Robert Matthew Johnson-Marshall & Partners (RMJM) in 1961. From this point the practice heavily focused on public-sector construction taking place as part of the large-scale urban renewal schemes, both within the UK and internationally.

60 Newman, p.200.

61 *Reports of the ... Development Corporations for the period ending 31 March 1975*, p.5.

62 Office of the Police and Crime Commissioner for Gwent, 'Contractors appointed to build next generation Police HQ' (press release), bam website <https://www.bam.com/en/press/press-releases/2017/11/contractors-appointed-to-build-next-generation-police-hq>.

63 Newman, p.200.

64 Phillip Riden, *Rebuilding a Valley* (Cwmbrân: Cwmbrân Development Corporation, 1988), p.78.

65 Riden, p.79.

66 Gwent Record Office, D 2603 003597: South Western Areas Development.

67 Gwent Record Office, D 2603 002620: Fairwater Shopping Centre.

68 Cwmbran Development Corporation, *Board Report 1954-55*.

69 Riden, p.83.

70 *Reports of the ... Development Corporations for the period ended 31 March 1965*, p.154.

71 Gwent Record Office, D 2603 000183: Monmouth House Official Opening; *Reports of the ... Development Corporations for the period ending 31 March 1977*, p.5.

72 Riden, p.147.

73 Richard Sheppard, Robson & Partners, now Sheppard Robson, was founded 1938 by Richard Herbert Sheppard, joined by Geoffrey Robson in 1950. The firm pioneered the use of technically innovative concrete-shell buildings and through the 1950s-1970s were renowned for their public and commercial buildings. More recently the firm has lead the way in sustainable architecture.

74 *Reports of the ... Development Corporations for the period ending 31 March 1973*, p.161.

75 Gwent Record Office, D 2603 000214: Town Centre Decorative Features.

76 Newman, p.203. Also, RIBA Journal, August 1986.

77 *Reports of the ... Development Corporations for the period ending 31 March 1955*, p.191.

78 *Reports of the ... Development Corporations for the period ending 31 March 1955*, p.186.

79 Riden, p.90.234.

80 Newman, p.201.

81 *Reports of the ... Development Corporations for the period ending 31 March 1956*, pp.196-97.

82 Newman, p.202.

83 Newman, p.202.

84 Newman, p.201.

85 *Report of the Cwmbrân Development Corporation for the period ending 31 March 1988*, p.10.

86 'Torfaen Learning Centre', Torfaen County Borough Council website <https://www.torfaen.gov.uk/lgsl/en/21st-Century-Learning/LearningCentre/Torfaen-Learning-Centre.aspx>.

87 'Grange University Hospital', BDP website <http://www.bdp.com/en/projects/f-l/specialist--critical-care-centre/>.

88 *Reports of the ... Development Corporations for the period ending 31 March 1960*, p.194.

89 Riden, p.55.

90 Riden, pp.54-55.

91 *Reports of the ... Development Corporations for the period ending 31 March 1951*, p.155.

92 Riden, p.57.

93 Riden, pp.58-59.

94 Gwent Record Office, D 2603 000141: Housing-Demonstration Types.

95 Cwmbran Development Corporation, *Board Minutes 8 March 1951*.

96 *Reports of the ... Development Corporations for the period ending 31 March 1954*, p.214.

97 Riden, pp.63-64.

98 Gwent Record Office, D 2603 000167: Housing Town Centre South now called Southville.

99 Gwent Record Office, D 2603 00019: Fairwater III.

100 Riden, p.131.

101 *Reports of the ... Development Corporations for the period ending 31 March 1969*, p.141.

102 *Reports of the ... Development Corporations for the period ending 31 March 1972*, p.163.

103 Gwent Record Office, D 2603 A 000135: Lands/Plots/Houses Quarterly Housing Returns 1979-1983.

104 *Report of the Cwmbran Development Corporation 31 March 1986*, p.9.

105 Gwent Record Office, D 2603 000137: Housing Services for the Elderly.

106 *Report of the Cwmbran Development Corporation for the period ending 31 March 1988*, p.9.

107 *Register of Listed Buildings*, Ref. No. 27026 <https://cadwpublic-api.azurewebsites.net/reports/listedbuilding/FullReport?lang=&id=27026>.

108 *Register of Listed Buildings*, Ref. No. 82034 <https://cadwpublic-api.azurewebsites.net/reports/listedbuilding/FullReport?lang=&id=82034>.

109 *Register of Listed Buildings*, Ref. No. 81859:Aqueduct over Dowlais Brook, Monmouthshire & Brecon Canal <https://cadwpublic-api.azurewebsites.net/reports/listedbuilding/FullReport?lang=&id=81859> and Ref. No. 82035: Aqueduct over Dowlais Brook, Monmouthshire & Brecon Canal <https://cadwpublic-api.azurewebsites.net/reports/listedbuilding/FullReport?lang=&id=82035>.

110 *Register of Listed Buildings*, Ref. No. 81862: Canal Bridge at Rachels Lock, Monmouthshire & Brecon Canal <https://cadwpublic-api.azurewebsites.net/reports/listedbuilding/FullReport?lang=&id=81862>, Ref. No., 81863: Canal Bridge at Shop Lock, Monmouthshire & Brecon Canal <https://cadwpublic-api.azurewebsites.net/reports/listedbuilding/FullReport?lang=&id=81863>, Ref. No. 81864: Canal Bridge at Top Lock, Monmouthshire & Brecon Canal <https://cadwpublic-api.azurewebsites.net/reports/listedbuilding/FullReport?lang=&id=81864>, and Ref. No. 81865: Canal Bridge at Tredegar Lock, Monmouthshire & Brecon Canal <https://cadwpublic-api.azurewebsites.net/reports/listedbuilding/FullReport?lang=&id=81865>.

111 *Reports of the ... Development Corporations for the period ending 31 March 1955*, p.190.

112 *The Architects' Journal* (May 1962) pp.1075 & 1081-1086.

113 *The Architectural Review* (August 1962) pp.130-131.

114 Riden, p.114.

115 *The Architects' Journal* (March 1966) pp.587-597.

116 Riden, p.199.

117 Riden, p.200.

118 Newman, p.207.

119 Riden, pp.222-25.

120 *Reports of the ... Development Corporations for the period ending 31 March 1972*, pp.161-62.

121 'Scene Cinemas', Cinema Treasures website <http://cinematreasures.org/theaters/22009>.

122 *Reports of the ... Development Corporations for the period ending 31 March 1973*, p.164.

123 *Reports of the ... Development Corporations for the period ending 31 March 1964*, p.157.

124 Riden, pp.152-53.

125 Riden, p.149.

126 *Reports of the ... Development Corporations for the period ending 31 March 1969*, p.142.

127 Newman, p.201.

128 *Reports of the ... Development Corporations for the period ending 31 March 1974*, p.11.

129 'Monmouth: Monastic Possessions of the Dissolved Abbey of Llantarnam', Kew, The National Archives, SC 6/HENVIII/2497 <https://discovery.nationalarchives.gov.uk/details/r/C5973279>.

130 Newman, p.335.

131 For background, see M. Port, *Six Hundred New Churches: The Church Building Commission 1818–1856*, 2nd edn (Reading: Spire Books Ltd, 2006).

132 Lambeth Palace Library, *Incorporated Church Building Society Files*, Ref. No. 5193.

133 Newman, p.198.

134 Lambeth Palace Library, *Incorporated Church Building Society Files*, Ref. No. 10498.

135 Newman, p.195.

136 Architectural History Practice, *Our Lady of the Angels: Statement of Significance* (2019).

137 Royal Commission on the Ancient and Historical Monuments of Wales, *Chapels Database*, NPRN 13147:Penywaun Independent Chapel <http://www.welshchapels.org/search/nprn/13147>.

138 *Chapels Database*, NPRN 13145: Bethel Independent Chapel <http://www.welshchapels.org/search/nprn/13145>.

139 *Chapels Database*, NPRN 10711: Elim Independent Chapel <http://www.welshchapels.org/search/nprn/10711>.

140 *Chapels Database*, NPRN 10724 <http://www.welshchapels.org/search/nprn/10724>.

141 *Chapels Database*, NPRN 13144: Siloam Baptist Chapel <http://www.welshchapels.org/search/nprn/13144>, NPRN 13150: Ebenezer Baptist Chapel <http://www.welshchapels.org/search/nprn/13150>, NPRN 10715: Mount Pleasant Baptist Chapel <http://www.welshchapels.org/search/nprn/10715> and NPRN 10729: Richmond Road Baptist Chapel <http://www.welshchapels.org/search/nprn/10729>.

142 *Chapels Database*, NPRN 13159: Hope Wesleyan Chapel <http://www.welshchapels.org/search/nprn/13159>, NPRN 10720: Wesley Street Chapel <https://coflein.gov.uk/en/site/10720/details/wesley-street-chapel-cwmbran>, NPRN 13143: Ebenezer Primitive Methodist Chapel <http://www.welshchapels.org/search/nprn/13143>, and NPRN 10733: Hope Primitive Methodist Chapel <http://www.welshchapels.org/search/nprn/10733>.

143 *Chapels Database*, NPRN 13161: Ebenezer Congregational Hall <http://www.welshchapels.org/search/nprn/13161>.

144 *Chapels Database*, NPRN 10710: Bethania Congregational Chapel <http://www.welshchapels.org/search/nprn/10710 and NPRN 13158: Pontnewydd Gospel Chapel <http://www.welshchapels.org/search/nprn/13158>.

145 Chapels Database NPRN 10731 Trinity Methodist Chapel<http://www.welshchapels.org/search/nprn/10731>.

146 Gwent Record Office, D 2603 001415 Churches: Cwmbran Assemblies of God.

147 The application was for an LDS church, a building for weekly worship. LDS Temples form a different class of building, used for specific ceremonies.

148 Gwent Record Office, D 2603 001414: Churches 1963 + Church Sites Committee.

149 The Evangelical Alliance, *Evangelical Strategy in New Towns* (London: Scripture Union, 1971) was set up to investigate the development of Christian activities in the New Towns.

150 Gwent Record Office, D 2603 001414: Churches 1963 + Church Sites Committee.

151 Gwent Record Office, D 2603 001415: Churches: Cwmbran Assemblies of God.

152 Gwent Record Office, D 2603 001414: Churches 1963 + Church Sites Committee.

153 Gwent Record Office, D 2603 001414: Churches 1963 + Church Sites Committee.

154 Gwent Record Office, D 2603 001455: Croesyceiliog South (Llanyravon) Site for Methodist church.

155 Gwent Record Office, D 2603 001666: Fairhill Methodist church.

156 Gwent Record Office, D 2603 001414: Churches 1963 + Church Sites Committee.

157 Gwent Record Office, D 2603 001414: Churches 1963 + Church Sites Committee.

158 For historical development, see Martha Sonntag Bradley, 'The Cloning of Mormon Architecture', *The Dialogue Journal*, 14: 1 (Spring 1981) <https://www.dialoguejournal.com/wp-content/uploads/sbi/articles/Dialogue_V14N01_22.pdf>; for current planning resources, see The Church of Jesus Christ of Latter-Day Saints website <https://aec.churchofjesuschrist.org/aec/home/>.

159 Architectural History Practice, *Our Lady of the Angels: Statement of Significance* (2019).

160 Architectural History Practice, *St David, Cwmbrân: Statement of Significance* (2019).

161 Gwent Record Office, D 2603 001414: Churches 1963 + Church Sites Committee.

162 Michael Quick, *Railway Passenger Stations in Great Britain: A Chronology*, 4th edn (Oxford: Railway and Canal Historical Society, 2009).

163 *Reports of the ... Development Corporations for the period ending 31 March 1966*, p.135.

164 *Reports of the ... Development Corporations for the period ending 31 March 1974*, p.7.

165 *Reports of the Cwmbran Development Corporation for the period ending 31 March 1982*, p.6.

166 *Reports of the ... Development Corporations for the period ending 31 March 1964*, p.154.

167 *Reports of the ... Development Corporations for the period ending 31 March 1968*, p.138.

168 *Reports of the ... Development Corporations for the period ending 31 March 1977*, p.7.

169 *Reports of the Cwmbran Development Corporation for the period ending 31 March 1983*, p.6.

170 *Reports of the Development Corporations for the period ending 31 March 1986*, p.8.

171 *Reports of the Development Corporations for the period ending 31 March 1988*, pp.6-7.

172 *Reports of the Development Corporations for the period ending 31 March 1988*, p.10.

173 Quarterly Meetings of the Cwmbran Urban District Council and the Cwmbran Development Corporation, 25 January 1957.

174 *Reports of the ... Development Corporations for the period ending 31 March 1971*, p.154.

175 Edward Proctor, 'The Topographical Legacy of the Medieval Monastery: Evolving Perceptions and Realities of Monastic

Landscapes in the Southern Welsh Marches' (unpublished PhD thesis, University of Exeter, 2019).

176 Proctor, p.367.

177 Proctor, p.381.

178 Proctor, pp.376-77.

179 Proctor, pp.449-54.

180 The *Itinerary of John Leland in Wales*, ed. by L. Toulmin Smith (London: G. Bell and Sons, 1906), p.50 and p.44.

181 Proctor, p.410.

182 Proctor, Appendix 4.

183 *Cwmbran New Town, CDC, The Official Handbook* (Ed J Burrow & Co ltd, Publishers, Cheltenham and London) p.31.

184 Minoprio & Spencely and Macfarlane, p.37.

185 *Reports of the Development Corporations for the period ending 31 March 1988*, p.11.

186 The other commission was for Pilkington's, St Asaph, 1966–67. This has been removed and its whereabouts are currently unknown. Information from Dr Dawn Pereira, author of forthcoming book on William Mitchell.

187 For more information on Polly Hope, see her website <http://www.pollyhope.com/about.html>.

188 *Reports of the ... Development Corporations for the period ending 31 March 1974*, fig.2.

189 E. Mason, 'Henry Collins and Joyce Pallot', *C20 Magazine*, Winter (2012), pp.22-23.

190 Site visit with representatives of Torfaen County Borough Council 12/12/2018.

191 Minoprio & Spencely and Macfarlane, pp.30-31.

192 *Reports of the ... Development Corporations for the period ended 31st March 1956*, p.196.

193 CDC Board Report 1954-55.

194 *Reports of the ... Development Corporations for the period ended 31st March 1955*, p.186.

195 Riden, p.83.

196 *Reports of the ... Development Corporations for the period ended 31st March 1960*, p.194.

197 *Reports of the ... Development Corporations for the period ended 31st March 1961*, p.200.

198 *Reports of the ... Development Corporations for the period ended 31st March 1961*, pp.153-154.

199 Gwent Record Office, D 2603 000183: Monmouth House Official Opening.

200 Gwent Record Office, D 2603 003325: Town Centre Central Building Gwent Square.

201 *Reports of the ... Development Corporations for the period ended 31st March 1973*, p.164.

202 Scene Cinemas, the Mall, Cwmbran Cinema Treasures Website.

203 David Horn, b.1937, grew up in Pembroke Dock before attending Chelsea School of Art and the Royal College. Teaching a various colleges, he became Head of Visual Art at Nottingham. *Dictionary of Artists In Wales* (Llandysul: Gomer Press, 2015).

204 *Reports of the ... Development Corporations for the period ended 31st March 1966*, p.138.

205 *Reports of the ... Development Corporations for the period ended 31st March 1973*, p.148.

206 Gwent Record Office, D 2603 001555: Town Centre – Civic Square (Including Water Gardens).

207 *Reports of the Development Corporations for the period ended 31st March 1983*, p.3.

208 *Reports of the ... Development Corporations for the period ended 31st March 1976*, p.9.

209 Gwent Record Office, D 2603 000214: Town Centre Decorative Features.

210 Gwent Record Office, D 2603 003329: Town Centre.

211 Gwent Record Office, D 2603 003596: Cwmbran Centre Offices.

212 Gwent Record Office, D 2603 000140: Open House Town Centre.

213 *Reports of the Development Corporations for the Period Ended 31st March 1986*, p.5.

214 Site visit with representatives of Torfaen County Borough Council 12/12/2018.

215 Gwent Record Office, D 2603 001746: Town Centre – Civic Square (including Water Gardens).

216 Monmouthshire XXIII OS Six Inch 1881.

217 Monmouthshire XXIII.11 OS 25 inch Revised 1917.

218 White Rose Cinema, Pontnewydd, Cwmbran, Cinema Treasures website <http://cinematreasures.org/theaters/51390>.

219 Monmouthshire XXIII.SE OS Six Inch Revised 1948-1949.

220 *Reports of the ... Development Corporations for the period ending 31st March 1951*, p.158: 8.5 acres at Tŷ Newydd, 86 acres at West Pontnewydd and 27 acres at Caerleon Road.

221 Gwent Record Office, D 2603 001448: Ty Newydd Housing.

222 Ministry of Health & Ministry of Works Housing Manual 1944.

223 Gwent Record Office, D 2603 003280: Pontnewydd West House Construction.

224 Gwent Record Office, D 2603 00014: Demonstration Housing. See Section 5.6 for further details.

225 *Reports of the ... Development Corporations for the period ending 31st March 1955*, p.184.

226 *Reports of the ... Development Corporations for the period ending 31st March 1960*, p.198.

227 Architectural History Practice, *St David, Cwmbran: Statement of Significance*, 2019.

228 *Reports of the ... Development Corporations for the period ending 31st March 1965*, p.195.

229 *Reports of the ... Development Corporations for the period ending 31st March 1960, p.197*.

230 2011 Census: Key Statistics for Pontnewydd Ward, Office for National Statistics website.

231 Gwent Record Office, D 2603 000166: Housing-Town Centre.

232 Riden, p. 71 / Gwent Record Office, D2603 000168: Submission Housing North of Town Centre.

233 Gwent Record Office, D 2603 000166: Housing-Town Centre.

234 Gwent Record Office, D 2603 000166: Housing-Town Centre.

235 Newman, p.202.

236 Riden, p.64.

237 Gwent Record Office, D 2603 000167: Housing TC South now called Southville.

238 Gwent Record Office, D 2603 000167: Housing TC South now called Southville.

239 John Boughton, *Municipal Dreams: The Rise and Fall of Council Housing* (London, 2018) p.107.

240 Gwent Record Office, D 2603 000167: Housing TC South now called Southville.

241 *Reports of the ... Development Corporations for the period ending 31st March 1964*, pp.157-158.

242 South Wales Argus ' Torfaen's newest school opens doors' <https://www.southwalesargus.co.uk/news/8375908.torfaens-newest-school-opens-doors/> [accessed 28/05/2020].

243 Minoprio & Spencely and MacFarlane, p.24.

244 *Apportionment of the rent-charge in lieu of tithes in the parish of Llanvrechva in the County of Monmouth*, 1842.

245 Monmouthshire XXIII Six inch to the mile OS mapping 1881. For discussion on the Jim Crow place-name see Footnote 77.

246 Church History <http://www.webster.uk.net/In-the-Community/St-Marys-Church/History.aspx> [Accessed 25/05/2020].

247 Monmouthshire XXIII SE Six inch to the mile OS mapping 1917, 1948-49.

248 Gwent Record Office, D 2603 001451: Croesyceiliog Areas General.

249 *Reports of the ... Development Corporations for the period ending 31st March 1952*, p.209.

250 *Reports of the ... Development Corporations for the period ending 31st March 1957*, p.209.

251 *Reports of the ... Development Corporations for the period ending 31st March 1959*, p.209.

252 Cwmbran Garden City of Wales Information Sheet no.HD4.

253 Cwmbran Garden City of Wales Information Sheet no.HD7.

254 Riden, p.197.

255 *Reports of the Cwmbran Development Corporation for the period ending 31st March 1980*, p.3.

256 Gwent Record Office, D 2603: Report on the Condition of Rented Houses.

257 *Reports of the ... Development Corporations for the period ending 31st March 1957*, p.209.

258 Gwent Record Office, D 2603 001451: Croesyceiliog Areas General.

259 Newman, p.201.

260 *Reports of the ... Development Corporations for the period ending 31st March 1959*, p.211.

261 Newman, p.201.

262 *Reports of the ... Development Corporations for the period ending 31st March 1974*, p.8.

263 Gwent Record Office, D 2603 001416: County Hall Site.

264 Gwent Record Office, D 2603 001414: Churches 1963 + Church Sites Committee.

265 Gwent Record Office, D 2603 001414: Churches 1963 + Church Sites Committee.

266 *Apportionment of the rent-charge in lieu of tithes in the parish of Llanvrechva in the County of Monmouth*, 1842.

267 The first reference found to the name of this cottage dates to the *Monmouthshire Merlin*, 21st July 1849, when the dwelling was owned by Benjamin Evans. The origin of the name in this instance is unclear, with local hearsay relating that the cottage was named after a seafaring friend of Evans. By this date 'Jim Crow' was a popular character in musical entertainments, a mocking characterisation of African Americans that originated in the US but is mentioned in newspaper reports within the UK and the Newport area in the 1840s/1850s. The name was later given to the laws of racial segregation in southern US states and remained a derogatory term for African Americans into the twentieth century.

268 Monmouthshire XXIII Six-inch OS mapping 1881 / Monmouthshire XXIIISE Six-inch OS mapping 1948/49 & Monmouthshire XXVIII Six-inch OS Mapping 1872 / Monmouthshire XXVIIINE Six-inch OS Mapping 1949.

269 Gwent Record Office, D 2603 000459: Report by Chief Architect on Preliminary Layout and House Types for Crown Road Area, Llanfrechfa.

270 Gwent Record Office, D 2603 000459: Report by Chief Architect on Preliminary Layout and House Types for Crown Road Area, Llanfrechfa.

271 *Reports of the ... Development Corporations for the period ending 31st March 1955*, p.185.

272 *Reports of the ... Development Corporations for the period ending 31st March 1959*, p.209.

273 *Reports of the ... Development Corporations for the period ending 31st March 1960*, p.193.

274 *Reports of the ... Development Corporations for the period ending 31st March 1959*, p.209.

275 Gwent Record Office, D 2603 001455: Croesyceiliog South (Llanyravon) – Site for Methodist Church.

276 Newman, p.202.

277 Minoprio & Spencely and MacFarlane, p.15.

278 *Reports of the ... Development Corporations for the period ending 31st March 1974*, p.11.

279 Minoprio & Spencely and Macfarlane, p.23.

280 Monmouthshire XXIII OS Six-inch 1881 & Monmouthshire XXVIII OS Six-inch 1881 / Monmouthshire XXIII.SE OS Six-inch 1899 & Monmouthshire XXVIII.NE OS Six-inch 1889.

281 Monmouthshire XXVIII.NE OS Six-inch 1938.

282 Monmouthshire XXVIII.NE OS Six-inch 1949.

283 Riden, p.62.

284 *Reports of the ... Development Corporations for the period ending 31st March 1953*, p.203.

285 *Reports of the ... Development Corporations for the period ending 31st March 1965*, p.153.

286 *Reports of the ... Development Corporations for the period ending 31st March 1957*, p.208.

287 Newman, p.201.

288 *Reports of the ... Development Corporations for the period ending 31st March 1974*, pp.9-10.

289 Riden, pp.229-30 / Report 31st March 1983 p.6.

290 Riden, pp.190-92.

291 *Report of the Cwmbran Development Corporation for the period ending 31st March 1986*, p.7.

292 *Report of the Cwmbran Development Corporation for the period ending 31st March 1988*, p.6.

293 Monmouthshire XXIII Six Inch OS Mapping 1899 / Monmouthshire XXVIII Six Inch OS Mapping 1899.

294 Monmouthshire XXIII SE Six Inch OS Mapping 1948/49 / Monmouthshire XXVIII NE Six Inch OS Mapping 1849.

295 *Reports of the ... Development Corporations for the period ending 31st March 1964*, p.152.

296 Gwent Record Office, D 2306 000149: Fairwater III.

297 Gwent Record Office, D 2603 003599: South Western Areas Fairwater III A&B.

298 Gwent Record Office, D 2603 003591: Fairwater 4.

299 Welsh Office Circular 42/75, 'Housing: Needs and Actions', 1975.

300 Gwent Record Office, D 2603 002620: Fairwater Shopping Centre.

301 *Reports of the ... Development Corporations for the period ending 31st March 1964*, p.153.

302 Gwent Record Office, D 2603 000150: Fairwater Shopping Centre.

303 Gwent Record Office, D 2603 000150: Fairwater Shopping Centre.

304 Gwent Record Office, D 2603 002620: Fairwater Shopping Centre.

305 Gwent Record Office, D 2603 000183: Monmouth House Official Opening.

306 Gwent Record Office, D 2603 000183: Monmouth House Official Opening.

307 *Reports of the ... Development Corporations for the period ending 31st March 1966*, p.136 & 1968 p.143.

308 Ian Nairn, 'Centre – and off-centre', *The Observer*, October 8th, 1967, p.28.

309 Gwent Record Office, D 2603 00150: Fairwater Shopping Centre.

310 *Reports of the ... Development Corporations for the period ending 31st March 1970*, p.152.

311 *Reports of the ... Development Corporations for the period ending 31st March 1971*, p.150.

312 *Reports of the ... Development Corporations for the period ending 31st March 1966*, p.140.

313 *Reports of the ... Development Corporations for the period ending 31st March 1973*, p.168.

314 *Reports of the ... Development Corporations for the period ending 31st March 1974*, p.10.

315 Monmouthshire XXIII 6 inch OS Mapping 1881 / 1899.

316 Monmouthshire XXIII OS six-inch 1881, 1948-49.

317 Minoprio & Spencely and Macfarlane, p.24.

318 Proctor, Appendix 4.

319 *Reports of the ... Development Corporations for the period ending 31st March 1956*, p.195.

320 *Reports of the ... Development Corporations for the period ending 31st March 1957*, p.211.

321 *Reports of the ... Development Corporations for the period ending 31st March 1959*, p.210.

322 *Reports of the ... Development Corporations for the period ending 31st March 1964*, p.152-153.

323 *Reports of the ... Development Corporations for the period ending 31ˢᵗ March 1965*, p.152.

324 VADS Online Database <https://vads.ac.uk/large. php?uid=67891&sos=0>

325 2011 Census: Key Statistics for St Dials, Office for National Statistics website.

326 Minoprio & Spencely and Macfarlane, p.23.

327 Proctor, Appendix 4.

328 Monmouthshire XXIII SE OS Six-inch 1899, 1916/1917, 1949 & Monmouthshire XXVIII NE 1899, 1917, 1949.

329 Minoprio & Spencely and Macfarlane, p.23.

330 *Reports of the ... Development Corporations for the period ending 31ˢᵗ March 1953*, p.200. and *1964*, p.152.

331 Riden, p. 106.

332 *Reports of the ... Development Corporations for the period ending 31ˢᵗ March 1969*, p.145.

333 *Reports of the ... Development Corporations for the period ending 31ˢᵗ March 1966*, p.136.

334 *Reports of the ... Development Corporations for the period ending 31ˢᵗ March 1977*, p.9.

335 *Reports of the ... Development Corporations for the period ending 31ˢᵗ March 1967*, p.135.

336 Gwent Record Office, D 2603 002620: Fairwater Shopping Centre.

337 *Reports of the ... Development Corporations for the period ending 31ˢᵗ March 1968*, p.138.

338 *Reports of the ... Development Corporations for the period ending 31ˢᵗ March 1973*, p.165, *1974*. p.5, *1975*, p.7.

339 *Reports of the ... Development Corporations for the period ending 31ˢᵗ March 1973*, p.165.

340 Gwent Record Office, D 2603 002620: Fairwater Shopping Centre.

341 *Reports of the ... Development Corporations for the period ending 31ˢᵗ March 1969*, p.145, *1973*, p168, *1974*, p.9.

342 *Reports of the ... Development Corporations for the period ending 31ˢᵗ March 1961*, p.201.

343 *Reports of the ... Development Corporations for the period ending 31ˢᵗ March 1969*, p.146.

344 Newman, p.202.

345 Minoprio & Spencely and Macfarlane, pp.22-23.

346 *Reports of the ... Development Corporations for the period ending 31ˢᵗ March 1964*, p.152.

347 Gwent Record Office, D 2603 A 000153: Housing Greenmeadow I.

348 Gwent Record Office, D 2603 000155: Greenmeadow I / Riden, p.,137.

349 *Reports of the ... Development Corporations for the period ending 31ˢᵗ March* 1968, p.138 / Gwent Record Office, D 2603 000155: Greenmeadow I.

350 Gwent Record Office, D 2603 000153: Housing Greenmeadow I.

351 *Reports of the ... Development Corporations for the period ending 31ˢᵗ March 1969*, p.142.

352 *Reports of the ... Development Corporations for the period ending 31ˢᵗ March 1972*, p.163.

353 *Reports of the ... Development Corporations for the period ending 31ˢᵗ March 1972*, p.163 & *March 1974*, p.5.

354 *Reports of the ... Development Corporations for the period ending 31ˢᵗ March 1968*, p.141.

355 *Reports of the ... Development Corporations for the period ending 31ˢᵗ March 1971*, p.145.

356 *Reports of the ... Development Corporations for the period ending 31ˢᵗ March 1975*, p.10.

357 Grade III Listing is no longer used at a national level, but such buildings are often represented on Lists of Buildings of Local Importance by individual authorities.

358 2011 Census: Key Statistics for St Dials, Office for National Statistics website.

359 Riden, p.182.

360 *Reports of the ... Development Corporations for the period ending 31ˢᵗ March 1975*, p.9.

361 Cwmbran Development Corporation, *Cwmbran: Garden City of Wales* Information Sheet no. HD6 1975 'Thornhill 1'.

362 Circular 24/75 was produced by the Department of the Environment in response to the growth of smaller households and the increasing need for smaller accommodation.

363 Cwmbran Development Corporation, *Cwmbran: Garden City of Wales* Information Sheet no. HD6 1975 'Thornhill I'.

364 Gwent Record Office, D 2603 003590: Thornhill Housing Phase II South.

365 *Reports of the Development Corporations for the period ending 31ˢᵗ March 1980*, p.5.

366 Gwent Record Office, D 2603 003589: Thornhill Housing Phase Three north.

367 Gwent Record Office, D 2603 003588: Thornhill IV.

368 *Reports of the ... Development Corporations for the period ending 31ˢᵗ March 1977*, p.6.

369 *Reports of the ... Development Corporations for the period ending 31ˢᵗ March 1977*, p.5.

370 *Reports of the Development Corporations for the period ending 31ˢᵗ March 1982*, p.4.

371 Gwent Record Office, D 2603 003589: Thornhill Housing Phase Three North.

372 Cwmbran Development Corporation, *Cwmbran Garden City of Wales* Information Sheet No.ID1 'Springvale'.

373 *Reports of the ... Development Corporations for the period ending 31ˢᵗ March* 1976, p.11.

374 *Reports of the Development Corporations for the period ending 31ˢᵗ March* 1980, p.6.

375 Cwmbran Development Corporation, *Cwmbran Garden City of Wales* Information Sheet No.OS1 'Springvale'.

376 *Reports of the ... Development Corporations for the period ending 31ˢᵗ March 1974*, p.9.

377 *Reports of the Development Corporations for the period ending 31ˢᵗ March* 1984, p.7-8.

378 Cwmbran Development Corporation, *Cwmbran: Garden City of Wales* Information Sheet no. R2 'Hollybush 2' (1975).

379 Cwmbran Development Corporation, *Cwmbran: Garden City of Wales* Information Sheet no.R1 'Hollybush 1' (1975).

380 *Reports of the ... Development Corporations for the period ending 31ˢᵗ March 1972*, p.163.

381 *Reports of the ... Development Corporations for the period ending 31ˢᵗ March 1974*, p.5.

382 Cwmbran Development Corporation, *Cwmbran: Garden City of Wales* Information Sheet no. R2 'Hollybush 2' (1975).

383 Gwent Record Office, D 2603 003587: Hollybush 3.

384 Gwent Record Office, D 2603 003591: Fairwater 4.

385 Monmouthshire OS XXIII.SW Six Inch, 1899.

386 Cwmbran Development Corporation, *Cwmbran: Garden City of Wales* Information Sheet no.HD3 'Maes-y-Rhiw' (1975).

387 *Reports of the ... Development Corporations for the period ending 31ˢᵗ March 1972*, pp.159-160.

388 Riden, pp.178, 181-183, 201-211.

389 *Reports of the ... Development Corporations for the period ending 31ˢᵗ March 1976*, p.8.

390 *Reports of the Development Corporations for the period ending 31ˢᵗ March 1984*, p.7.

391 *Reports of the Development Corporations for the period ending 31ˢᵗ March 1985*, p.7.

392 *Reports of the Development Corporations for the period ending 31ˢᵗ March 1987*, pp.6 & 8.

393 Monmouthshire XXVII.NE Six-inch OS mapping, 1899.

394 *Reports of the ... Development Corporations for the period ending 31ˢᵗ March*, 1970.

395 Riden, p.183.

396 Riden, pp.210-13.

397 Newman, p.207.

398 *Reports of the Development Corporations for the period ending 31st March 1979*, p.7.

399 *Reports of the ... Development Corporations for the period ending 31st March 1982*, p.4.

400 Lewis Silkin, The New Towns Act 1946 (foreword).

401 *The New Towns of Britain: Central Office of Information Reference Pamphlet 44* (HMSO), London, 1969) p.1.

402 Parker and Unwin were architects and planners with a close association to Ebenezer Howard and instrumental in the design and building of Letchworth.

403 The Tudor Walters Report outlined recommendation for standards, design, and location for the building of public housing; the 1919 Addison Act, properly known as the Housing, Town Planning etc... Act 1919, enacted this report for a wide-scale programme of council house building.

404 Vining, p.40.

405 Katy Lock & Hugh Ellis, *New Towns: The Rise, Fall and Rebirth* (London: RIBA Publishing, 2020) pp. 8-9.

406 Nicholas Bullock, *Building the Post-war World: Modern architecture and reconstruction in Britain* (Abingdon; Routledge, 2002) p.132.

407 Alexander, p.21.

408 Lock & Ellis, p.9.

409 *The New Towns of Britain: Central Office of Information Reference Pamphlet 44*, pp.5-6.

410 Mark Clapson, 'The English New Towns since 1946: what are the Lessons of their History for their Future?' in *Société française d'histoire urbaine* (2017) p.93.

411 Lock & Ellis, p.19.

412 Clapson, p.94.

413 Bullock, pp.131-33.

414 Alexander, pp.23-24.

415 *The New Towns of Britain: Central Office of Information Reference Pamphlet 44*, p.2.

416 Alexander, p.20.

417 *The New Towns of Britain: Central Office of Information Reference Pamphlet 44*, p.2.

418 Clapson, p.103.

419 Alexander, p.42.

420 Otto Saumarez Smith, *Boom Cities: Architect-Planners and the Politics of Radical Urban Renewal in 1960s Britain* (Oxford: Oxford University Press, 2019), Chapter 1.

421 Frederick Gibberd in Gibberd, Hyde Harvey and White, *Harlow: the Story of a New Town* (Stevenage: Publications for Companies, 1980), p.32.

422 Lock & Ellis, pp.11-13.

423 CDC Board Report, 1954–55.

424 Emily Cole, with Elaine Harwood, 'The New Town Centre, Stevenage, Hertfordshire: Architecture and Significance', *Historic England Research Report series* no.267-2020, p.13.

425 Wilfred Burns, *British Shopping Centres: New Trends in Layout and Distribution* (London, 1959), p.5.

426 Gwent Record Office D 2603 000214.

427 Clapson, p.108.

428 Torfaen County Borough Council.

429 *The New Towns of Britain: Central Office of Information Reference Pamphlet 44* p.13.

430 For example, Goldie Lookin Chain in the song 'Fresh Prince of Cwmbrân'.

431 Cole, pp.6-7.

432 Lock & Ellis, p.17.

433 Clapson, p.102.

434 Clapson, p.103.

435 Department of Planning Oxford Brookes University, *Transferable Lessons from the New Towns* (Department for Communities and Local Government: London, 2006).

436 *The New Towns of Britain: Central Office of Information Reference Pamphlet 44*, p.19.

437 Ministry of Town and Country Planning, *Final Report of the New Towns Committee*, Cmd. 6876, (London: Her Majesty's Stationary Office, 1946), p.30.

438 The Radburn system is named after the Radburn Estate, New Jersey, where Clarence Stein developed the first 'Garden City for the motor age'. This estate used a pedestrian network independent of the vehicular road system, allowing pedestrians to walk anywhere on the estate without the need to cross a road.

439 Ministry of Town and Country Planning, *Final Report of the New Towns Committee*, Cmd. 6876, (London: Her Majesty's Stationary Office, 1946) p.28.

440 John Grindrod, *Concretopia* (Brecon: Old Street Publishing, 2013) p.67.

441 J M Richards, 'Failure of the New Towns', *Architectural Review*, July 1953.

442 *The New Towns of Britain: Central Office of Information Reference Pamphlet 44*, p.19.

443 *Report from the Cwmbran Development Corporation ending March 31st 1988*, p.11.

444 Grindrod, p.50.

445 *Wellbeing of Future Generations (Wales) Act 2015: guidance*, p.24.

446 NHLE 1449625: <https://historicengland.org.uk/listing/the-list/list-entry/1449625>.

447 Cole, pp.21-23.

448 AHP, p.3.

449 *New Towns Committee (Chairman: Lord Reith), Final Report*, Cmd. 6876, (London, 1946), para. 201.

450 Lock & Ellis, p.ix.

451 *The New Towns of Britain Central Office of Information Reference Pamphlet 44*, p.1.

452 Lock & Ellis p.66.

453 In February 2014 the TCPA published 'New Towns Act 2015?' a report into how Garden Cities and New Town planning could be reinvigorated for the 21st century https://www.tcpa.org.uk/Handlers/Download.ashx?IDMF=a1abf968-2127-4e0c-a04d-fbed529fb230.